The Piano

SMITHMARK

The Piano

JEREMY SIEPMANN

This edition published in 1996 by Smithmark Publishers, a
division of U. S. Media Holdings, Inc., 16 East 32nd Street,
New York, NY 10016

SMITHMARK books are available for bulk purchase for
sales promotion and premium use. For details write or call
the manager of special sales, SMITHMARK Publishers,
16 East 32nd Street, New York, NY 10016; (212) 532-6600

Produced by Carlton Books Limited
20 St Anne's Court, Wardour Street, London W1V 3AW

ISBN 0 7651 9833 9

Printed and bound in Dubai

10 9 8 7 6 5 4 3 2 1

Contents

The story of the piano is the story of a superstar. Like most superstars of a certain age, it has had its fair share of face-lifts, and more than its fair share of implants. Unlike the average superstar, however, it has stubbornly refused to be type-cast. What, after all, *is* the piano but the plaything of kings, and the bottle-scarred veteran of cheap saloons and dockland brothels (where Brahms earned his keep as a boy); the tender confidante of well-bred maidens, and a notorious agent of seduction; the fire-breathing dragon of the super-virtuoso, and the infinitely subtle voice of the poet; the very ornament of middle-class respectability, a triumph of industrial technology, a money-spinner in a million, and a victim of mass burnings in the streets (in New Jersey in 1904, the sentence being passed by the annual congress of American piano retailers on all instruments deemed to be 'out of date')? In the latter part of the 19th century, the world was in the grip of an epidemic to which there seemed to be no end. In Cuba, America's sleepy-eyed matinée idol Gottschalk mounted a concert for 40 pianos. In New York an architect designed an apartment block with an upright piano built into the wall of each unit. At one point the United States had more pianos than bathtubs.

A view from

From the 1830s right up to the First World War, concert pianists on both sides of the Atlantic were the pop idols of their day, and their love affairs were the talk of high society and low. Piano teachers swarmed like ants, and of their even more numerous pupils, nine out of ten would themselves become teachers. Publishers, of course, cleaned up. In the living-rooms, salons and parlours of the world, pianos groaned beneath the weight of accumulated sheet music, 90 per cent of which has long since turned to dust. In the more sophisticated homes, however, that music included some of the greatest ever conceived. It was for the piano that Mozart wrote his 27 piano concertos, most of which are widely held to be his finest instrumental music; that Beethoven wrote his epoch-making sonatas; that Schubert wrote his beautiful waltzes and impromptus; that Chopin and Liszt wrote music which opened up a whole new world of sound and raised virtuosity to heights never before imagined; that Mendelssohn wrote his 'Songs Without Words', and that Schubert, Schumann, Brahms and Wolf wrote the greatest songs with words ever written. And where would the world of chamber music be without the piano? Without the duo sonatas, the piano trios, quartets and quintets of Mozart, Haydn, Beethoven, Schubert, Schumann, Mendelssohn and Brahms, for a start.

And can anyone imagine ragtime and jazz without Scott Joplin, Jelly Roll Morton, 'Fats' Waller, Art Tatum, Count Basie, Duke Ellington, Bill Evans and Oscar Peterson? Or popular song without Gershwin and his fellow song pluggers in New York's Tin Pan Alley? What would the cinema (and particularly the silent cinema) have been without the piano, or today's pop world be without the electronic keyboard? The piano has been at the centre of almost every musical development in Western music since the last quarter of the 18th century. It has weathered political and industrial upheaval, world wars and the computer revolution. Yet with the advent of electricity, the gramophone record, the radio and the cinema, there was no shortage of critics who were writing its obituaries.

When we talk of 'the piano', however, we are not talking about one instrument but many. Even today it is still evolving, though now very slowly, but with the potential alliance of the traditional piano and the computer, no-one should write it off as having reached the end of the line at last. What began, in the very early 18th century, as a lightweight contraption that could be carried about by a single person has reached its maturity as a gleaming black titan, nine and a half feet in length and weighing more than a ton. In the following pages we will encounter it at many of its intervening stages, but with minimum attention to technical detail. Readers wanting more specific information about the actual mechanics involved can turn profitably to Professor Cyril Ehrlich's scholarly but rather academic *The Piano: A History* or to the voluminous but invaluable *Men, Women and Pianos: A Social History* by Arthur Loesser, a great pianist and scholar who laboured over his magnum opus for more than thirty years. Add to these Rosamund Harding's *The Piano-Forte: Its History Traced to the Great Exhibition of 1851* and you should have all the information on the subject that any but the most case-hardened pianophile could possibly want or hope to find.

the summit

More than any other instrument, the piano has relied for its extraordinary success not only on its musical merits and uses but on its acceptability as an item of furniture in homes ranging from those of the humblest labourer to the salons and palaces of the unimaginably wealthy. In the case of the former, a fantastic amount of ingenuity and expertise has gone into effectively 'shrinking' the piano to the point where there was scarcely a household in the industrialized world that could not accommodate it. At the other extreme, the casework has received if anything even greater attention than the mechanism housed within it. Spouting gargoyles, bow-clutching Cupids, intertwining serpents, flute-playing automata, paintings by some of the best artists of the day, nothing has been considered too much for the adornment of this uniquely potent instrument – potent not only as a musical phenomenon and article of furniture, but as a spur to the imagination and aspiration of many different classes of many different societies, and, hardly less, as a symbol of social and industrial standing. The sheer snobbery (both horrifying and hilarious) that has been lavished on the piano, like the unscrupulousness of its shabbier manufacturers and salesmen, is sometimes breathtaking. So, too, as we shall see, is the astounding inventiveness of some of its more eccentric pioneers, of whom there were more than a few.

Many spirits, then, inhabit the pages ahead, but the journey, for all its byways, is first and foremost a musical one, your guide being himself a musician. The star of the show, after all (and we should not forget it) is first, last and always a 'musical' instrument. Enjoy!

JEREMY SIEPMANN, STONESFIELD, OXFORDSHIRE, *JUNE 1996*

The Piano

I N OR AROUND 1709, IN FLORENCE, THE ITALIAN HARPSICHORD MAKER BARTOLOMEO CRISTOFORI CONSTRUCTED THE WORLD'S FIRST PIANO, TO WHICH HE GAVE THE GRAND BUT RATHER CUMBERSOME TITLE OF *GRAVICEMBALO COL PIANO E FORTE* (LITERALLY, 'HARPSICHORD WITH SOFT AND LOUD'). THIS WAS NOT, HOWEVER, SIMPLY A HARPSICHORD IN WHICH THE QUILL PLECTRA HAD BEEN REPLACED BY HAMMERS, BUT AN INSTRUMENT WHICH THROUGH AN INGENIOUS ESCAPEMENT MECHANISM GAVE TO THE FINGERS THE POWER OF VARYING THE LOUDNESS BY MEANS OF TOUCH ALONE.

Small Beginnings

8

Far from being just a rickety experimental contraption, the instrument was already highly developed and its essential principles remained the basis for all subsequent developments during the next hundred years. Strange though it seems for a country which nurtured vocal art from birth to decadence, the earliest sounds of the most expressive keyboard instrument yet devised fell largely on deaf ears – and so they continued to. Cristofori was both the first and the last great Italian piano maker. Indeed, he appears to have been an isolated phenomenon. After a brief flurry of attention, commemorated by a series of pieces whose sole distinction is that they were the first to be composed expressly for the new instrument (by Lodovico Giustini), the Italians turned their backs on the piano.

It was in Germany that the piano first made significant headway, pioneered by the renowned clavichord- and organ-builder, Gottfried Silbermann. He made the acquaintance of a man who knew of Cristofori's work in Italy. In 1730, effectively 'borrowing' Cristofori's mechanism wholesale, Silbermann built the first piano in Germany. Like Cristofori's piano, it took the form of a wing-shaped grand. Six years later his handiwork was scrutinized by none other than Johann Sebastian Bach, whose criticisms – that the action was heavy and unreliable, and the tone of the treble too weak – predictably enraged him. But the justice of Bach's comments could not be ignored. (Well into the 18th century, the piano was closer in sound and construction to the harpsichord than to the instrument we know today. The strings were both fewer and thinner, the frame of the instrument was of wood,

as with the harpsichord, and the hammers were both lighter and harder. For some considerable time, the piano was less brilliant and powerful in sound than the biggest harpsichords of the period.) Eleven years later, at the court of Frederick the Great in Potsdam, Bach encountered Silbermann's most recent instruments and proclaimed himself well pleased.

So closely was Silbermann's name associated with the instrument, indeed, that he was commonly believed to have invented it. Silbermann's renown, Frederick's custom and Bach's widely reported approbation did nothing to harm the piano's progress in Germany. By 1752, the piano's superiority over the harpsichord and clavichord was being trumpeted by the highly esteemed Johann Joachim Quantz (with C. P. E. Bach the most famous musician in Frederick's retinue) in one of the major treatises in musical history – *Versuch einer Anweisung die Flöte traversiere zu spielen*, otherwise known as 'Essay on the Instruction of How to Play the Transverse Flute'.

No instrument succeeds, however, without musicians to champion it. Of these, the most influential by far was Carl Philipp Emanuel Bach, the second son of the great Johann Sebastian. As well as being the most important German composer in the transition from the Baroque to the Classical era (and hence from the harpsichord to the piano), he was a revered performer and the greatest 18th-century authority on keyboard style. His exhaustive and penetrating *Essay on the True Art of Keyboard Playing* is one of the few books on music whose quality, as distinct from its significance, has stood the test of centuries. While directed specifically at harpsichord and clavichord players,

it clearly acknowledges the power in the wings. "The more recent pianoforte," he writes, "when it is sturdy and well built, has many fine qualities, although its touch must be carefully worked out, a task which is not without its difficulties." In the years between 1762 and his death in 1788, Bach became one of the few unarguable masters of the new instrument, and saw it transformed, partly through his own efforts as a composer, from an exotic upstart into the heir apparent of the great keyboard tradition into which he himself had been so favourably born.

During his long service at the court of Frederick the Great (an

The earliest surviving Cristofori piano (with 54-note keyboard), dated 1720.

A Silbermann piano of c. 1745. Silbermann established Cristofori's piano action in Germany.

accomplished musician and composer himself), he had had ample opportunity to study the piano and had witnessed dramatic improvements in the instruments supplied by Silbermann, of whose pianos the King harboured no fewer than fifteen when Johann Sebastian Bach paid his now famous visit to the court in 1736.

In C. P. E. Bach's keyboard music the rise of the piano and the fall of the harpsichord are played out in a series of tableaux that are as rich in character as they are in

significance. It was not for their significance, however, but for their art that they were deeply admired by Mozart, Clementi and Beethoven, among many other composers. "He is the father," said Mozart, "and we the children." (Strange to say, it was not until 1782, when he was already 26 years of age, that Mozart came to know the works of Johann Sebastian Bach.) Clementi went even further. "Whatever I understand of the pianoforte," he wrote, "I learned from his book."

The Piano Goes Public

For all its cultivation by socially aspiring Germans, the piano achieved its first spectacular successes in England. Silbermann's pupil Johannes Zumpe may have been no match for his master when it came to craftsmanship and professional integrity, but he, too, had a shrewd head for business, and within only a little time of his arrival in London in 1760 he was making a fortune, which he retired to enjoy at an early age. The keyboard market in London at that time was dominated by the firms of Shudi, Broadwood and Kirkman, whose instruments were made exclusively for the moneyed aristocracy, and priced accordingly.

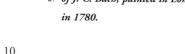

Thomas Gainsborough's portrait of J. C. Bach, painted in London in 1780.

Zumpe, sensing a growing demand among the ascending middle classes, decided to make and market pianos at a price they could afford. To this end,

he simplified Cristofori's action and adopted the 'square' (literally, rectangular) form of the clavichord developed in Germany in the 1740s (see pages 12–13). His success was instantaneous and he entered the history books, where he has remained unchallenged, as 'the father of the commercial piano'. With Zumpe, the craft of piano-making became a business to an extent unmatched by any of his colleagues or predecessors. His instruments could hardly compare in quality with those of his rivals, but they were simple to make, cheap to buy and quickly delivered (by a solitary, foot-weary porter).

It was Zumpe's 'square' that afforded the piano its first great rise to the pinnacles of fashion: on 2 June 1768, when it made its solo debut in London at the hands of the fashionable Johann Christian Bach. With his friend and

An early pianoforte 'concert', given in a well-to-do 18th-century household.

compatriot Carl Friedrich Abel, Johann Christian pioneered the just-emerging institution of the public concert, dominating London's musical life for the best part of twenty years. The youngest son of J. S. Bach, Johann Christian was born in 1735, only fifteen years before Sebastian's death. While his early training was certainly overseen by his father, it was Carl Philipp Emanuel, the third son, under whose guidance he became a keyboard player of considerable distinction. Unusually for the far-flung musical Bachs, J. C. travelled to Italy in 1754 where he studied composition with Padre Martini, perhaps the most famous teacher in Europe, and became a skilled and successful composer of Italian opera (though not without getting himself banned from the stage of Milan's San Carlo Theatre for his conduct with a young ballerina). In 1761 he left Italy for England, produced two operas there and rapidly became a favourite at the court of George III, where he was soon appointed music master to the Queen.

Strangely for so accomplished and popular a virtuoso, Bach wrote relatively little for keyboard alone. His main contributions to the repertoire are two sets of six sonatas, Op. 5 (1767) and Op. 17, published posthumously. The first of these had been seen in manuscript by the eight-year-old Mozart, whose visit to London in 1764 resulted in one of the most touching friendships in musical history. Mozart spoke of Bach throughout his life with affection and admiration, and paid double tribute to their friendship (embracing an age gap of 21 years), first by arranging some of these sonatas as concerto movements, later by basing the slow movement of his A major Concerto, K. 414, on a theme of Bach's.

Both sets of sonatas are well worth exploring, though the opening work is negligible at best (technically easy and musically vapid, it seems likely that Bach was simply using it as bait with which to catch the attention of aristocratic young ladies whose minds and fingers might be taxed by the

remainder of the volume). Bach was always a shrewd and unapologetic businessman. As he characteristically said of Carl Philipp Emanuel, "My brother lives to compose; I compose to live." His music – the last sonata of Op. 5 being one glaring exception – is generally lightweight and unassuming, designed to charm rather than to challenge, but it is supremely professional and finds him writing quite idiomatically for the inflective properties of the piano. His Op. 13 concertos may say on the title-page that they are suitable 'for Harpsichord or Piano Forte', but the style of the keyboard writing shows no such ambivalence.

Bach's concert has frequently been cited as the instrument's first solo outing, but this was in fact its third. The first, seldom noted, took place in Vienna in 1763, when it seems to have made little impression. A fortnight earlier than Bach's momentous display, a Mr. Henry Walsh had played the instrument at a concert in Dublin. But Mr. Walsh was no Bach, and Dublin was not London.

It must be remembered, however, that for all the success it enjoyed in the wake of its London unveiling the piano at this point was hardly an instrument without its limitations. Its tone was thin and brittle, its mechanism noisy and unreliable, and for a considerable time it continued to be outshone in brilliance by the harpsichord and could only hint at the tenderness and subtlety of the clavichord. Yet, once launched on its dizzying spiral of success, there was no stopping it. More than fifty years after the instrument's invention, the age of the piano finally and irrevocably dawned. By the mid-1780s such was the growth in the piano's popularity that most of the great harpsichord makers had hung up their quills and either retired or turned their attention to the new king of instruments.

11

The Zumpe square on which J. C. Bach gave his celebrated London recital of 2 June 1768.

The Square and the Upright

As we have seen, until the introduction of the 'square', all pianos were of the 'grand' type. A really viable upright did not arrive on the scene until 1795, when the Englishman William Stodart effectively stood a grand piano on its end and adjusted the keyboard and hammers accordingly.

The Square Piano

The so-called 'square piano' is actually rectangular and is closer in shape and overall impression to a large clavichord. The recessed keyboard is set into one of the long sides of the rectangle, and at one end rather than in the centre. The strings are stretched horizontally down the length of the casing, at right angles to the keys. With the lid closed many an early square looks more like a sideboard than a musical instrument. Largely because of its economical use of space and the lower price accruing to its relatively simple mechanism, the square was particularly favoured in the middle-class home up until about 1830, after which it yielded to the upright – except in the United States, where it dominated the domestic market for most of the 19th century.

The earliest extant square piano was made as early as 1742 by the German

A clavicytherium, in essence an up-ended harpsichord, shown in Cassells Magazine, 1888; see page 15.

12

maker Johann Söcher, although Silbermann's pupil Christian Ernst Friederici is often credited with its invention. The close similarity in appearance between the square piano and the clavichord was no coincidence, particularly in Germany, where the clavichord was most prized, and where the piano, in any case, was seen as a kind of super-clavichord rather than a reincarnated harpsichord. Indeed, in form and general construction they were little different from their predecessors, save for the metal strings, a considerably strengthened frame necessitated by the resulting increase in tension, and of course the hammer action.

Around 1763 Johannes Zumpe, a German emigrated to London, produced the first English square piano – an instrument so light and compact that it was carried to the homes of its purchasers on the back of a single porter. Zumpe's instruments were elegantly made but mechanically unreliable and hardly bear comparison, in sound, with the later models of Broadwood, Clementi and Hawkins, yet it was on an instrument by Zumpe that J. C. Bach gave his historic solo performance of 1768.

Having more or less cornered the market for several years, Zumpe was later overtaken by John Broadwood, whose first square pianos date from 1771 and whose clients were to include some of the greatest musicians of their day, Beethoven foremost among them.

By 1775 Johann Behrend had exhibited a square piano in Philadelphia, and within a year of that event Sebastian Erard in Paris produced

13

Zumpe's rectangular invention found great popularity on the Continent. This example of the type was made by Pohlmann in 1769.

14

the first French model, so close in design to Broadwood's that it bordered on grand larceny, but then the same could be said of Broadwood's with regard to Zumpe's. Despite its evident success in marketing terms, the instrument left a good deal to be desired. Its tone, in particular, was weak and rasping and was hardly to be compared with that of the grand. In the early 1780s, however, Broadwood hit on the idea of moving the wrest-plank from the right hand side (its traditional siting in the clavichord) to the back of the case. The consequent improvement in tone and volume exceeded his best hopes and transformed the construction of square pianos from that day forward. Within a short time Broadwood's innovation was universally adopted, and with it, strange to say, the European contribution to the instrument's evolution came unexpectedly to a halt.

Thereafter, all significant improvements came from America, where the square piano enjoyed a unique popularity for the best part of a century. The variation in quality between the various makes was immense, but the best squares had a delicate, mellow sound, rather like a cross between a small grand piano and a harp. As time passed, and the century of Romanticism began to take wing, serious composers were increasingly writing music that lay beyond the capacities of the average domestic square.

In rising to meet the challenge, far and away the most significant development was the introduction, by Alpheus Babcock in 1825, of the full iron frame. Now, at last, the instrument could support the heavier stringing required if it was to meet the ever-increasing demand for a stronger, fuller tone. But there were snags. The earliest pianos using Babcock's frame, and even the radically improved version patented by Jonas Chickering in 1840, suffered from an unpleasantly metallic tone. This was not fully rectified until Steinway's epoch-making introduction, in 1855, of the so-called Overstrung Scale, a system whereby the bass strings crossed over the others in a fan-like pattern.

Barring one or two late improvements, the American square piano had now reached the apex of its development. In sound and mechanism, it could rival the standard grand being manufactured in Europe. But its days were numbered and by 1880 it was as good as dead.

A giraffe piano, a form of very tall upright, now obsolete, this example dating from the first half of the 19th century.

The Upright Piano

No such fate awaited the upright, which flourishes to this day. It owes its invention and evolution to the simple, practical desirability of saving space – or, to be more precise, of exchanging floor space for wall space, because in its infancy the upright was the Tyrannosaurus Rex of keyboard instruments, looming high above the heads of its players. The idea was first applied to pianos, albeit without much success, as early as the 1730s, but its origins go back as far as 1480, when the harpsichord was up-ended (its keyboard and action suitably adapted) and imposingly rechristened as the Clavicytherium. Strange to say, it was not until almost at the end of the 18th century that the idea was successfully applied to the grand piano (by William Stodart of London in 1795). Three years later William Southwell of Dublin followed suit with a square piano. In both of these cases, however, the instrument rested on a stand of table height, bringing the end of the now L-shaped grand within a few inches of the ceiling. Not until the turn of the 19th century was the stand dispensed with, allowing the instrument to rest squarely on the floor as it has done ever since (give or take a set of casters), and from that point onwards, the upright's future was assured.

It was many years, however, before its shape became standardized. Many early models retained the lyre-shape of the harpsichord and grand piano, the long bass strings stretching to their highest extension on the left-hand side,

the case then tracing the downward curve of the shortening strings to the right. The tall end was sometimes decorated with a scroll, and for obvious reasons these instruments, often attaining a height of seven feet plus, came widely to be known as 'Giraffes'. In Austria, particularly, they enjoyed a prolonged vogue and became a fixture in well-to-do Viennese apartments. More often, in the rest of Europe and the United States, the up-ended grand was enclosed in a rectangular cabinet, sometimes fitted with doors that, when open, revealed in the aperture one or two tastefully occupied shelves, be it with books, crystalware, spirits or statuary.

Not everyone could afford such instruments, nor would the dimensions of their rooms necessarily accommodate them. With a rapidly expanding market, the manufacturers now gave a high priority to what might be described as instrumental shrinkage. To achieve this without an unacceptable drop in quality it was necessary to house the requisite number and length of strings within a smaller space. As early as 1802 Thomas Loud of London had experimented with stretching the long bass strings from the lower left to the upper right of the instrument, but another decade was to pass before the battle was won. With Robert Wornum's diagonally strung 'cottage' piano of 1813, standing less than four feet in height, 'the piano for the people' had arrived.

A 19th-century upright. By the second half of the century, it had replaced the square as the people's piano.

15

The Grand Piano

In the grand, which derives its wing-shape from the harpsichord proper, the strings and sounding-board are laid out horizontally rather than vertically – that is to say, parallel with the keyboard and the floor, not the wall. This construction has given it advantages in sonority which have helped to ensure its supremacy, as have some major innovations introduced during the development of the square and the upright.

The Concert Grand

Today's magnificent instruments are the unchallenged lions of the pianistic kingdom and in almost every sense dwarf their more unassuming ancestors. Unsurprisingly, they do not come cheap. These are high precision instruments, with almost 1,000 working parts and a wide variety of ingredients.

The vital statistics of the contemporary concert grand include the following:

AVERAGE WEIGHT: *1,060 lbs (480 kilograms)*
AVERAGE LENGTH: *9 feet (274 centimetres)*
HEIGHT: *3 feet 2 inches (965 millimetres)*

Parts and materials:

FRAME: *Cast iron*
CASE: *Laminated mahogany or maple*
WHITE KEYS: *Formerly ivory, now plastic*
BLACK KEYS: *Formerly ebony, stained pear wood*
HAMMERS (OUTER): *Lamb's wool*
HAMMERS (INNER): *Mahogany*
STRINGS (UPPER): *Steel*
STRINGS (LOWER): *Steel, wrapped in copper*
ACTION (MECHANISM): *Steel, copper, wood, felt, leather*
PEDALS: *Steel, wood, brass*
SOUNDING BOARD: *A variety of woods (aged c. 70-100 years); glues*
FINISH: *Ebonized, high gloss*

The concert grand accounts for only 18 per cent of the grand piano market, no doubt due to its high price (c. £70,000/$100,000). On the other hand, the so-called 'baby' grand, tucked away at the opposite end of the range at an average cost of £28,000/$40,000, accounts for less than 2 per cent. Weighing in at a mere 252 kilograms (554 pounds) and stretching to a modest 155 centimetres (a little over 5 feet), the 'baby' grand is now beginning to look like an endangered species. Even in its heyday, it was more a piece of furniture than a serious musical instrument, and it has seldom equalled

the quality of a good upright. Its survival reflects the fact that, even today, the term 'grand' has an air of leisured elegance about it, though the baby of the family has now been more or less relegated to the night club and the cocktail lounges of luxury liners and minor grand hotels. The vast bulk of the piano market comprises the middle-range of instruments, five to six feet in length, such as one generally finds in the normal musical household.

PRINCIPAL PARTS OF THE GRAND

The Keys *Each key is essentially a lever, operating on the principle of the see-saw. When one end is pressed down, the other comes up, sending a hinged hammer flying upwards (or in the case of an upright, forward) towards the string. The strength of the sound is determined by the speed of the hammer immediately preceding the moment of impact. At the same time, the key lifts the damper (see below), enabling the string to vibrate freely. The keyboard of the standard grand piano contains 88 keys.*

The Hammers *Originally covered with soft but resilient leather (usually deerskin), the hammers of the modern piano have generally been covered with hardened felt of carefully graduated thickness throughout the instrument's compass. The making of piano hammers is a highly specialized independent trade and as with the action (the mechanism of the keyboard), few piano manufacturers make their own, even today.*

The Escapement *A device which allows the hammer to fall back immediately after impact, thus enabling the string to continue vibrating while the key remains depressed or the dampers raised. This ingenious mechanism was one of the most revolutionary features of Cristofori's instrument. Between 1809 and 1823 the French maker Erard introduced his double-escapement action, enabling rapid repetition of notes and paving the way for the present-day action of the grand piano.*

The Dampers *Pads of felt, mounted on wood, which prevent each string's vibration except when lifted by the key or the sustaining pedal. Until John Broadwood invented the 'sustaining pedal' (see below), the action of lifting the damper on early square pianos was achieved by means of a hand-stop similar to that found on the organ.*

The Strings *The strings of the modern piano are made of high-tension steel and except for the bass register are apportioned at the rate of three strings per note. The bass strings are of steel, tightly wrapped in coiled copper. The pitch of a string depends on its length, its diameter, the density of its metal and the tension to which it is subjected. The tension of a single string today may be as much as 200 lb, and the strings of a modern concert grand may have an overall tension of more than 30 tons.*

The Frame *Prior to the introduction of the iron frame by Alpheus Babcock of Philadelphia in 1825, all piano types had a wooden frame. Babcock's invention can thus be seen as perhaps the single most significant development in the history of piano technology. Chickering and, finally,*

A detail of the strings
of a Bösendorfer grand.

A modern Imperial concert
grand (with 8-octave keyboard), by
the Viennese makers, Bösendorfer.

Steinway improved on
Babcock's frame (see
page 14).

🎵 The Pedals

All grand pianos have at least
two pedals, all concert
grands three. Of these
the most important is
the 'sustaining pedal',
which keeps the dampers raised
above the strings for as long as the
pedal is held down. This wonderful device, which was
introduced by John Broadwood in 1783, has often been
called 'the soul of the piano'.

The 'soft' (or 'una corda') pedal shifts the entire action
(keyboard, hammers and all) to the right so that the hammers
strike one less string than normally. The term 'una corda' (literally, 'one
string') dates from the period in the 18th and early 19th centuries when there
were only two strings per note. The function of the 'una corda' pedal is not,
however, primarily to reduce the actual loudness of tone but to alter its quality
of tone.

The third pedal, when fitted, is placed between the other two and is known
as the 'sostenuto' pedal – a confusing term, in view of the fact that the word is
merely the Italian for 'sustaining'. This pedal keeps the dampers lifted only over
those notes whose controlling keys are depressed at the moment when the pedal
is applied. Apart from a few works by the French 'impressionists' (Ravel, Debussy,
for example) and a handful of others, this pedal is not required for the proper
playing of the piano repertoire as a whole.

🎵 The Soundboard

As with every stringed instrument, the
sound is amplified by the sympathetic vibration of another surface, generally of
wood. In the grand piano, the soundboard lies below the strings and is
buttressed by a series of wooden bars glued to its underside. The size and
deployment of these bars has a very significant bearing on the overall sound of
the instrument and partially accounts for the different 'characters' of various
pianos and national manufacturing traditions.

The Piano as Object

Like the rest of its large and venerable family, the piano has always lived a double life: as a musical instrument on the one hand, and as an item of furniture on the other – in the 18th century often doubling as a tea table, writing desk or sewing table.

Hardly less care and ingenuity have been devoted to its casing than to its mechanism. From its very earliest days, sculptors and painters have lavished nymphs, shepherds, wood sprites, serpents, dolphins and many other figures on its legs and sides. Alessandro Trasunti and other Italian makers went so far as to make detachable casings which could thus ennoble successive instruments of steadily improving quality. Fallboards and music desks were inlaid with gold and ivory, lids were decorated on both sides by exquisite paintings, including some by the greatest masters of the day, the pedals were supported by puttos and dolphins – the sky, almost literally, was the limit.

Naturally, these instruments did not come cheap. In the early years of the 20th century, a Mr. Frederick Marquandt of New York parted with more than $40,000 for an artified Steinway grand that was five years in the making. Today, such a price would be laughably low for a straight, basic, slimline concert grand; then it was an almost unimaginable fortune. At the opposite end of this spectrum is the piano which Blüthner encased entirely in leather for its lofty but brief career aboard the ill-fated *Hindenburg* airship.

For rooms too small even to accommodate an upright, the early 19th-century shopper could purchase a small triangular piano, purpose-built to fit snugly in the corner. Pape of Paris could provide you with pianos of almost any size and shape. Round, oval, hexagonal, pyramidic, concealed within a table or a writing desk, or brazenly displayed as a trendy conversation piece.

Among the items on display at the Great Exhibition of 1851 were J. Champion Jones's 'Double or Twin Semi-Cottage Piano', featuring "two fronts and sets of keys, one on either side, suitable for any number of players from one to six", and William Jenkin's "Expanding and Collapsing Piano for Gentlemen's Yachts, the saloons of steam ships, ladies' cabins etc., only 13 1/2 inches from front to back when collapsed." At around the same time, Broadwood's offered the potential buyer a mind-spinning choice of styles, including "Sheraton, Jacobean, Tudor, Gothic, Louis XIII, XIV, XV and XVI, Flemish Renaissance, Elizabethan 'cinquecento', Queen Anne, Empire and Moorish."

Wherever the piano has flourished, a cluster of curious mutations has inevitably arisen, featuring such improbable items as the 'Portable Grand Pianos' marketed by London's Longman & Broderip in 1789, or their smaller cousins which could be "conveyed and even played on in a coach". Mozart's friend, the Irish tenor Michael Kelly recalled that the Duke of Queensbury owned one of the latter and was seldom seen to travel without it. From other sources we learn of carriages with mini-pianos fitted under the seats,

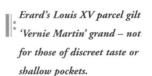

Erard's Louis XV parcel gilt 'Vernie Martin' grand – not for those of discreet taste or shallow pockets.

to be withdrawn and played at opportune moments, just as we hear of other diminutive pianos accompanying singers on the waterways of Venice.

Adorned with cast bronze statuettes, this Bösendorfer of 1867 was made for Empress Eugenie.

Unusual Shapes

Among the more eccentric approaches to the piano's appearance are some of the earliest uprights of Christian Friederici. One, dating from 1745, abandons the wing-shaped casing, determined by the respective lengths of the strings inside, in favour of an equilateral triangle – a procedure requiring a diagonal rather than a perpendicular stretching of the strings. Still more challenging to the builder's ingenuity, however, is a later model in which the strings, while arranged perpendicularly, are deployed so that the longest, lowest sounding ones were in the middle, and the shortest, highest sounding ones at either end. This freakish layout meant that keys on the extreme right controlled strings on the extreme left, and vice versa, hence their elaborate connection to long metal rods, activating hammers which could be as much as two feet away. There is perhaps no more tortuous a demonstration of the musical sacrifices made on the altar of an instrument's appearance. But there were other altars.

The last third of the 18th century saw a great upsurge of interest in furniture and other items which behind a graceful exterior fulfilled a dual purpose. Thus we find as examples of the so-called 'harlequin' style, stepladders concealed in library tables, dressing tables disgorging camouflaged washstands, mirrors resplendently concealing dressing cases (sometimes, even pianos). The concept of the dual-purpose piano reached its apex, however, with a patent filed in London in 1866 by a certain Mr. Milward. In addition to being a fully fledged piano, this one came complete with a hidden couch, mounted on rollers for easy access should the over-zealous practicer succumb to fatigue, a closet specially designated for the bedclothes, a tastefully finished bureau with drawers, a wash-basin flanked by a jug, towels "and other articles of toilet", a music stool so arranged that it contained, in addition to the usual conveniences, a work-box, a looking-glass, a writing desk or table, and a second, though smaller, chest of drawers.

The Piano and Big Business

In the 18th century, piano building was a craft. In the 19th it became a business. In 1827, Pleyel of Paris employed approximately 30 workers and produced an average of 100 pianos a year. Within less than a decade, the work force had risen to 250 and the annual output to nearly 1,000 – an increase of 900 per cent. Nor was this anything like an isolated phenomenon. With the spectre of supply outstripping demand hovering over their shoulders, the manufacturers grew increasingly dependent on successful marketing. And the competition was fearsome. In one memorable encounter in the corridors of a Philadelphia hotel, the piano-movers of two rival makes met in battle, using as weapons the unscrewed legs of their respective instruments. Remarkably, there were no fatalities. But in the market outside the stakes were high, and the salesmen run ragged. Their approaches were several, but beneath the fancy language of the advertising men the principles of the salesmen were broadly speaking much the same.

In America, particularly, quantity was easily, if not habitually, confused with quality. In the 1870s, potential buyers were inundated with sales and manufacturing statistics as though popularity was synonymous with value. One make bureaucratically announced that "The sale of Weber pianofortes has increased in four years by 368 per cent, as per Internal Revenue returns, while the other leading Pianoforte Houses have increased by only 20 to 25 per cent." Haines countered by proclaiming themselves "The largest manufacturers of square pianos in the U.S.," and boasted, by way of proof, that they were "now producing forty pianos per week." Steinway were unimpressed. They, after all, were producing "One new piano every working hour! Ten pianos every day!" Chickering, taking a longer perspective, modestly revealed in 1873 that "Forty-one thousand Chickering pianofortes have been made and sold since 1823!" Work it out by the week, and it comes to a mere fifteen, lagging behind Weber's weekly output by fully 25, and leaving Steinway with a commanding lead of 35 per week (their annual output being 2,600).

It must not be thought, however, that an obsession with large numbers is a purely American phenomenon. In Britain, too, both public and press were subject to fits of advanced numeritis. The soaring popularity of the piano reflected in part its status as a marvel of industrial technology. One writer eagerly informed his readers that the action for a single Broadwood piano boasted no fewer than "3,800 separate pieces of ivory, woods, metals, cloth, felt, leather and vellum", while another marvelled that "a grand piano passes under the hands of upwards of forty different workmen".

In the 20th century, a similar approach was adopted to boost the sales of hamburgers by a well-known fast-food chain,

Pleyel's factory in 1870, by which time piano making was big business in Europe and the USA.

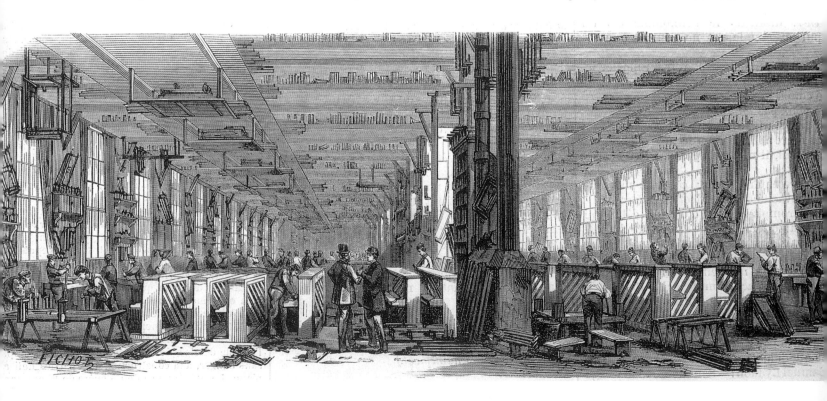

now well past its billionth burger. Other nutritious products seem likewise to have taken a leaf out of the piano salesmen's book, adopting a sensuous verbal approach which had been applied to the sale of pianos as long ago as 1789, when a German maker described a typical product as "a construction whose accuracy and care gives the case the smoothness of seamless marble, a keyboard that is a delight to look upon and whose unsurpassed mechanism is receptive to the gentlest finger-play, a tone which rivals the bassoon in the bass and the sweetest fluting in the treble, one that can be raised from the softest breath of a 'pianissimo' to a smashing 'fortissimo'. These are, very shortly, the qualities of Schiedmayer's fortepianos, which may be purchased, though hardly paid for, with 40 louis d'or."

Terms of Endorsement

Among the most successful (and sometimes the most expensive) sales ploys is the suggestion of quality through association, a system of tacit endorsement which is most conspicuously applied today in the realm of sports and athletics. The practice of paying a commission to famous musicians for lending their names to the sale of a particular make was already in full swing by the end of the 18th century, not least in Vienna, a city of relatively modest size which harboured a record number of pianists and piano teachers and no fewer than ten rival manufacturers. Beethoven was besieged with offers of complimentary pianos in exchange for his endorsement, and not by Austrian makers alone. Among his favourite pianos was an instrument shipped to him at enormous expense, of money and effort alike, by John Broadwood of London. Nor was Beethoven alone. Erard of Paris, quite unsolicited, sent complimentary pianos not only to Beethoven but to Haydn and the then highly esteemed but now largely forgotten Leopold Kozeluch, but not before doing the same for Napoleon Bonaparte. The practice continues to this day, with many a famous pianist tied to a particular make – 'Sviatoslav Richter plays only the Yamaha', 'Alfred Brendel plays only the Steinway' and so on. No make, however, could compete in testimonials with Steinway, whose roster reads like a Who's Who of pianists. The association game was by no means confined to famous musicians. Among Steinway's much-touted 'conquests' in the 19th century were the Queen of Spain, the Empress of Russia, the Sultan of Turkey, Queen Victoria, and a bevy of Rothschilds, to cite only a few.

The third great pillar in the big-time showcasing of pianos was the rash of industrial trade fairs and international expositions which cropped up regularly in the last century, most notable among them being the Great Exhibitions of 1851 and 1867. Steinway and Chickering, the two leading American firms, invested many thousands of dollars each on promotions, hiring famous pianists to demonstrate their wares, issuing glossy brochures and cultivating the press for all they were worth. The rich and famous, however, constituted a mere fraction of the piano market, then as now. At the same time, they helped beyond measure to fix the piano in the public eye as a badge of distinction, an emblem of social superiority. Throughout the Victorian era pianos remained high on the shopping lists of those who were out to keep up with the Joneses, never mind the crowned heads of Europe, and the manufacturers catered for every level. At the bottom end of the market, too, competition was fierce, with ethics high on the list of casualties.

Fast Buck Enterprises

Perhaps the most shameless and cynical of all pianistic sales ploys was the great stencil racket, the widespread application, principally in America, of a simple ruse by means of which inferior instruments, often little better than high-class junk, had stencilled on their fallboards the names of fake pianomakers calculated to sound like real ones: Steinmay or Stemway, for instance, instead of Steinway, Bachstein instead of Bechstein, Pickering instead of Chickering and so on. The arch-perpetrator of this (amazingly enough, legal) technique was a New England businessman, one Joseph P. Hale, who knew as much about music and pianos as the Statue of Liberty. Such was the fashion for the piano that he reasoned, quite rightly, that many, perhaps even most, of his potential customers knew even less about pianos than he did. If it had the right appearance, if it had keys activating hammers activating strings, it was a piano. What did his dupes know of the myriad refinements that separated genuine Steinways from Steinmays?

Another ploy was to blind the buyer with technology and a meaningless, grandiloquent vocabulary. One maker offered 'a semi-grand on the principle of the speaking trumpet', perhaps hoping to upstage another whose instruments claimed to be 'backed on the principle of the violoncello'. And what was one to make of a 'Registered Tavola Pianoforte' in which "a drawing room table stands upon the centre block or pedestal and contains a pianoforte (opening with spring bolts) on the Grand principle."? The clincher here would seem to have been the inclusion of an irresistible extra, namely "a closet containing music composed by the inventor."

Elsewhere the bemused shopper was assailed by a range of instruments variously labelled 'Michrochordan', 'Acrosonic', 'Console', 'Harmomelo', 'Registered Compensation', 'Lyra Cottage', 'Microphonic', 'Utiliton', 'Vertichord' and many other similar and equally empty names. One maker offered his interesting 'compressed pianofortes', another a politically correct 'Piano for the People', while Mr. J. H. R. Mott of London was pleased to announce his 'Patent, Everstanding and "Ne Plus Ultra" Pianos', clearly not intended for the same market as another maker's 'Artisan Piano', meekly sporting a truncated compass and plain wooden keys. One Harrison's 'Piccolo Utilitarian Boudoir Pianoforte' economized on strings, having only one per note in place of the usual three. Minimalism was not born yesterday: other popular pianistic midgets included 'Pianettes', 'Boudoir Cottages', 'Piccolos', 'Pianinos' ... and one maker was given and publicly congratulated on his 'little Quaker-like pianos', offered to "the public of small means – the needy clerk, the poor teacher, the upper class mechanic."

One of the strangest episodes in the marketing of pianos occurred in America in the last quarter of the 19th century. In the aftermath of the Civil War, an unlikely alliance was formed between the makers of pianos and the manufacturers of sewing machines. Both were products widely used by women at home, both were widely seen as triumphs of American engineering and industrial enterprise, and both could be had for a roughly similar price. G. E. Van Syckle Co. of Bay City, Michigan, manufactured both, and itinerant sales representatives in far-flung rural districts frequently carried both in their wagons. Further east, a firm in Connecticut, spotting a gap in the market, made a combination sewing-machine and melodeon. There was even a publication, launched in 1880 and entitled the *Musical and Sewing Machine Gazette*. But all good things must come to an end. After only nine issues, the journal folded and was reborn as the *Musical Courier* – with nary a sewing machine in sight.

THE PIANO MAKERS

♪ *Baldwin*

In March 1866, one D. H. Baldwin, a music teacher and piano salesman, hired a young assistant by the name of Lucien Wulsin. Within seven years, Wulsin had been transformed from a lowly clerk, book-keeper and general dogsbody into a major partner in Baldwin's firm, which began to manufacture pianos of its own in 1889. With Baldwin's death in 1899, Wulsin and his fellow partner G.W. Armstrong were dismayed to discover that their former colleague had left most of his substantial fortune for missionary purposes. Together they contrived to buy up all the stock of the Baldwin estate and that of the only remaining partner, A. A. Van Buren. From then on, the Baldwin Piano Company became a byword for everything that was most enlightened in industrial management. To provide their workers with the optimum comfort and encourage their aspiration to the highest quality, Wulsin and Armstrong had their factories designed for beauty as well as efficiency. The walls were decorated with pictures of Greek and Roman masterpieces, designed to instil in the workers a reverence for classical forms and proportions, the light, spacious offices and workrooms were surrounded by flower beds and ornamental paths, and the factory windows themselves were graced by floral window boxes. Everything conspired to establish a mood of refinement and artistic enterprise. Workers were treated as craftsmen, not as human cogs in the industrial treadmill, and their devotion to quality paid rich dividends. At the great Paris Exposition of 1900, Baldwin took the Grand Prix, and Wulsin was decorated with the Cross of the Legion of Honour. From the mid-20th century onwards, Baldwin has been the principal American rival to the ubiquitous Steinway, and has earned the advocacy of such outstanding musicians as Leonard Bernstein and André Previn.

♪ *Bechstein*

No European maker exceeded the skill, imagination and business acumen of the German Carl Bechstein, whose rise to market supremacy was immeasurably aided by the committed, persistent and well publicized advocacy of Hans von Bülow. One of the greatest pianists of the century, Bülow was also a conductor of genius and the one-time son-in-law of Liszt (a familial tie severed when his wife abandoned him for Wagner). With Bülow's unflagging support, Bechstein became the undisputed emperor of European piano manufacturers. He was also among the first to establish prestigious concert halls in several cities. By 1913 the firm he had founded in 1853 was employing 1,200 workers, though their average output of 5,000 pianos a year (half of them destined for England) was surprisingly low by the standards of other big manufacturers, the more so for the size of his workforce. The quality of the product, on the other hand, was generally held to be peerless, rivalled only, in the public mind, by Blüthner and the American giant Steinway, though Bechstein's prices undercut the latter's by more than fifteen per cent. Bechstein enjoyed, too, a social position which set him apart from virtually all of his rivals. A respected friend of many renowned artists and writers, he became the principal supplier of pianos to most of the crowned heads of Europe, and was personally decorated by many of them.

♪ *Blüthner*

Born in Germany in 1824, the generously bewhiskered, severely professorial looking Julius Blüthner was, in fact, almost entirely uneducated, at least in any formal sense. As well as building up one of the biggest and most admired manufacturing firms in the world (founded in Leipzig in 1853), Blüthner contributed to the piano's tonal armoury the so-called 'aliquot system', whereby the tone, duration and power of the upper notes were enhanced by unstruck, resonating strings set in motion by sympathetic vibration. Despite this imaginative device, his instruments had a generally lighter, more silvery tone than those of his principal rivals.

♪ *Bösendorfer*

Bösendorfer of Vienna (founded 1828) are responsible for some of the biggest pianos ever to go into mass production, their full-size concert grands exceeding ten feet in length and encompassing more than eight octaves (including unstruck, resonating bass strings à la Blüthner and his 'aliquot system'). In 1872, and in common with a number of other major manufacturers, Ludwig Bösendorfer, the son of the firm's founder, Ignaz, opened a concert hall (the Bösendorfersaal) which soon became the principal Viennese venue for chamber music concerts and solo recitals.

♪ *Broadwood*

The London firm of John Broadwood & Sons is the oldest piano manufacturer in existence. Founded in 1728 by the Swiss-born harpsichord maker Burkhard Tschudi, later anglicized to Burkat Shudi, it passed into the hands of the Scots-born John Broadwood (his son-in-law and partner from

1769 and 1770 respectively) on Shudi's death in 1773. In that year, the firm's first pianos appeared, with little to distinguish them from Zumpe's save the name. Not until seven years later did Broadwood produce a square piano of his own design (this including the transplanted wrest-plank, as discussed on page 14) which was followed a year later by his first grand. From then on, many of his innovations, like those of his sons and further descendants, were widely adopted, in some cases near-universally. A noteworthy feature of his 1783 patent was the inclusion of pedals for

Inset: Blüthner's 'aliquot system', in which the upper register was enriched by applying a sympathetically vibrating fourth string to each trichord treble.

23

The fortepiano which Broadwood sent to Beethoven in 1818. This incorporates a split damper pedal mechanism independently controlling bass and treble. Broadwood patented foot pedals in 1783.

raising the dampers and shifting the action sideways (the so-called sustaining pedal, frequently mis-called the 'loud' pedal, and the 'una corda' or 'soft' pedal).

🎵 *Chickering*

The piano-building firm founded in 1823 by a New England cabinet maker, Jonas Chickering, was the first to rival in quality and enterprise the greatest of the European houses. Chickering's partner John McKay was a born businessman, and the first to make maximum use of America's burgeoning canal and railway networks. Chickering's first significant coup in the way of design came with his patenting in 1840 of a single cast-iron frame for the square piano which was a marked improvement on that first patented by Alpheus Babcock in 1825. It was his patenting of a similar frame for the grand piano in 1843, however, that ensured him a prominent place in the pantheon of piano makers. It would be only a slight exaggeration to say that the success of this design caused a revolution in piano-building. Here, at last, was a grand piano that could support the heightened tension and thicker strings required to meet the resilience and richer tone increasingly demanded by the greatest virtuosos and composers. The importance of Chickering's innovation was formally acknowledged in Europe with the award of the Gold Medal at the Universal Exposition held in Paris in 1867. An interesting later development was the founding in 1905 of a subsidiary department, under

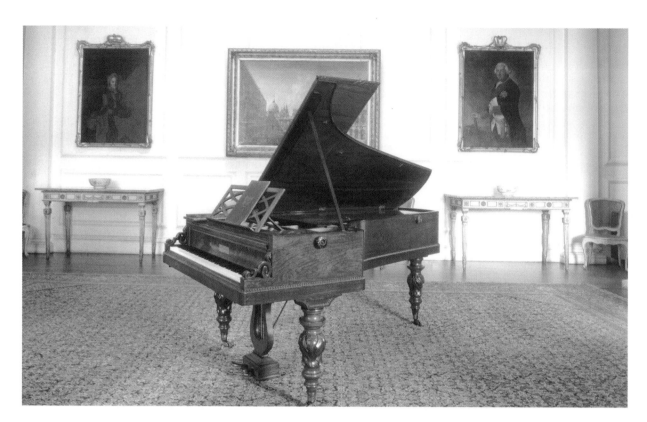

A 19th-century Pleyel grand. All the greatest virtuosi played in Pleyel's Paris concert hall.

the direction of Britain's Arnold Dolmetsch, devoted to the manufacture of harpsichords, clavichords, viols and lutes. The world, however, was not yet ready for such antiquarian pursuits and the experiment was terminated five years later. The last of Chickering's most noteworthy innovations was the introduction, in 1926, of a freely vibrating soundboard suspended independently of the piano's rim.

🎵 *Erard*

One of the greatest names in the history of piano building, Sébastien Erard first came to public attention with his construction of a mechanical harpsichord in 1776. Among his earliest patrons was the Duchesse de Villeroi, who allotted a workshop to him in her château, where in 1777 he produced the first piano ever made in France – a square, with a compass of five octaves, based on similar models imported from England and Germany. On establishing his headquarters in Paris, he excited the jealousy of the Parisian instrument-building fraternity, belonging improbably to the Fanmaker's Guild, who seized his workshop, only to be out-manoeuvred by Louis XVI who in 1785 formally conferred on Sébastien the right to build fortepianos independently of the guild. With the outbreak of the French Revolution and the ensuing Terror, Erard found it prudent to remove himself to London, where he had opened a branch as early as 1786. The firm's patronage flourished on both sides of the English Channel, clients including such diverse luminaries as Marie Antoinette, Napoleon and George IV. Erard's most important

contribution to the piano's evolution was the perfecting of the so-called 'double-escapement' action (see page 16). The firm enjoyed the patronage of many great pianists and reached the formal apex of its fortunes with the award of a gold medal at the great Paris Exposition of 1855. Thereafter, its chronic conservatism led to a dramatic decline, with pianists turning increasingly to German and American instruments. Wealthy amateurs remained faithful on the whole, and the standard of workmanship and exterior design was maintained, but by the end of the century the great days of Erard were over. The London branch was closed down, and the firm's output failed to expand, despite the pianomania which had by then spread to every region of the globe.

🎵 *Pleyel*

Ignaz Pleyel was the 24th of 38 children in the family of an understandably impoverished schoolteacher. As a composition student, he was apprenticed to Haydn and lived with him for five years, developing a style so close to his teacher's that their works have frequently been misattributed to one another. With the single exception of Clementi, he was musically the most overqualified piano manufacturer in history, with sixty symphonies, still more string quartets, eight concertos, chamber works of almost every kind and two operas to his credit. He had the additional and unusual distinction of having composed hurdy-gurdy pieces for performance by Ferdinand IV, the 'Lazzarone' King of Naples.

In 1795, Pleyel opened a music shop in Paris and founded a publishing house which flourished for the best part of forty years, issuing some four thousand works, including many by Boccherini, Beethoven, Clementi, Haydn, Dussek and others, and establishing a nationwide network of agents for the sale of same. He was also the first to publish miniature scores, leading off with four Haydn symphonies and going on to publish ten volumes of his string quartets, as well as works by Beethoven, Hummel and the now largely forgotten George Onslow.

It was in 1807 that he began the piano business which would carry his name well into the 20th century, long after his compositions had been forgotten.

In 1815 the firm was joined by Pleyel's son Camille, an accomplished musician like his father, and a future friend of Chopin, who gave his first and last Paris concerts at the Salle Pleyel, opened by the firm in 1830, a year or so before Chopin's arrival in the city. The family's contribution to the fast-developing story of the piano was augmented in 1831 by Camille's marriage to his Christian-namesake, the pianist Camille Marie Moke.

◗ *Steinway*

If the name of any make has come to be synonymous with the piano itself, that name is Steinway. The dynasty, still going strong, was founded in 1836 by Heinrich Engelhard Steinweg of Wolfshagen in Germany. Within five years of his emigration to the United States in 1850, his squares won him a prize at the great fair of the American Institute – this at a time when squares had fallen from fashion in Europe. More significant in its ramifications for the industry at large was the iron-framed, overstrung grand of 1859 and the similarly based upright of 1863. With their massive iron frames, their

fanlike disposition of heavy strings at unprecedented tensions and their machine-covered hammers of thick felt, Steinway's instruments inaugurated a new era, revolutionizing concepts of piano design and tone worldwide. Never before had pianists been able to command so great a range of tone and volume. Steinway's innovations, comprising more than 40 patents in 20 years (1865–85), were widely adopted, first in Germany, where Steinway established its own Hamburg branch in 1880, and then almost universally. In the years since the Second World War, Steinway's American and European models have diverged somewhat in character, the American instruments being generally brighter, more brilliant, more metallic in tone, the Hamburg pianos retaining more of the warmth and tonal depth associated with Steinways of pre-World War One vintage, and to this day with Bechsteins.

◗ *Yamaha*

The first Japanese pianos appeared in Europe as early as 1878, and were slow to make any significant inroads into the Euro-American hegemony. Yamaha, now famous for its motorcycles, hi-fi equipment and other electronic products, began life in 1887, as a musical instrument maker. Its first product was a modest harmonium and it was not until 1900 that it built its first upright piano. Astonishingly, a full half-century elapsed before this was joined by the Yamaha grand. Since then the Yamaha has gained steadily in quality and reputation and is now numbered among the top makes in the world, and has won the unstinting advocacy of such keyboard legends as Sviatoslav Richter and the late Glenn Gould.

A decorative Steinway grand. Steinways have a compass of 7-and-a-quarter octaves.

Entertainments and Entertainers

In every age there have been those who deplore the taste and lack of discrimination shown by the multitude. They hold that music is a high art and that to give it anything less than our complete attention is tantamount to blasphemy. They throw up their hands in horror at the suggestion that music as wallpaper is a defensible proposition. Some scorn the very concept of music as entertainment. Yet that one, curiously tainted term sums up what may well be the most important, and the most abused, of all music's functions – and particularly, perhaps, of music in the home.

Before the advent of mass communications it was music, more perhaps than anything else, which kept us entertained in company. 'Great' music has always been the exception, never the rule. For every masterwork there are a million lesser diversions whose only purpose is to pass the time. And unlike television, perhaps the most passive form of entertainment yet devised, they entertained by actively enlisting the imagination – never more so than in programme music, where the images exist solely in the listener's mind. In a Europe rent by political and military strife, and later in the Americas, whose independence of Europe was achieved by the shedding of much blood, one particular kind of programme music has always held pride of place.

Pianistic Battles

Ever since Tudor times, composers had occasionally amused themselves by depicting celebrated battles, but by the end of the 18th century and the start of the 19th – the Age of Revolution – this tendency had become a 'craze'. Parlours on both sides of the Atlantic resounded to the din of pianistic cannonfire, composers sometimes calling for the use of the whole forearm (and in at least one case of both forearms) on the keyboard. The most famous and durable of these, by far, was *The Battle of Prague*, composed in 1790 by an otherwise obscure Bohemian, Frantisek Kotzwara, who hanged himself in a London brothel with no inkling of the posthumous fame that awaited him. In the United States and throughout the British Empire, this noisy but undistinguished warhorse was to become, for more than half a century, the best known

and most frequently played of all extended piano works, blasting its way even into Windsor Castle, where it was applauded (and perhaps secretly played?) by Queen Victoria herself. Despite such occasional social coups, however, these battle pieces were generally the musical equivalent of pulp fiction, and they were aimed frankly at the parlour rather than the salon.

The higher reaches of the aristocracy and nobility traditionally preferred their musical combatants to be of genuine human flesh and blood. A favourite, though necessarily occasional diversion in the royal suites was the instrumental duel. Musical duels have a long and distinguished pedigree, dating back at least as far as the battle of Phoebus and Pan in ancient Greek myth. The Pythian Games in the sixth century B.C. were predominantly musical, and as Wagner makes plain in *Tannhäuser*, the Minnesingers were at it full tilt in the 13th century. At the end of the 16th century there was the celebrated 'duel of two organs' in Venice, when Claudio Merula and Andrea Gabrieli battled it out in St. Mark's Basilica. In 1708 Scarlatti and Handel faced each other in a showdown organized by Cardinal Ottoboni in Rome, and nine years later the incomparable J. S. Bach routed Louis Marchand in Dresden, courtesy of the King of Poland.

Of the many specifically pianistic duels, two stand out above all others: the battle of Mozart and Clementi in 1781 and that between Liszt and Thalberg in the mid 1830s. Both contests, in keeping with long tradition, were conceived and sponsored by royalty, the first being the brainchild of the Austrian Emperor Joseph II, who had made a bet with the Grand Duchess that Mozart would prove himself superior to Clementi. The two men duly joined battle, improvising individually, playing works of their own, sight reading sonatas by Paisiello and then improvising together at two pianos on a theme taken from these works. The verdict was characteristically vague, but the Emperor won his wager, it being agreed that "while Clementi had only art, Mozart had both art and taste". Clementi was fulsome in his praise of Mozart, and derived long-term benefits from the

The 19th century was an age of vainglorious heroics at the keyboard as well as on the battlefield.

encounter, as his subsequent compositions demonstrate; Mozart was typically nasty about Clementi, but thought highly enough of his Sonata in B flat, Op. 6 No. 2 (Clementi's contribution to the proceedings), to pinch one of its themes for his own *Magic Flute* overture.

Beethoven, too, being in some ways a natural bully, went in for a number of these pianistic cockfights, and predictably won them all hands down, though none of his victims was remotely of Clementi's calibre. Josef Wölffl, Joseph Gelinek and Daniel Steibelt are remembered today almost entirely for having been soundly trounced by the bruiser from Bonn.

The odds were more even in the case of the famous Liszt/Thalberg duel, organized as a charity event in 1836 by the expatriate patriot Princess Christina Belgioso of Italy. Her verdict ranks among the best examples of the royal cop-out: "Thalberg," she said, "proved that he was the best pianist in Europe, Liszt that he was the only one."

Paris at that time, for all its political upheavals, was widely considered to be the cultural capital of Europe and of the world. In the aftermath of the French Revolution, painters, writers, poets, playwrights, many of the world's most famous and brilliant musicians all converged on the city, so that one might run across at (or en route to) one salon in a single evening such luminaries as Ingres, Delacroix, Stendahl, Victor Hugo, Heine, Balzac, Rossini, Cherubini, Liszt, Berlioz, Mendelssohn, not to mention a

host of lesser celebrities. The aristocrats of Paris, French or otherwise, were very much more than merely wealthy; they were highly educated, broadly cultured and uniquely cosmopolitan in both outlook and experience. They had their counterparts, however, in other cities, other countries: in Vienna, London, New York. In many of these, pianists were numbered among the most prized of social ornaments. Dowagers, and dowagers-to-be, held court in drawing-rooms, from townhouses to palaces, and were only too pleased to lay on an evening featuring the talents of Mr. Moscheles, Monsieur Chopin or "that nice Mr. Mendelssohn," as Queen Victoria called him. Only in the highest society were musicians accepted as anything approaching social equals. In the more pretentious establishments, they were ushered in at the back door and sometimes literally cordoned off from the guests of the evening. As recently as the 1920s, one duchess of ostentation sought the services of the great violinist Fritz Kreisler (also, incidentally, a remarkable pianist). Taken aback by the great man's fee, she pondered for a moment. "That's a great deal of money, Mr. Kreisler," she said, "but you shall have it ... on condition that you will not attempt to mingle with my guests." "Ah," replied Kreisler, "in that case I shall be happy to do it for half the amount."

A concert en famille, c. 1830, providing a light accompaniment to easeful contemplation.

'Proper' Entertainment

Despite the extraordinary proliferation of the piano in the 19th century, there was a feeling in some quarters that the piano alone was inadequate to the demands of really 'proper' entertainment. As a result, particularly in England, it was withdrawn from the front and reduced to providing illustrative accompaniments to poetical words which actually told a story.

In the homes of genteel Victorians the most popular after-dinner entertainment was the so-called 'Drawing-Room Ballad'. The participants in these were not, on the whole, professional musicians brought in from outside but enthusiastic (if not particularly accomplished) amateurs, drawn from the assembled company or the host's family. They were generally sentimental numbers of polite character but little substance, furnished with piano accompaniments that any moderately accomplished daughter could play. Their composers were often women, as were the bulk of their *ad hoc* accompanists, but their singers were predominantly male. Perhaps the most famous of all drawing-room ballads was *The Lost Chord* by Sir Arthur Sullivan, which sold well over 500,000 copies in England alone, and was frequently played in arrangements for solo piano.

An interesting though peripheral adjunct of such after-dinner entertainment was the curious medium of ballads composed not for singers at all but for speaker and piano. Accompanied recitations they might be called, although they were sometimes in the nature of unaccompanied stanzas interspersed with pianistic illustrations. Schumann and Richard Strauss both contributed to the medium, Schumann in his rarely (if ever) performed 'Ballads for Declamation' and Richard Strauss in his setting of Tennyson's *Enoch Arden*, entertainingly and colourfully exhumed by the ever-unpredictable Glenn Gould in his recording with Claude Rains. The latter, however, belongs more properly to the realm of melodrama as initiated by Jean-Jacques Rousseau in his *Pygmalion* of 1762, and exemplified at its most effective by Beethoven in the dungeon scene of *Fidelio* and Weber in the Wolf's Glen scene in *Der Freischütz*. Early in the 20th century a wide range of such melodramas for speaker and piano was readily available for domestic use on both sides of the Atlantic.

"That Nice Mr. Mendelssohn" playing for Victoria and Albert at Buckingham Palace in 1842.

Multipiano Jamborees

The child Mozart and his sister were among the first (and certainly the smallest) pioneers of a new medium: the piano duet. Wolfgang himself later expanded the concept with his Concerto in E flat for Two Pianos and Orchestra, and the Concerto in F for Three Pianos. Little can he have imagined, however, the lengths to which his successors would carry such procedures. The 19th century, often referred to as the Romantic Century, was an age obsessed with size and grandeur. Composers like Berlioz, Wagner, Mahler, Bruckner and Alkan wrote works of gargantuan proportions, dwarfing in size even Beethoven's grandest conceptions. Among the less exalted manifestations of Romantic gigantism was a vogue for multipiano jamborees which flourished for a good quarter of the 19th century, most extravagantly in the Americas, but in Europe, too.

Multiple keyboard works as such were nothing new. Well before Mozart, Bach had written splendid concertos for two, three and even four harpsichords. Only in the 19th century, however, did the practice run riot. In Vienna, the normally sober and morally upright Czerny betrayed a taste for extravagance which contrasted oddly with his austere and self-disciplined lifestyle – witness, for example, his arrangement of Rossini's *William Tell* Overture for sixteen pianists playing four-hands on eight pianos (and for that deprived multitude who boasted but one piano per household, Czerny provided alternative arrangements for only three pianists playing six-hands on a single keyboard). Friedrich Kalkbrenner, too, was an apostle of the pianistic orgy. While never matching Czerny's record, he made up in personnel what he may have lacked in hardware, securing for one concert a line-up including, as well as himself, Chopin, Mendelssohn and Ferdinand Hiller (one of the most admired pianists of the day).

The self-styled king of the multipiano 'monster concert', however, was Louis Gottschalk, whose previous high of ten pianos, in Madrid in 1852, was eclipsed by his subsequent assemblage of forty pianists for an extravaganza in Havana. Eight years earlier, in Philadelphia, Henri Herz had announced an equally populous cast but in the event sadly failed to muster more than eight.

A soirée of 1908. By this time the piano alone was thought inadequate to the demands of 'proper' entertainment. It was relegated to the role of providing accompaniments to balladeers.

Child Prodigies

One particular form of musical entertainment has held its own through many generations of changing fads and fashions, and its fascination remains timeless. Curiously enough, however, the high-pressure marketing of child prodigies seems only to have started with Mozart (and, coincidentally, with the rise of the piano), around the middle of the 18th century. Of earlier prodigies we know next to nothing. Today the traffic in child wonders is as crowded as ever, though their commercial exploitation is mercifully on the wane.

Perhaps the most remarkable in recent memory is the Russian-born Evgeny Kissin, who was already among the truly great pianists by the time he reached his teens. Unlike many former prodigies he has made the transition from *Wunderkind* to mature artist with no apparent trouble. The Greek-born Dimitri Sgouros enjoyed a considerable flurry of attention in the 1980s, playing some of the most demanding showpieces in the repertoire after hearing or seeing them only once. He made some impressive recordings, too, and then receded until recently from public view, as has the diminutive

A quartet of Bechsteins giving a flavour of the multiple keyboard concerts that were all the rage in the mid 19th century.

Spaniard Leandro Aconcha, who in 1972, when he was all of five, made sold-out debuts all over Europe, playing Mozart's most taxing piano sonata and some of Chopin's most fearsome études. The mysteriously neglected English pianist Michael Roll (a great artist) was playing Schubert Impromptus at the same age, and at twelve made his London debut at the Royal Festival Hall, playing the Schumann Concerto. Such things are far more common than we tend to realize, and to a large extent are more or less taken for granted among pianists. Of great modern-day virtuosos, many, including Daniel Barenboim, Peter Serkin, Vladimir Ashkenazy and Shura Cherkassky, were seasoned performers, and in some cases worldwide celebrities, before they reached their teens.

But consider some of their predecessors: Camille Saint-Saëns (1835–1921) was playing and composing at three, and when at the age of ten he made his official recital debut, he offered to play as an encore any of the 32 Beethoven Sonatas. At the age of eight, Felix Mendelssohn (1809–47) could play all of the Beethoven symphonies on the piano, from memory, except for the Ninth, which had not yet been written. Much later in the century came the Polish-born Mieczyslaw Horszowski (1892–1992). At

three, though not yet able to read music, he played some of Mendelssohn's Songs 'Without Words', and at five could play all of Bach's Two and Three Part Inventions from memory and transpose them into any key at a moment's notice. He was also able to take down in dictation anything he heard, no matter how complex, and had embarked on his own (short-lived) composing career with a number of piano pieces, including two sonatas, and a meticulously scored work for full symphony orchestra.

The greatest genius of them all, however (some believe, the greatest genius in human history), was Wolfgang Amadeus Mozart. In 1763, when he was seven years old (admittedly elderly by Horszowski's standard), he was carted around Europe by his father and deliberately exploited as a highly lucrative commodity, tastefully presented at the royal courts, but sinking almost to the level of a vaudeville act when performing for the rising bourgeoisie. Their success generated a bandwagon, and in 1791 we find a certain 'Miss Hoffmann', aged six, performing concertos on the piano and the harp, assisted on the kettledrum by her brother, who had at the time advanced to the imposing age of three-and-a-half.

Far more numerous than any of these artists, however, are those who have failed to mature into great or even moderately distinguished musicians. Too often, these have been the hapless victims of parental ambition, forced into exceptional accomplishments by mental and sometimes physical cruelty (Ruth Slenczynska's autobiography *Forbidden Childhood* makes depressing reading). Others have been casualties of social prejudice. Fanny Mendelssohn and Anna-Maria Mozart, sisters of Felix and Wolfgang respectively, were also remarkable prodigies, but a time when it was thought 'unseemly' for respectable young ladies to be professional musicians. So much so, indeed, that several of Fanny Mendelssohn's highly accomplished songs and piano pieces were published under her brother's name. Felix himself believed that his sister's gifts were greater than his own.

A roll call of spectacular prodigies would have to include the names not only of those mentioned above but of Chopin, Liszt, Anton Rubinstein, Karl Tausig, Ferrucio Busoni, Josef Hoffman, Artur Rubinstein, Claudio Arrau, Julius Katchen and Martha Argerich, but there are many more.

Nine-year-old Daniel Barenboim practising before a concert in Vienna in 1952.

31

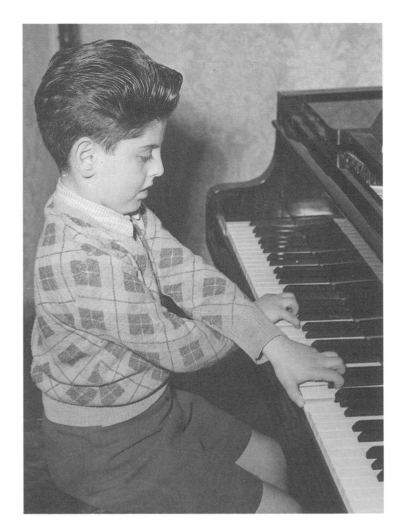

Home, Sweet Home: The Piano and Popular Music

Throughout the 19th century, and acceleratingly so after around 1850, the standard domestic fare for the piano had little to do with the 'quality' output of the great composers. The piano works of Schubert, Chopin, Schumann, Weber, even Mendelssohn, had never really held a candle, in terms of sales, to pieces like *Flower Song, Shower of Pearls, Edelweiss* (way before Rodgers and Hammerstein), *Dance of the Demons, Alpine Maid's Dream, Simple Confession, Monastery Bells,* and so on, with a special place of honour held for such hardy standards as *The Battle of Prague, The Maiden's Prayer, The Last Hope* and *The Dying Poet.*

Dances, as ever, ranked high in the literature of the parlour, and as ever they incurred the alarmed disapproval of upstanding moralists on both sides of the Atlantic. The waltz craze had been bad enough (comparable in notoriety with the advent of rock 'n' roll in the 1950s), but this had been succeeded by the rage for the polka – scorned in the *New York Herald* for its "low origin" and branded as "indecent, immodest and scandalous." Another self-appointed guardian of the nation's moral fibre castigated it as "a kind of insane Tartar jig performed to disagreeable music of an uncivilized character." Such attacks, of course, only served to further the cause of this disreputable foreign import, and the family piano now groaned under the weight of the sheet music devoted to it.

It was not, however, the piano piece, whatever its source or kind, but the popular song with piano accompaniment that constituted the greatest weight. Indeed, the song sheets outnumbered purely pianistic numbers by a ratio almost impossible to calculate. To begin with, they mimicked or duplicated the after-dinner ballads so popular in England, but as the century wore on, the balance shifted increasingly to home-grown products.

Particularly successful were the songs of grocer-turned-composer Stephen Foster (1826–64), the first authentically

Greengrocer-turned-songwriter Stephen Foster was the first truly popular American composer.

popular American composer. Many of his songs, all with piano accompaniment, broke all sales records for music in the United States. Although Foster valued his drawing-room ballads most highly, it was his pseudo-black 'minstrel' songs that made his name immortal, among them *Oh Susanna!, Camptown Races, Old Folks at Home* (or *Swanee River*) and *My Old Kentucky Home.* In addition to his songs (175 in all), Foster wrote twelve purely instrumental works and made numerous arrangements, but these were often embarrassing efforts, and none of them has stood the test of time. Foster's success reflected a trend which was still gathering force in the second decade of the 20th century, namely the true popularization of popular music. The ascending 'lower' classes, particularly in America but to a significant extent in Britain too, increasingly rejected the long tradition of aping their social 'betters'. The fact is that a new kind of folk music was emerging, perhaps the last we shall ever see in this remorselessly electronicizing world. Now known generically as jazz, it represented a trend of downward social mobility in which, to a degree unknown even in the days of Rousseau's 'noble savage' in the 18th century, society's 'betters' now aped their social 'inferiors'. The titles and lyrics of the songs told their own story, as songs like *I Dream of Jeannie with the Light Brown Hair* were gradually supplanted by such hitherto uncouth and unabashedly plebeian conceptions as *Bedelia, I'd Like ta Steal Ya, Who Threw the Overalls in Mrs. Murphy's Chowder* and *Guess I'll Have to Telegraph Ma Baby.* Where once operatic tunes and medleys had ruled the domestic roost, now the hit numbers from blackface 'minstrel shows', vaudeville entertainments and musical comedies all but eclipsed them. Their unprecedented popularity, however, was not a reflection of their quality alone, which was often minimal; it owed much to new and aggressive forms of marketing. Not only were songs advertised in print and widely distributed in shops, but

phalanx upon phalanx of sheet music salesmen were dispatched into the country at large, selling their wares in face-to-face confrontations not entirely unlike those engineered by various evangelical religious groups.

The sheet music industry had become very big business indeed, and its unchallenged capital was a small pocket of New York city which came picturesquely to be known as Tin Pan Alley. Its name was well earned. When George Gershwin was hired by one Tin Pan Alley publisher to 'plug' his songs in 1914, he found himself confined to a cubicle with a pile of Remick's latest offerings on the piano, which he was expected to pound out all day long for the benefit of potential customers. His was only one of several identical cubicles on that particular floor, and none of them was sound-proofed. Nor did work stop with the close of the formal business day. Gershwin and his fellow pluggers were often despatched to nearby towns and cities as well as to vaudeville theatres in Brooklyn and Manhattan.

The 'minstrel' songs, depicting the lives of Southern blacks, were the most popular of Foster's output.

With its brash sales techniques and its unprecedented turnover, it achieved profits hitherto undreamt of, a single song often selling as much in a year as previous 'hits' had sold in a quarter-century. As a contributor to the *New York Times* put it in 1914, "The consumption of songs in America is as constant as the consumption of shoes, and the demand is similarly met by factory output." And every one of these sales betokened a home or institution boasting at least one piano, or occasionally its humbler cousin, a harmonium. In the decade between 1895 and 1915, the piano, in addition to its long-established role in the family, became a frequent focal point for teenage socializing in which the latest hit tunes were pounded out, sung and often danced to. In many ways this marked the highpoint of the piano's popularity, as it marked the swan song of the home as a social centre. The advent of the cinema, and the 'liberation' of women after the First World War were to usher in a new order, but the story of the piano itself was by no means over.

Will they, won't they? Punters listen to a tune hot off the song-sheet press in Tin Pan Alley.

From Piano Player to Player Piano

To have music without effort is one of humanity's oldest dreams. Even in the age of CD-ROM we continue to try and perfect its fulfilment. Where keyboard instruments are concerned, the search goes back at least to Tudor times. Henry VIII had a self-playing virginal, quaintly noted in the inventory of his possessions as "an instrument that goethe with a whele without playinge uppon." By the beginning of the 19th century, a number of instrumental craftsmen and chronic gadgeteers were investigating methods of applying similar principles to the now fast-evolving piano.

In 1825 a man named Courcel came up with a device which led, though at a snail's pace, to a revolution in home music-making. In effect, it was a piano-playing robot: a multi-fingered creature in a cabinet, which was wheeled up to an ordinary piano and let loose on the keys. Like most other bits of 19th-century pianistic hardware, it went by an impressively Greek-sounding name, the 'Cylindrichord'. It was operated by a crank at the side, and it won fulsome praise from a respected English musician, Dr. Thomas Busby, who rather blew his cover by declaring "The Cylindrichord is an admirable and efficient substitute for a first-rate performer on the pianoforte."

From this description the Cylindrichord sounds uncannily like the player pianos which seriously threatened to put the conventional piano out of business at the start of the 20th century, except that it was operated by means of a clockwork mechanism whereas they worked on the pneumatic principle of the automatic loom, first demonstrated by its inventor in 1801. This pneumatic principle involved a perforated card on a cylinder, which allowed certain needles to pass through it (hence the perforations) while rejecting others. It was only a matter of time before someone realized that the same principle could be applied to air pumped by a bellows. By this means, musical instruments, too, could be controlled. In the case of a keyboard instrument – the piano or the organ – the pressure of the air would control the movement of the keys. All that was necessary was to put the right size and shape of hole in the right place and the puff of air would play whatever notes were desired.

It was not until 1863 that the first complete pneumatic piano-player was built and patented, and even then it was a failure. By the late 1870s the idea had begun to intrigue tinkerers on both sides of the Atlantic, but the public steadfastly refused to take it seriously. Ten years later

Taking the mediocrity out of interpretation – recording music for use on the player-piano, 1909.

An advertisement of October 1901 extolling the virtues of the Apollo piano player.

there were a number of machines on the market whose sophistication left the Cylindrichord far behind, yet still the great consuming public proved unready. By the turn of the century, however, both machinery and public had begun significantly to change.

In the case of the machines, the crank, which was all too suggestive of a kitchen meat-grinder, was replaced by a twin-pedalled footpump, leaving the operator's hands free to manipulate other controls, which affected speed and volume. The feet, too, acquired versatility, one operating the footpump controlling the bellows, the other controlling the piano's sustaining pedal. In theory, at least, the consumer could now be offered a virtuoso finger-technique, unlimited repertoire and a high degree of interpretative control – and at no expense of effort. It was a turning point, with grave implications for the traditional piano industry. The manufacturers had finally found the public's Achilles' heel, and now moved rapidly into high gear. "Perfection without practice" became the slogan of the day, and there was no shortage of customers who swallowed the bait whole.

The player piano, or pianola as it was variously called, certainly eliminated wrong notes and the need for finger exercises, and it could play as fast and as loudly as any human being without tiring. But perfection, as promised in the advertisements, required more than that. To most musically sensitive ears, the player piano continued to sound as mechanical as it unarguably was.

Having taken the effort out of technique, the manufacturers now addressed a subtler problem. If they were to capture the widest possible public they would have to take the effort out of interpretation as well. The merely perforated rolls of paper controlling the selection of notes left too much to the purchaser's imagination. As a result, the rolls began to appear with specific guidelines, printed on the paper of the rolls and indicating exactly how the tempo and rhythm of any piece should be controlled Rolls with ready-made interpretations authorized by world-famous pianists began to appear. Follow their guidelines and you would produce a reasonable facsimile of their own performances – so ran the theory. The reality was all too evidently otherwise. Now came the breakthrough.

In 1904 a German called Welte invented a device by means of which a piano roll, properly perforated, could record with a high degree of fidelity performances given by living pianists. Welte called his invention the Mignon and soon persuaded many of the greatest pianists and composers of the day to record on it. It was a turning point in musical history.

In 1905, six per cent of the pianos sold in the United States were player pianos. Within a decade the percentage had more than quadrupled, and a mere five years after that the figure had risen to seventy per cent. Accordingly, fewer and fewer people learned to play the conventional piano. There was no doubt about it. The institution of genuinely home-made music was in a state of alarming decline.

His Master's Voice

With Welte's invention of the so-called 'reproducing piano' (as distinct from the mere player piano), the piano entered its final phase of development. Almost at once, rival systems began to appear: the German firm Hupfeld's DEA in 1905 and, most significantly, two American variants in 1913 which were effectively to corner the market from then on. These were the Duo-Art, made by the Aeolian Company, and the acronymic Ampico system from the American Piano Company. Hupfeld countered with the 'Duophonoloa' and 'Triphonola', which held their own in the European market for some time.

The basic technology behind all of these makes was much the same. The artist, by means of his or her touch, would complete an electrical circuit by way of sensitive contacts placed just beneath the key. This in turn activated a set of lead pencils to record varying patterns of longer and shorter marks on a piano roll revolving at the standard speed. The length and spacing of these marks corresponded exactly (according to theory, at least) with the player's every nuance of tone, articulation and phrase. In fact, the earlier rolls required another musician to mark every detectable nuance into a copy of the music as the pianist played, these later being translated into meticulously cut perforations, designed to control the flow of air to correspond as accurately as possible to the pianist's actual performance. Needless to say, the pianist was invited to collaborate in these post-production sessions, thereby overcoming the notational limitations inevitably encountered by the 'secretarial' musician, whose taxing job it was to mark the score during the recording.

All of these systems, of course, claimed to reproduce with perfect fidelity any performance recorded on them, whether by a rank beginner or a world-famous soloist. Testimonials tumbled from the lips and pens of countless virtuosos, all stating unequivocally that their finest renderings had now been replicated in every detail. Some were prepared to back their claims in public. There was one occasion in London when the great Alfred Cortot, as subtle and poetic a player as ever lived,

Every home should have one – the Duo-Art pianola made by the American Aeolian Company.

performed a Liszt rhapsody, dovetailing, in alternation, his own 'live' performance with that preserved on a Duo-Art roll. No less sophisticated a critic than the razor-sharp Ernest Newman later swore that "with one's eyes closed it was impossible to say which was which." In New York, Mischa Levitzky, one of the most popular virtuosos of the day, did the same thing, again with a Liszt rhapsody. The Aeolian Company, in particular, induced most of the important American orchestras to mount special concerts featuring 'invisible' soloists (the piano's keys moving up and down with startling rapidity, as though the ghost of Liszt himself were sitting there, unseen).

Within a short time of its unveiling, the reproducing piano was disgorging performances by such eminent artists as Busoni, Debussy, Grieg, Mahler, Richard Strauss, Paderewski, Pugno, Saint-Saëns, Carreño, Artur Rubinstein, Gershwin, Harold Bauer and many others. From the artists' point of view, the reproducing piano had many advantages over the gramophone (Rachmaninov was still making piano rolls as late as 1933, seven years after the introduction of electrical recording). For a start, it was not limited in duration to the four-and-a-half minutes per side allowed by the 78 rpm gramophone record. The sound quality was as good as the piano on which the roll was being played, and vastly preferable, in the view of many listeners, to the distorted sound of the piano as captured by the microphone, let alone all the hiss and crackle through which it had to struggle en route to the ear. Also, wonder of wonders, any wrong or missing notes could be corrected before the roll was released. But are these rolls really as accurate as claimed by the artists themselves? This remains a contentious issue, and it has been pointed out many times that the artists had a vested interest in the sales of the rolls, which in no way threatened their livelihood. In most cases, comparison of an artist's piano roll with his or her gramophonically recorded performance of the same work leads to a measure of scepticism.

Reproducing mechanisms could be fitted to any piano, and were frequently added to otherwise conventional instruments by

such makers as Steinway, Chickering, Broadwood, Knabe, Weber and Steck. The Welte-Mignon mechanism alone was available at one time in 115 different makes of piano.

The recording process itself could be long, laborious and expensive. The Duo-Art and Welte's Duophonola were appropriately named, since the normal procedure required the making of two different recordings, one of the notes and pedalling, the other of the dynamics and shading. The Duo-Art used a finely-tuned mechanical device to measure the rebound of the hammer from the string, while the Ampico employed a special 'spark chronograph' to record the speed of the hammer during its last quarter-inch of travel prior to impact, with a trace on a revolving cylinder to record the degree of power applied by the pianist. In the case of Duo-Art rolls, there were sixteen degrees of dynamic intensity deemed to be sufficient to cover all extremes, and the most sensitive and finely graded 'crescendos' and 'diminuendos' in between. When this information was proudly revealed to the great pianist Artur Schnabel, in a bid to

secure his participation, he shook his head regretfully. "Unfortunately," he replied, "I use seventeen."

A further bonus of the reproducing piano was its liberation of composers from the hitherto insuperable limitations of a pianist's ten fingers. Among noted figures who took advantage of this to write directly for the new instrument were Stravinsky, Hindemith, Malipiero, Herbert Howells, and the American Conlon Nancarrow, who decided to devote his entire output to the medium.

Almost from its very beginnings, the expensive fashion for reproducing pianos was living on borrowed time. While it was to be some decades before the gramophone could rival the actual sonority of the instrument, it could catch details and subtleties of nuance more convincingly than all but the best piano rolls. What effectively killed off the reproducing piano, however, was not the gramophone but the radio, whose fidelity exceeded all recordings throughout the first half of the century.

The reproducing piano was the acme of the automatic piano (pianola) medium.

At the Movies

With the advent of the cinema in the late 1890s the piano acquired a new, indeed a leading role. The besetting irritant of the silent film, ironically, was the din made by the early projectors. The piano was conscripted to drown them out. Keyboard hacks would show up, sit down, pound away indiscriminately until the film was over, and then go home. Strange to say, the idea of matching the music to the images on the screen was originally of secondary importance. Pianists who were clever improvisers found a stimulating new forum for their talents, and were much in demand, but they were always in the minority. For those less gifted, the music of the masters was mercilessly plundered in the name of entertainment. Nothing was sacred. Bach chorales, speeded up or slowed down as required by the circumstances on the screen, rubbed shoulders with equally elastic bursts of Verdi operas, which were then supplanted in their turn by puffs of Offenbach or slabs of Wagner, and so it went, the music being pulled about to fit the pictures with no regard to its claims on art. As the industry gained ground, works by Beethoven, Schubert, Brahms and Tchaikovsky were chopped up, reconstituted and widely distributed to cinemas as being "suitable for scenes such as tree-felling, aeroplane dives and Red Indian chases". Other works, similarly dismembered, found themselves retitled: 'Sinister misterioso' by Mozart, 'Weird moderato' by Mendelssohn, 'Victorious allegro' by Grieg. Wagner's and Mendelssohn's famous wedding marches were used not only for screen marriages but for fights between spouses, acrimonious divorce scenes, and so on. As one veteran cinepianist put it, "We had no mercy. Finales from famous overtures, with *William Tell* and *Orpheus* the favourites, became *galops*, Meyerbeer's *Coronation March* was slowed down to a majestic *pomposo* to give proper background to the inhabitants of Sing-Sing's death-house, *The Blue Danube* was watered down to a minuet by a cruel change in tempo."

As early as 1909, certain film companies began to issue 'specific suggestions for music', and by 1913 there were bulky catalogues catering to the needs of every conceivable mood or circumstance. *The Sam Fox Moving Picture Music Volumes* by J. S. Zameenik were pioneers in the field, but the standard text for years to come was Giuseppe Becce's *Kinothek* of 1919. Perusers of the *Handbook of Film Music*, in which Becce had a hand, were offered numerous menus, such as the following:

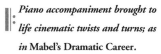

Piano accompaniment brought to life cinematic twists and turns; as in Mabel's Dramatic Career.

DRAMATIC EXPRESSION
(MAIN CONCEPT)

① CLIMAX (SUBORDINATE CONCEPT)
  (a) Catastrophe
  (b) Highly dramatic *agitato*
  (c) Solemn atmosphere; mysteriousness
    of nature

② TENSION – *Misterioso*
  (a) Night: sinister mood;
  (b) Night: threatening mood
  (c) Uncanny *agitato*
  (d) Magic: apparition;
  (e) Impending doom: 'something is going
    to happen'

③ TENSION – *Agitato*
  (a) Pursuit, flight, hurry;
  (b) Flight
  (c) Heroic combat
  (d) Battle
  (e) Disturbance, unrest, terror;
  (f) Disturbed masses, tumult;
  (g) Disturbed nature: storm, fire

Tyrone Power as Eddy Duchin, trying to keep at least one hand on the keyboard while falling under Kim Novak's spell.

Less taxing to decode were the short and atmospheric compositions purveyed by the rash of original composers that emerged to satisfy the cinema's musical needs. Among the suggestive titles on offer were *Heavy, Tragic, Suspense, The Slimy Viper, Ashes of Vengeance, Help! Help!, The Lure of Crimson, The Drug, Frowsy Freddie, Gruesome misterioso, The Crook's Shadow, Dark Intruder* and *Broken Vows*.

The success of the piano in cinemas led to its widespread adoption in other public places – in shops, schools and even, occasionally, in factories, where it fulfilled the function now played by recorded Muzak.

With the advent of the sound film, or 'talkie', in 1927, however, the age of the cinema pianist came to an abrupt end. In the lavish Hollywood film scores that set the tone of the new era, the piano itself hardly got a look in, save for a handful of so-called biopics ostensibly portraying the lives of various great composers, such as *Song of Norway* (Grieg), *A Song To Remember* (with Cornel Wilde as Chopin), *Song Without End* (featuring Dirk Bogarde as Liszt, with Jorge Bolet doing the actual playing), and *Rhapsody in Blue*, with Alan Alda's father as George Gershwin. Then, too, there has been the occasional feature whose storyline involves pianists of one kind or another: *The Seventh Veil* (with Ann Todd at the mercy of the sinister James Mason), *The 5,000 Fingers of Doctor T, Moonlight Sonata*, featuring the legendary Paderewski, *The Alien Corn*, starring Dirk Bogarde as a young pianist of decidedly un-Lisztian talent, *The Eddie Duchin Story, The Competition* (Richard Dreyfuss and Amy Irving bidding for keyboard stardom under the stern eye of teacher Ann Bancroft), and *Madame Sousatska* (with Shirley MacLaine as an eccentric old-world piano teacher).

Very occasionally, a film score will contribute an item to the mainstream concert or record repertoire, as in the case of Richard Addinsell's *Warsaw Concerto* (composed for the 1941 film *Dangerous Moonlight*) or, some fifty years later, Michael Nyman's score for Jane Campion's *The Piano* subsequently moulded by the composer into a fully fledged concerto which was recorded with Kathryn Stott as the outstanding soloist. Conversely, the use of an established concert work as a film score has sometimes introduced millions not only to the work in question but to the world of classical music generally. This happened with the use of Rachmaninov's Second Piano Concerto (the model for Addinsell's *Warsaw Concerto*) in Noel Coward's *Brief Encounter*, starring Trevor Howard and Celia Johnson as the star-crossed middle-aged lovers. And although the revival of interest in the ragtime composer Scott Joplin was already well underway by 1973, *The Sting* (with more than a little help from Paul Newman, Robert Redford and pianist-composer Marvin Hamlisch) turned *The Entertainer* into Joplin's biggest worldwide hit.

The Gadgeteers

To this day, there is no keyboard instrument that will serve all needs equally. The clavichord, for instance, was touch-responsive almost to a fault. In terms of the subtle rises and falls of the human voice, no other keyboard instrument, even today, can match its range – extending even to the use of a vibrato on a single note. But, even supposing that one finds its tone satisfactorily refined, its dynamic range is miniscule compared to any of its keyboard siblings. In strength, it can barely make it across a large room, much less a concert hall. The harpsichord, by contrast, can produce the most splendid sonorities, and has a precision of 'attack', so-called, unsurpassed by even the most up-to-date concert grand piano. But it cannot inflect; the subtle contours of human song are beyond the reach of its mechanism, and of all keyboard instruments it sounds (because it is) the most unequivocally mechanical. A similar shortcoming afflicts the organ, though not as much as is generally believed. But what instrument can sustain so rich a panoply of sounds in perpetuity? Certainly not the piano, whose tone, acoustically speaking, declines at a dramatic pace immediately after its initial impact. Needless to say, the search for a keyboard instrument that can combine all the above virtues, but with none of their drawbacks, has exercised the minds of

A boon to players, the six-manual Janko keyboard was a threat to piano makers; see page 43.

instrumental craftsmen for centuries. The problem was particularly acute in the days when the piano had not yet triumphed over the harpsichord.

Combinations and Couplers

No-one was more tireless in his efforts to secure the best of both world's than Johann Stein of Augsburg. In 1769 he devised a combined harpsichord and fortepiano to which he gave the modest name of 'Polytoniclavichordium'. This was soon exceeded in complexity by two further hybrids, the 'Vis-à-vis Flügel', a one-manual piano faced by a three-manual harpsichord, and requiring two players to operate it, and the 'Melodika', a combination piano and touch-sensitive reed organ.

Not to be outdone, the Still Brothers of Prague produced in 1796 a combination piano and organ, housing 230 strings, 360 pipes and 105 different tonal accoutrements, including bells, drums, cymbals, triangles and other ephemera. It was three feet nine inches in height, seven feet six inches long, three feet two inches wide, had two keyboards, one above the other, and no fewer than twenty-five pedals, designed to unleash a further armoury of special effects, including lute, flute, bassoon, viola da gamba, French horn, clarinet and a battalion of others too numerous to list.

Some makers, harking back to the use of octave couplers found in organs and some of the larger harpsichords, tinkered with ways of applying the same mechanism to the piano. Thus, octave passages could be played perfectly synchronized without requiring a second's practice. Technical difficulties were all but eliminated, and the full resonance of an orchestra could, or so the sales pitch suggested, be unleashed by a single player. While most of these devices were confined to the piano's lower registers, some couplers were made to duplicate the upper registers as well, as in Johann Streicher's example of 1824. Among the great pioneers of the 'orchestral' coupler were Erard Frères of Paris, whose first model, produced in 1812, comprised two independent soundboards, one above the other and each with its own separate action and strings. The upper set was tuned an octave higher than the lower. Both sets of strings could be combined or separated at will by means of a pedal. In 1845, Benjamin Nichels took a new approach to the idea by combining an upright with a grand (horizontal), each provided with its own separate keyboard, action and strings. Inevitably, the practical cost of all this ingenuity was to make the touch intolerably heavy, which explains why these thrilling but unwieldy mutations never caught on.

A more viable proposition was the so-called 'Duo-clave' (literally, 'double-keyboard') piano, designed to enhance the

fashion for piano duets. In effect it was basically two pianos in one, two separate keyboards and actions being placed opposite each other within a single case. In 1800 the Viennese Matthias Müller devised a small upright with keyboards on both sides, the main disadvantage here being that players of small stature were unable to see one another. In some cases, as in Erard's Duoclave of 1812, the extra keyboard came as an optional extra.

Many of the most ingenious modifications of the piano were those designed to sustain the sound after the initial impact, on the model of the organ. Indeed, some of these experiments aimed at a (theoretically) straightforward combining of the two instruments. One example, from Mainz in Germany, confronted the player with no fewer than 250 different stops, but even this was eclipsed by a Bohemian machine combining in a single case a concert grand piano and an organ of some 360 pipes.

More intriguing, as well as more challenging, than these outright hybrids were a number of devices aimed at actually bowing the strings, these being applied to both the harpsichord and the piano. The earliest known example dates from as early as 1570. In 1742 a Frenchman called le Voir incorporated into a harpsichord a cello and viola, the bowing of which was controlled by treadles, the 'bows' consisting of rollers wrapped in horse-hair. Seven years on, he had

expanded his cabinet orchestra to include two violins and a drum. Another harpsichord, from 1764, included a built-in lute and consort of viols. This, however, was thoroughly upstaged by a Moravian instrument of 1730 which boasted 790 strings and 130 different registrations.

Heavy, hopelessly complex and unreliable, these ingenious and daring inventions soon withered on the vine – as did a series of automatic transposing devices, whereby the player could theoretically play Chopin's 'Black Key' Etude in the right key without ever leaving the white keys.

Unusual Keyboards

The layout of the keyboard itself has been the subject of much experimentation. From time to time, attempts have been made, for instance, to adapt it to the natural, lateral movement of the arms, that is to say in a curved line rather than a straight one. Despite the successive failures of all such aberrations, the idea has been floated in one generation after another, ever since the Viennese piano maker Neuhaus first wheeled it out in 1780. Two other Austrians, Staufer and Haidinger, took out a patent on their own variant in 1824, to be followed by other inventive hopefuls in 1840, and again

Professional duo Nettle & Markham with their 1920s Pleyel double concert grand.

42

Kate Ryder 'preparing' a piano for a performance of John Cage's **Sonatas and Interludes.**

in the late 1860s. It was not until the second decade of the 20th century, however, that the day of the concave keyboard looked like dawning at last. In 1910, a German named Clutsam succeeded in persuading a number of leading manufacturers to adapt and market his own version, which enjoyed a flurry of celebrity when certain reputable artists played on it in public, leading to its eventual, if brief, adoption by the Königliche Hochschule für Musik in Berlin. As its only real beneficiaries were children and diminutive women (who could now reach octaves and tenths with ease), it soon fell out of favour and joined its predecessors on the scrap heap.

More fruitful, and marginally longer-lived, have been the various attempts at extending the piano's range and versatility by means of pedal keyboards, on the model of the organ. The Metropolitan Museum in New York houses one such instrument, built by Andreas Stein of Augsburg as early as 1778, and in the first half of the 19th century in Paris the firms of Erard and Pleyel separately experimented with the idea. It enjoyed a sufficient vogue in the United States to become the house speciality of the Henry F. Miller Piano Company, and on both sides of the Atlantic it attracted some distinguished advocates. In 1843, Louis Schöne constructed

a pedal piano for Felix Mendelssohn, comprising 29 notes and connected to a separate action, placed at the back of an upright, where a special soundboard covered with 29 strings was built into the case. Whatever its virtues, however, this promising hybrid was never a really viable proposition, and would probably have sunk without trace had Robert Schumann not written some of his loveliest pieces for it. No serious lover of piano music should be ignorant of his beautiful Etudes in the Form of Canons, or of Debussy's equally beautiful arrangement of them for two pianos. Their neglect by duo-piano teams is hard to understand.

Far and away the most imaginative and truly musical experiment with the keyboard was conducted by a fiercely moustachioed Hungarian nobleman in the 1880s. Paul von Janko was himself an accomplished pianist, a graduate both of the Vienna Conservatory and the Polytechnicum and the possessor of a restless and enquiring mind. Far from being a dotty gadgeteer, he was the first man thoroughly to re-examine the very principles of the conventional keyboard, whose layout had been essentially unchanged for more than four hundred years – four centuries of almost cataclysmic change in the evolution of European music. Moved by a desire to bring the most difficult modern works within the grasp of the serious amateur, he devised a multiple keyboard of several tiers, similar in appearance to that of the organ, but closer in principle to the then new-fangled typewriter (invented in Milwaukee, Wisconsin, in 1867). With this ingenious device, adaptable to any piano with a normal action, such wide-spanned intervals as the tenth and even the twelfth could be played with ease, simply by moving a finger to the rank immediately above or below the principal keyboard in use at the time.

Making child's play of virtuoso barnstorming, however, posed a dangerous threat to business. If Granny or little Emma could dash off Liszt's *La Campanella* in the family parlour after tea, what price the heroic accomplishments of a Rubinstein, Tausig or Bülow? The publishers, fearing that widespread adoption of the Janko keyboard would depreciate their stock, since naturally everything would have to be refingered, implacably opposed the invention. Hordes of potentially imperilled teachers equally deplored it. Piano manufacturers, too, were thrown into a quandary. The chips were down. Despite sympathetic advocacy by no less a manufacturer than Blüthner, Janko's brainchild did not stand a chance. By the outbreak of World War I, it was all but officially declared dead. By the time the German Paul Perzina devised his brilliant Reversible Key-Bottom (by means of which the Janko as well as the conventional keyboard could be used on the same piano), it was too late. Janko adjourned to Constantinople, where he died a disappointed man in 1919. But as one commentator put it at the time, he had got his bearings wrong. The commonest failings of pianistic lions were not technical but musical. What was called for was "a patent mind attachment for brainless virtuosi". (For the curious, a working example of Janko's invention may be seen at the National Museum in Washington D. C.)

Like Janko, Emanuel Moór was both Hungarian and an accomplished, even distinguished musician – a pianist and a prolific composer who had works commissioned by the likes of Ysaÿe, Casals and Flesch. His Duplex Coupler Grand Piano, unveiled in 1921, was effectively two pianos in a single case, tuned an octave apart, with two manuals, as on the harpsichord, which could be played separately or in combination, thus enabling the pianist to play such masterworks as Bach's 'Goldberg' Variations (written for double-manual harpsichord) without recourse to tricks and compromise. The inventor's British wife, Winifred Christie, made an excellent recording of Bach's famous Toccata and Fugue in D minor on the Moór Piano, as it was more simply known, but despite such convincing evidence of its merits and the warm recommendation of Sir Donald Tovey, the instrument was too limited in scope, too ungainly to behold and too difficult to play.

The Prepared Piano

Where the piano is concerned, almost all of these experiments have one thing in common: they subscribe to a fundamental concept of the instrument as a kind of surrogate orchestra, designed, in earlier times, as much for the domestic performance of symphonic and operatic reductions as for the interpretation of original keyboard works, idiomatically conceived for the unique properties of the piano as it had then evolved. In the 20th century, blessed with an extraordinary range of electronic miracle-workers, the need for such instruments disappeared, but the story of the piano was far from dead. Nor, as demonstrated by a number of well-known composers, did its radical modification require vast expense and technical wizardry.

As the 20th century got underway in earnest it looked as though the piano had been exploited to its full potential. From the crystalline clarity and precision of Bach and Scarlatti to that Debussyan wash of overtones suggesting "an instrument without hammers", from the 'orchestral' sonorities of Beethoven and Liszt to the percussive ferocity of Bartók and Prokofiev, the piano looked to have yielded up its every secret. And if you confined your demands of the instrument to the keyboard, perhaps it had. It was thus a natural progression of evolution when the American composers Henry Cowell (1897–1965) and John Cage (1912–92) took to exploring the insides of the piano. In Cowell's *Sinister Resonance* of 1930, the strings are strummed while certain keys are held down but never struck, and in the weird but rather wonderful *The Banshee* (1925) he ignores the keyboard altogether, employing the pianist's hands exclusively on the strings, sweeping over them in gliding wails and occasionally plucking them, harp-style, while an assistant looks after the pedals to great colouristic effect. It was also Cowell who first took to modifying the piano's innards with various foreign objects placed on or between the strings – an innovation taken up and expanded by Cowell's pupil Cage in his Sonatas and Interludes for Prepared Piano, in which rubber erasers, nuts, bolts, screws, mutes are called for. The 'prepared piano' has also been employed by Lou Harrison, Christian Wolff and Toshiro Mayuzumi. Certain of Cage's innovations bypass strings, keys and pedals altogether, requiring the pianist to 'play' only the instrument's outer casing, or merely (in the famous *4'33'*) to sit facing the keyboard for the specified duration without once coming into contact with the instrument. Nor did Cage rest content with such passivity: in his *Water Music* of 1952 the pianist is required to pour water from pots, blow whistles under water, use a radio and a pack of cards, and other similar diversions.

Means and Expression

I T WOULD BE POINTLESS TO TRY TO SEPARATE THE EVOLUTION OF THE PIANO ITSELF FROM THE MUSIC WRITTEN FOR IT. EACH HAS NURTURED THE OTHER AT EVERY STAGE OF THEIR JOINT DEVELOPMENT. WHERE FORM IS CONCERNED, VERY FEW ARE PECULIAR TO THE PIANO, AND THOSE THAT MAY AT FIRST SPRING TO MIND (THE CONCERT STUDY, OR ETUDE, SAY, OR THE OPERATIC PARAPHRASE), THERE IS HARDLY ONE THAT COULD REALLY BE DEFINED AS A FORM. STUDIES, FOR INSTANCE, HAVE NO PREDETERMINED STRUCTURE AND EXIST IN MANY FORMS, WHEREAS THE PARAPHRASE OR FANTASY IS A LARGELY IMPROVISATORY CONCEPT, EACH INDIVIDUAL EXAMPLE DEFINING ITS OWN FORM FROM WITHIN. EVEN FUGUE IS NOT SO MUCH A FORM AS A TEXTURE, A TECHNIQUE.

STYLE IS SOMETHING ELSE AGAIN. ALL GREAT COMPOSERS BRING TO THEIR WORK A CHARACTER AND 'ACCENT' ALL THEIR OWN. SOME, LIKE CHOPIN, LISZT AND DEBUSSY, HAVE A KEEN SENSE OF INSTRUMENTAL IDIOM – CHOPIN'S WORKS, IN PARTICULAR, ARE ALMOST INCONCEIVABLE FOR ANY INSTRUMENT OTHER THAN THE PIANO – WHEREAS OTHERS, LIKE SCHUBERT, WROTE GREAT MUSIC WHICH IS OFTEN SURPRISINGLY AWKWARD TO PLAY AND EASILY RECAST IN 'ORCHESTRAL' TERMS. GREAT COMPOSERS HAVE RARELY USED ESTABLISHED 'FORMS' IN THE SAME WAY AS ONE ANOTHER. INDEED, THEY MAY NEVER HAVE USED A GIVEN FORM TWICE IN QUITE THE SAME WAY. NO TWO OF BEETHOVEN'S 32 PIANO PIANO SONATAS, FOR INSTANCE, ARE FORMALLY IDENTICAL. WHAT FOLLOWS, THEN, IS AN OVERVIEW OF THE MAIN FORMS AND STYLES USED BY THE GREAT COMPOSERS FOR THEIR KEYBOARD WORKS, AND OF THEIR HISTORICAL EVOLUTION.

Accompaniments

In the 17th and 18th centuries the reputation of a keyboard player often rested as much on his ability to improvise as on the performance of fully notated solo pieces. At this time it was customary to write out only the bass line and to indicate the required harmonies by means of various figures, Arabic and Roman. The means of their fulfilment were left to the player, who could respond with anything from simple block chords to considerable elaboration. The ability to do this required a very thorough knowledge of both harmony and counterpoint. The latter was especially important in comparatively thin or exposed textures, such as a duo or trio sonata, in which the melodic line improvised by the keyboard player must avoid duplication of the melodies written out by the composer for the other instruments. The use of a keyboard instrument as a standard part of the Baroque orchestra arose largely from a need to supplement the often anaemic string tone and to provide a harmonic (essentially chordal) backdrop to the melodic intertwinings of the contrapuntal weave. It also served to provide a precise rhythmic framework, marking the beginnings of beats rather like a super-musical metronome. The term 'continuo' for this part derives from the fact that while other instruments may drop out and re-enter, the keyboard accompaniment continues throughout. Another term used for this system is 'thorough bass', a corruption of 'through bass'; that is, a bass which continues or goes 'through' the whole composition. Readers who want to pursue a hands-on approach to this technique can turn profitably to the four-pages which Bach devotes to it in the musical 'notebook' he compiled for his second wife, Anna Magdalena.

Schubert by Klimt. Schubert's songs present considerable difficulties for accompanists.

This learned, sophisticated, 'aristocratic' art increasingly fell by the wayside with the rise of a mercantile middle class in the 18th century, as the long reign of polyphony gave way to the simpler textures of accompanied melody, known in the trade as 'homophony'. The upward social mobility of the emerging bourgeoisie brought a new market with a taste for ease. The challenges of the old figured bass were replaced by simple harmonic accompaniments which lent themselves to a stock set of formulas, of which the most famous is the routine spelling out of three-note chords (bottom-top-middle-top), known as the Alberti bass. For those to whom even the Alberti bass was too challenging, there was a still more simplified accompaniment-figure called the 'murky' (pronounced 'moorky'). This consisted of a continuous waggling back and forth of simple broken octaves – a kind of monotonously rhythmic counterpart to the drone bass of the bagpipes.

There was, however, one sphere in which the old continuo tradition held its ground. For many decades, the orchestral 'conductor', insofar as there was one, directed the performance from the keyboard (usually sharing the burden with the First Violinist). This practice persisted well into the 19th century, long after thorough bass had become effectively a forgotten art. As orchestras grew bigger, and more massive in their sonority, the relatively weak-toned harpsichord yielded to the steadily increasing power of the piano. Haydn directed all his symphonies from the keyboard, and Mozart in his piano concertos expected the soloist to play continuo throughout the orchestral *tutti*.

The Piano and Song

Well before their use in orchestras, indeed from the time of their invention onwards, keyboard instruments have been used to accompany the human voice or some other solo instrument. Here, too, the figured bass was widely employed, but by the time of Bach's death in 1750 it had largely disappeared. The rise of the middle-class, and the place of women in it, can be charted by even a quick look

at the catalogues of contemporary music publishers, which boasted such conspicuously un-aristocratic titles as *Melodious Songs for the Fair Sex*, *Little Songs for Little Girls*, *Little songs for children for the encouragement of virtue* and *Lullabies for German Wet-Nurses*. But the breadwinner himself was not to be left out. He could give voice to *Joyful Songs for German Men*, join his best beloved in *Songs for the Family Circle*, *Songs for Innocent Pastime*, or best of all, in *Songs Sacred to Burgherly and Domestic Happiness, to Amiable Morality, and to Guiltless Pleasure*. The printed music gave two lines only, the melody for the right hand, the generally scanty bass line for the left, with the texts of the songs printed in between. The right hand invariably doubled the melody in unison with the voice. In some cases, even the text was dispensed with. A typical publication of the day made it plain that "such songs need not be sung, but may be played on the keyboard alone".

By the beginning of the 19th century, the more sophisticated among the middle class had advanced well beyond *Lullabies for German Wet-Nurses*, and were now singing songs by Mozart, Haydn and Beethoven, soon to be joined by Schubert, by general consent the greatest songwriter ever. In these the 'murky' played no part, and Alberti a very small one. In many cases, the accompaniment was not only of very considerable difficulty (in the case of Schubert's *Erl King*, one of the major hurdles of a pianist's repertoire), but more important to the impact of the song than the melody itself. And in Schumann, another of the very greatest songwriters, the singer is often still less crucial than the piano since the accompaniment frequently doubles the voice part.

45

Music written for the domestic market in the late 19th century had to be easy and tuneful.

Variation Forms

Variations have been among the staples of the keyboard literature for almost as long as there have been keyboards. Where the piano repertoire is concerned, there are four basic types:

Melodic Variation

In this form the original tune is decked out in a sequence of stylistic and textural dresses (ornamental turns, decorative scale passages, rhythmic, textural and tempo alterations and so on) while the chief outline of the melody, the original harmonies and the overall form of the theme are preserved, though the mode (major or minor) may sometimes be altered. The same techniques of variation can be applied, within the given limits, even to those elements which are retained from the original theme. The bass line, for instance, may be amplified by a trill, fast or slow, or be doubled in octaves, and the basic chords of the original harmonies may be 'seasoned' with decorative notes adjacent to those of the original. Almost all variation sets of the Classical period (loosely, 1750 to 1820) are melodic variations, Mozart's being perhaps the best known.

Harmonious Alliances

Those in which the harmonic pattern of the theme is preserved while melody, tempo, rhythm, texture (chords or intertwining melodic lines) and mode (major/minor) may change beyond recognition. The most famous, and the greatest, keyboard example of this type is the monumental set of 30 by J. S. Bach popularly known as the 'Goldberg' Variations. Thereby hangs a tale. The work was commissioned by the insomniac Count Kaiserling to ease and occupy his mind during his long, undesired periods of wakefulness. Contrary to widespread belief, it was never intended as a soporific. It derives its nickname from the name of the Count's harpsichordist Johann Goldberg, whose forcibly sleep-denying task was to perform it. Lasting more than an hour if all the indicated repeats are observed, the work is a miracle of beauty, ingenuity, refined complexity and technical brilliance. Originally composed for a double-manual harpsichord, it poses particularly challenging problems for the pianist when the hands cross or effectively play on top of one another, as they frequently do.

Passacaglia or Chaconne

In this type the theme is not a self-sufficient melody but either a constantly reiterated bass line, above which the upper parts may change, or a series of chords, whose harmonic sequence and unvarying rhythm is reiterated, unchanged, throughout the composition. This form of variation is called both 'passacaglia' and 'chaconne' (in the Baroque era the two names were used interchangeably). Unusually, it seems to have been imported to Europe from Mexico in the 16th century. It enjoyed enormous popularity in the Baroque era. Handel left two remarkable keyboard chaconnes, both in G, one sporting no fewer than 63 variations and being in effect a guided tour through every kind of keyboard figuration then in use. The most famous passacaglia for the piano is the set of 32 Variations in C minor by Beethoven.

Fantasia-variation

In this type only a part of the original theme (a single melodic phrase, a motto rhythm, a structural form) is retained as a basis for variation, all other aspects and parts being subject to very considerable transformation. The Fantasia-variation will often have a recurring theme or fragment that serves as an agent of unity. It reached the peak of its development in the 19th century, particularly in the piano works of Schumann and Liszt

Variation Techniques

For much of the 18th century, variation-making was a fairly stereotyped business, in which a few standardized techniques were applied in rather the same way as a shop window mannequin is draped in a series of skirts, blouses, jackets and trousers as the seasons go by. In the case of piano variations, these include such handy, ready-made garments as the following (and a veritable bucket-full of rhythmic alterations):

◑ Neighbouring, auxiliary notes (jargon: appogiaturas), or a collection of same, turning the original single-note into a decorous, elliptical turn of four.

◑ Repeated notes, by means of which 'la la' might be rhythmically livened into 'la ta-dada, la-ta-dada'.

◑ Decorative scale passages, whereby a single 'c' might be transformed into an eight-note glide up or down the octave from one 'c' to another.

◑ Rolled or rhythmically unfurled chords (jargon: *arpeggios*; ie, harp-like), whereby a single melodic 'c' would be turned into a 'c' chord.

◑ A breaking up of the original melody in a sequence of right-hand/left-hand alternations, giving a somewhat hiccuping effect.

◑ The simple transformation of a single note into a prolonged trill, with or without a connecting 'turn' into the next note.

◑ A change of mode, from major to minor (or, more rarely, *vice versa*) for one variation.

◑ A change of tempo. Most sets will include at least one slow variation.

◑ A change (almost always in the last variation) of metre, from duple to triple or *vice versa*)

◑ Alternating right-hand and left-hand variations, often followed by variations in both simultaneously.

◑ Changes of key (rare, although in Beethoven's so-called Variations in F major, Op. 34, no two variations are in the same key).

Left: The composer and publisher Anton Diabelli, who in 1819 asked 50 composers to contribute a variation apiece to his waltz.

The struggles of Prometheus, mythical champion of mankind, inspired Beethoven to write his Variations in E flat, Op. 35.

Mozart's Variations on *Ah, vous dirai-je, Maman* ('Twinkle, Twinkle, Little Star') provide an excellent introduction to these techniques, partly because the theme is so familiar and thus easy to keep track of. It also provides an excellent example of the stereotyped layout of late 18th-century keyboard variations.

There was a time when many of Mozart's sets of variations were among the most popular items in the repertoire. Today, only two remain anywhere near the centre: the one just mentioned, and another on an aria by Gluck *(Unser dummer Pöbel meint)*. After Bach's 'Goldberg' Variations, the most famous sets in the piano repertoire are Beethoven's 'Eroica' and 'Diabelli' Variations (the latter leaving no variational stone unturned), Brahms's great sets on themes by Handel and Paganini, Schumann's Symphonic Etudes and *Carnaval* (an excellent example of 'fantasia-variations'), Liszt's *Totentanz* (variations on the medieval chant Dies irae) for piano and orchestra, Rachmaninov's Rhapsody on a Theme of Paganini (the same theme used by Brahms) and Dohnanyi's Variations on a Nursery Song ('Twinkle, Twinkle' again). Many more examples may be found within larger sonata designs. No great composer was more intensively concerned with variations than Beethoven. They occur repeatedly in his sonatas and reach their highest peak in the outer two of his last three Sonatas, nos. 30 and 33 (Opp.109 and 111, respectively).

Dance Forms and the Suite

Suite is a common name for any instrumental work in several movements, especially, as in the Baroque era, a sequence of dances. The standard order of movements in the 17th and 18th centuries was 'allemande', 'courante', 'sarabande' and 'gigue', with a host of optional extras, such as the 'gavotte' and 'minuet', commonly inserted between the 'sarabande' and the 'gigue'. The most famous Baroque suites to have become part of the central piano repertoire are the six Partitas, the six English Suites and the six French Suites by Bach. Where the piano is concerned, Handel's many keyboard suites have fallen into almost total neglect, although isolated movements still surface occasionally, especially the theme and variations known as 'The Harmonious Blacksmith'.

The suite by name plays a relatively slight part in the piano music of the 19th and 20th centuries. Among the best-known are Grieg's delightful, deliberately archaic 'Holberg' Suite (more often heard in the arrangement for string orchestra), and Debussy's 'Children's Corner' and *Suite bergamasque*. Important suites in all but name abound, however, prominent among them being most of Schumann's so-called piano 'cycles', of which the most significant are *Papillons*, the *Davidsbündlertänze*, *Carnaval*, the *Humoreske*, *Kreisleriana*, and *Faschingsschwank aus Wien*, Brahms's cycle of sixteen waltzes, Op. 39 (designed for performance as an integrated set, several have come to be known on their own), Mussorgsky's 'Pictures at an Exhibition' (better known in Ravel's orchestration, it was originally written for piano), Ravel's own *Tombeau de Couperin* and *Valse nobles et sentimentales*.

ALLEMANDE A rather stately dance of German origin, it became the standard opening movement of the Baroque suite, and was frequently used as such by Bach and Handel, whose suites are the earliest to have secured a place in the modern piano repertoire. In moderate tempo, it has four beats to the bar and is generally initiated by an introductory note (or 'upbeat') before the first accentuated note, producing the same rhythm as the word 'begin'.

BOUREE A brisk French dance in duple metre, dating from the early 17th century and one of the optional movements of the Baroque suite. As such, pianists may occasionally encounter it in Bach, more seldom in Scarlatti, and once only in the case of Chopin, whose solitary contribution rates as little more than a curiosity.

COURANTE One of the standard movements of the Baroque suite, the dance exists in several different forms, differentiated by national traditions. The Italian 'corrente' is in quick, triple time, with continuous running figures in a straightforward melody-and-accompaniment texture. The French 'courante' is a more sophisticated version, characterized by a teasing rhythmic ambiguity (resulting from changes of metre within the dance, so that the emphasis changes from three to two accented beats in a bar) and a greater contrapuntal weave (the intertwining of two or more melodic strands). In his suites and partitas, many of them now firmly established in the central piano repertoire, Bach uses both forms, but favours the French (most ingeniously, perhaps, in the second English Suite, where the rhythmic ambiguity is uppermost). The Italian type crops up in the French Suites Nos. 2, 4, 5 and 6, and in the Partitas Nos. 1, 3, 5 and 6.

GAVOTTE A 17th-century French dance in duple metre, it was one of the most popular optional numbers in the Baroque suite. Bach was particularly fond of it and used it frequently in his keyboard works. In moderate tempo and duple metre, it often has a two-note upbeat figure rhythmically analagous to the word 'tambourine'.

An engraving by Duclos of an 18th-century ball. Suites were made up of various dance-style movements. In the 17th and 18th centuries the structure was allemande, courante, sarabande and gigue, with other dance types inserted between the sarabande and gigue.

GIGUE Traditionally the final movement in Baroque suites, it concludes virtually all of Bach's, and derives originally from the 16th-century Irish or English 'jig'. In triple time, it frequently uses fugal techniques, dotted rhythms (uneven: long, short-long, short-long) and inversion (the beginning of the second half often being the opening tune upside down). The gigue from Bach's fifth French Suite has become particularly popular.

MINUET A French dance, originating in the folk tradition, it can be seen as an ancestor of the waltz, sharing with it the triple metre and moderate tempo, and an elegance born of long cultivation by the royal courts of Europe. It became one of the most popular optional dances of the Baroque suite (examples abound in Bach) and is the only one to have survived the decline of the suite in the middle of the 18th century. It was widely used in the piano music of Mozart, Haydn and Beethoven, and after lying more or less dormant through most of the 19th century, it was briefly revived by Debussy (*Suite bergamasques*, 1890), Fauré, Bartók, Schoenberg and Ravel (*Menuet antique*, 1895, *Sonatine*, 1905, *Menuet sur le nom d'Haydn*, 1909)

SARABANDE A stately dance of Spanish origin, it became the standard slow movement of the Baroque suite, and is thus present in all of Bach's and Handel's fully-fledged suites. In triple metre, its most obvious characteristic is an accent or prolonged tone on the second beat of each bar. Although there is no hint of such things in its Baroque manifestation, it began life as a wild and wanton love dance. As one 17th-century treatise put it, "it is a dance and song so lascivious in its words, and so ugly in its movements, that it is enough to inflame even very honest people." After a hundred years or so of neglect, the sarabande staged a modest comeback in the late 19th and early 20th centuries, when its champions included Brahms, Debussy (*Pour le piano*, *Images*, *Hommage Rameau*), Satie (*Trois sarabandes*, Busoni (*Sarabande und Cortège*, Op. 51), Saint-Saëns, Reynaldo Hahn, Albert Roussel, Germaine Tailleferre and Henry Brant (Two Sarabandes for Keyboard, 1931). There are many examples of 'covert' sarabandes, masquerading under other names, notably the theme of Bach's 'Goldberg' Variations, where it is identified only as 'Aria'.

The minuet and gavotte (the latter a favourite of Marie Antoinette) were among the many regional country dance styles that were 'civilized' by becoming popular at court and in the houses of the nobility.

Popular and National Dance Forms

The dance is as old as music itself, and most of those dance forms which have flourished in the realm of piano music have their origins in folk tradition. While some, like the waltz, have become universal, most have been closely identified by their composers with specifically national characteristics. In many cases, their relative 'exoticism' is a large part of their appeal. They form part of that magic carpet of the imagination which is one of music's most precious attributes. And, like us, they exist both individually and in families (see Dance Forms and the Suite).

CAKEWALK Originating with black American slaves in the 19th century, this was a brisk, sassy, syncopated dance closely related to ragtime. It was popularized in blackface minstrel shows and later in vaudeville and burlesque, and became a craze in both America and England. The cakewalk found its way into European concert life by way of the 'Golliwog's Cakewalk' in Debussy's 'Children's Corner Suite' of 1908.

DUMKA Bohemian dance originating in Ukraine and characterized by sudden mood changes, from the deeply melancholy to the wildly exuberant. The most famous pianistic *Dumky* are those used by Dvořák in his Piano Quintet and the so-called *Dumky* Trio, Op. 90.

ECOSSAISE Not in fact Scottish, despite its name, this is a quick, brisk dance in duple metre which enjoyed a great vogue in the early 19th century. Beethoven wrote a celebrated set, and Schubert many.

FANDANGO A triple metre Spanish dance of moderate to quick tempo, it is traditionally danced by a pair to the accompaniment of castanets and guitar. Stylized piano fandangos include examples by Granados (in *Goyescas*) and Falla (transcribed, from 'The Three-cornered Hat').

FARRUCAS A lively, exciting dance in duple metre, immortalized by Manuel de Falla in 'The Miller's Dance' from his ballet 'The Three-cornered Hat'. It has often been played in Falla's own transcription for piano.

The cakewalk – an invention of black American slaves in the 19th century, its rhythms were immortalized by Debussy in the 20th.

FURIANT Of Bohemian origin this is one of the most exciting dance types anywhere, in brisk triple-metre and characterized by exhilarating cross-rhythms.

JOTA This is an exception to the pervasive influence of flamenco, coming from the north of Spain and associated

50

The polka has been a source of endless inspiration to composers of dance music.

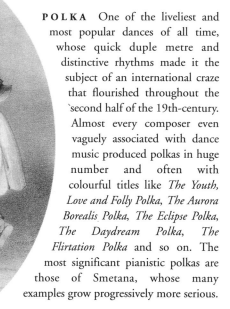

with the region of Aragon. It has been memorialized in piano music by de Falla, and by Liszt in his *Rhapsodie espagnole*.

LANDLER A country cousin (and precursor) of the Viennese waltz, it smacks more of hob-nailed boots on the village green than of chandeliered ballrooms. It has a somewhat slower pace than the waltz but is easily confused with it. Mozart, Beethoven, and, particularly, Schubert, wrote many pianistic examples.

MAZURKA A Polish sung folk dance (or rather a family of three different but closely related dances), it frequently sounds like a rather rough-shod form of the waltz, with its triple metre and its characteristic accent on the second or third beat of each bar – not entirely unlike the Ländler. Contrary to widespread belief, it was cultivated outside Poland well before Chopin popularized it throughout the Western world. In the 18th century it enjoyed considerable favour, albeit in a very urbanized form, among the aristocracy of Europe and by 1830 it had made its way into drawing rooms in both Russia and the United States. Chopin alone, however, transformed it into an art form of the greatest subtlety and range. His 50-odd mazurkas contain much of his most inspired and original music, and their emotional range is immense. Of his followers, only Karol Szymanowski (1882–1937) wrote mazurkas of even vaguely comparable quality, although there are isolated examples from Glinka, Tchaikovsky and Borodin.

POLKA One of the liveliest and most popular dances of all time, whose quick duple metre and distinctive rhythms made it the subject of an international craze that flourished throughout the `second half of the 19th-century. Almost every composer even vaguely associated with dance music produced polkas in huge number and often with colourful titles like *The Youth, Love and Folly Polka*, *The Aurora Borealis Polka*, *The Eclipse Polka*, *The Daydream Polka*, *The Flirtation Polka* and so on. The most significant pianistic polkas are those of Smetana, whose many examples grow progressively more serious.

POLONAISE Like the mazurka, the polonaise was originally a sung dance, or rather a whole family of them, and by the late 16th century it had found its way out of its native Poland and into neighbouring countries, becoming particularly popular in Scandinavia. It remained, however, in the realm of folk music and might have continued in relative obscurity for centuries if it had not been taken up by the Polish nobility, in whose hands it began rapidly to evolve into the distinctive and representative dance that it is today. During this transitional period it continued to be sung, though its words naturally underwent considerable sophistication and its rhythms began to approach those of the courtly polonaises to come. Strictly speaking, the polonaise is not so much a dance as a kind of processional – a *march dansante*, despite its triple metre. Its most outstanding feature was its insistent, rather martial rhythmic motto, and it was this purely musical property that recommended it to non-Poles such as Bach, Mozart,

51

Spanish dances like the fandango are of gyspy origin and accompanied by guitar and castanets. All self-concsiously 'Spanish' keyboard music, from Scarlatti to Rodrigo, features guitar imitation.

Beethoven, Weber, Schubert, Field and Schumann. It fell to the Polish-born Chopin to infuse the form with a nationalism which resounds to this day. In his hands the polonaise became a blazing, patriotic tone-poem in which the fearsome, the tender and the grandiose combined to unique effect and lifted it into the highest realms of art.

RAGTIME For many years the terms 'ragtime' and 'jazz' were used interchangeably, suggesting that they were synonymous. The confusion is easy to understand since virtually all of the early jazzmen also played ragtime, but the differences betwen them were significant. Ragtime, in its purest sense, was never improvised but, like jazz, rather composed, often with considerable exactitude, by literate musicians reared in the Western 'classical' tradition. Like jazz, it had important origins in the musical styles of black plantation workers, many of them former slaves, but was equally influenced by the hymns, dances and marching bands of the white community. The particular 'feel' of ragtime, however, can be strongly discerned in the music of the white American composer-pianist Louis Moreau Gottschalk (1829–69), especially in the piano pieces *Bamboula, Le Bananier*, and *Le Banjo*, composed many years before ragtime was heard of. The term itself is descriptive of the music's 'ragged' rhythms, though the syncopations in early ragtime were very mild compared to what they later became. The first published piece bearing the name 'rag' was *Mississippi Rag* by Kerry Mills (1897), but the uncrowned king of ragtime composers was Scott Joplin (1868–1917). His *Maple Leaf Rag* of 1899 became the most famous of all piano rags, and his music, strongly classical in its leanings, was the subject of a major revival during the 1970s. Few now dispute his place in the pantheon of American music. As one historian put it, Joplin's rags are "the precise American equivalent, in terms of

The waltz has attracted composers of almost every kind. Waltz kings of the keyboard have ranged from Schubert and Liszt to Poulenc and Stravinsky.

53

SEGUIDILLA An Andalusian dance in fast triple metre, sung to the accompaniments of castanets and guitars, with four bars of castanet rhythm recurring after each verse.

TANGO The origins of this dance are still disputed, but it is generally accepted as a Latin American (and specifically Argentinian) dance, which is said to have developed in the slums of Buenos Aires. With its catchy, slinky, sexy rhythms ('*dash*, dot-*dash*-dash' or '*dot*-dash, dot-*dash*-dash'), it became one of the most popular dance forms of the 20th century.

TWO-STEP A quick-tempo ballroom dance of American origin but similar in many respects to the polka, it enjoyed great popularity on both sides of the Atlantic before being ousted by the foxtrot during the 1910s.

WALTZ Very probably the most famous dance in the world, it has attracted composers of almost every kind since its meteoric rise in the early 19th century. The composers who have contributed most to the piano waltz in particular (as opposed to the glittering orchestral waltz sequences by the Strauss family and others) are Schubert, Chopin, Liszt, Brahms and Ravel, but there are delightful, polished and masterly piano waltzes, too, by Weber, Anton Rubinstein, Chabrier, Fauré, Glazunov, Godowsky, Poulenc, Stravinsky and many others, including such disparate sources as Gershwin, Hans von Bülow, Donizetti and Britten.

Like many folk dances, it was in triple time with a characteristic emphasis on the second beat. Emanating originally from Austria and southern Germany, the taste for the waltz swept across Europe like a virus and it was soon as at home in Paris as in Vienna.

No form more typified the glitter and grace of 19th-century Parisian salons than the waltz, and the Chopin waltz in particular. Chopin's early, Polish waltzes have little of the dash and the bejewelled elegance of his Parisian works, and unlike most of their later siblings could easily be danced to (the notion of the idealized 'concert' waltz then being in its infancy). They retain something of the formalized grace and slower speeds of the minuet, with its courtly undertones, and follow its simpler structure.

With few exceptions, Chopin's mature waltzes are sparklingly extroverted, pianistically elegant and emotionally refined. Shrewdly designed for the ears of Parisian *salonistes* and the fingers of the more advanced dilettantes, they assured the composer's success both socially and commercially, and have enjoyed a popularity which shows no sign of abating.

Liszt's many waltzes have been almost entirely ignored with the single and striking exception of his famous 'Mephisto' Waltz, No.1. Brahms's waltzes are altogether briefer than any of Chopin's or Liszt's and were intended to be played as a self-contained sequence. They exist in two versions for one pianist (the second a simplified version of the first) and one version for two.

The Boston two-step enjoyed great popularity before being ousted by the polka, an enthusiasm fuelled by the welter of tunes produced in its honour.

native dance music, of minuets by Mozart, mazurkas by Chopin, or waltzes by Brahms." The basic structure of the mainstream rag – an introductory section, normally little more than a fanfare, followed by several contrasting sections – is very close to that of the typical Viennese waltz or military march of the period.

The ragtime craze spread to Europe in the first two decades of the 20th century and attracted a number of well-known concert composers such as Satie, Stravinsky, Hindemith and Milhaud, who left some of the more curious examples of early 'crossover' music.

In the 1970s, such classically trained and sophisticated musicians as Joshua Rifkin, William Bolcom and William Albright demonstrated in their own compositions that the ragtime idiom was far from exhausted, Bolcom, in particular, finding a style very much his own in such seductive pieces as *The Graceful Ghost* and *Seabiscuits*.

Free Forms

Prelude and Fantasia

The terms 'prelude', 'fantasia' and 'fantasy' are basically interchangeable. Originally, as its name implies, a prelude was a movement which served as a kind of introduction to another movement, generally a fugue (and to this day 'prelude' and 'fugue' go together like bread and butter, Romeo and Juliet, Night and Day or Laurel & Hardy). But formal preludes may also precede not merely one movement but several, as in the suite or partita. Then, too, there are many self-contained preludes that precede nothing but each other. This is true of many preludes by Bach, and all of those by Hummel, Chopin, Alkan, Rachmaninov, Szymanowski, Debussy and Scriabin. In general, when it does precede another movement, the prelude is relatively short, though there are a number of examples in Bach where the prelude is far weightier and more expansive than the succeeding fugue. In most preludes and fugues, there will be some common, unifying feature, even if only of mood. An interesting departure from this approach was the publication in 1837 by the then very famous pianist and composer Ignaz Moscheles of '50 Preludes in major and minor keys, intended as short introductions *to any movement*'.

Preludes originated with the tuning of instruments just prior to a performance, and developed into an improvisatory preamble. The improvisatory element is still evident in early keyboard preludes, which are without time-signatures and bar-lines. In the story of the piano, it survives more elaborately in the fantasy or fantasia, which may or may not exist on its own. As the term implies, the emphasis here is on the rhapsodic, colourfully imaginative, subjective element and the movement often ranges freely through a number of keys, and draws on different elements of style: aria, virtuoso keyboard writing, operatic-style recitative and so on. A good, early example of this approach can be clearly heard in Bach's famous 'Chromatic Fantasy and Fugue'. For players of reasonable advancement, the emotionally adventurous fantasies of Bach's son Carl Philip Emmanuel are well worth looking through. Of Mozart's three piano fantasies, the most dramatic is the clearly sectionalized C minor, K. 475, composed as an extended prelude to his great C minor Sonata and is frequently heard both in that context and on its own. The D minor Fantasy, K. 397, is very much slighter and considerably easier to play.

Among the most notable examples from the 19th century are Beethoven's highly improvisational, not to say bewilderingly eccentric Fantasy in G minor, Op. 77, the magnificent

Liszt's piano transcription of Isolde's 'Liebestod' from Wagner's opera Tristan und Isolde *is wonderfully realized.*

Fantasia in C minor for piano, chorus and orchestra and the two *Sonatas alla Fantasia*, Op. 27 (No. 2 being the famous 'Moonlight' Sonata); Schubert's four-movement 'Wanderer' Fantasy and the still greater Fantasy in F minor for piano duet, and Schumann's Fantasia in C, Op.17 (though in keeping with the much-expanded Romantic notion of the concept, this is a highly organized, beautifully disciplined work which is really closer to the world of sonata). The commonest forms of fantasy in the 19th century, however, were highly virtuosic reworkings and elaborations of popular and operatic tunes, such as those of Liszt, Thalberg, Kalkbrenner. Some of Liszt's operatic fantasies (from Bellini's *La Sonnambula*, Donizetti's *Lucia di Lammamoor*, Verdi's *Simon Boccanegra* and Wagner's *Flying Dutchman* and *Tristan*, for example) are counted among the most important works of his output.

Toccata

Closely related to the basic concept of prelude and fantasia is the keyboard toccata, whose forms are many and whose definitive characteristic is a degree of keyboard virtuosity. Bach's early toccatas are not among his greatest works, but the C minor in particular still finds its way fairly regularly into piano recitals. In the 19th century the toccata became an endangered species, the only great example being Schumann's early Toccata in C, Op. 7 – a formidably difficult and, in the right hands, very exciting one-movement work in sonata form. In the 20th century, the only notable toccata to find its way into the central repertoire is Prokofiev's lone example.

Fugue

With the fugue, so often preceded by the above forms, we come to one of music's most needlessly off-putting terms. Today, the very name has imposing, academic connotations. It represents the cerebral, intellectual, mathematical side of music, whereas words like 'song', 'romance', 'aria', 'duet', 'dance' and 'rhapsody' conjure up less forbidding images, altogether more immediate and expressive. Even a term as drily descriptive as 'variations on a theme' has a more welcoming ring to it. Fugue is music for the head. Fugue is highbrow. Fugue is discipline. Fugue is 'them' not 'us'. Fugue is rules. Fugue is polysyllabic polyphony. But fugue is also Bernstein's *West Side Story*, Britten's *Young Person's Guide to the Orchestra*, the Alec Templeton/Benny Goodman jazz hit *Bach Goes to Town*. Above all, fugue is musical conversation.

The basic principle of the fugue is found in the simplest children's round, such as Nous n'irons plus au bois.

Fugue is melody. And, contrary to widespread belief, fugue is not a form, but a particular texture, a procedure by which different melodies, or fragments of melody, intertwine to become greater than the sum of their parts.

Most children from musical families unknowingly encounter the basic principle of the fugue in the simplest rounds: *Frère Jacques*, *London's Burning*, *White Sands and Grey Sands* and so on. A melody, or a fragmentary melodic idea, is answered by another voice singing the same tune while the original voice sings a kind of counter-melody. Fugues, like rounds, can be for two voices, or for three or four voices, the main difference being that fugue allows for a far greater range of variation. It is indeed a form of 'theme and variations', except that the themes varied will be at least two: the initial 'subject' and the counter-melody accompanying the repetition of the subject by the second 'voice'. Fugues may be short (a number of keyboard fugues by Bach barely exceed one page) or long (the final movement of Beethoven's towering *Hammerklavier* Sonata occupies roughly 11 minutes in performance); they may be straightforward (as in Bach's more elementary examples) or strenuously complex – *Hammerklavier* again).

During the Baroque era, fugues were a dominant feature in the musical landscape. By Mozart's time, they were on the wane; Mozart's own fugues could be numbered on the fingers of one hand. Of Baroque fugues which have held a central place in the piano literature, far and away the most famous are those of Bach's 'Well-Tempered Clavier' – two books of 24 Preludes and Fugues, one in each key. As these rely heavily for their effect on the clear delineation of several melodic strands at once, the piano, with its fantastic dynamic range and potentially infinite variety of shadings, is felt by many people to be the ideal instrument for them, although in the last quarter of our century this has become an increasingly unfashionable view. Among the most compelling advocates of the 'Well-Tempered Clavier' have been Edwin Fischer, who made the first complete recording of 'The 48', Rosalyn Tureck, Glenn Gould, Tatiana Nikolayeva, Sviatoslav Richter and Andras Schiff.

Of the fugues written expressly for the piano, the most famous are those by Beethoven (in the sonatas Opp. 27 Nos 1, 106 and 110, and in the 'Diabelli' and 'Eroica' Variations); Schubert (in the final section of the great 'Wanderer' Fantasy); Mendelssohn (Six Preludes and Fugues); Liszt (Prelude and Fugue on B-A-C-H); Brahms (Variations and Fugue on a Theme of Handel); Franck (Prelude, Chorale and Fugue); and Shostakovich (24 Preludes and Fugues).

The Principles of Sonata Form

The Classical concept of sonata form is intrinsically dramatic, relying on the opposition and eventual reconciliation of conflicting states of being. The most basic confrontation is between one key and another, related but distinct, and existing in a state of mutual tension. No technical knowledge on the part of the listener is required to appreciate this relationship. Anyone whose musical interest has got them as far as this page can savour it while being in ignorance of the concept it embodies. This holds true for all music. Indeed, if technical knowledge were required for its enjoyment, the names of Bach, Handel, Mozart, Beethoven, Schubert, Brahms, Fats Waller, Elvis Presley and the Beatles would be no more than footnotes in human history.

This contrast of key, consciously perceived or otherwise, is demonstrable through the joint sciences of mathematics and acoustics, and belongs firmly, at one level, to the world of objectivity. It forms the background against which a sonata movement is unfurled, in much the same way as the scenery and lighting, within the clear-cut boundaries of the stage, provide the backdrop to a play. The presence in the stage-set of a door and a double bed is an objectively verifiable fact. The drama that can take place between the one and the other is potentially infinite, but until sound or movement (an offstage scream or the entry onto the stage of an actor, for example) is introduced we have no play. The set itself is no more than a three-dimensional picture. There is one crucial difference, however, between the stage set and the phenomenon of key. While there is no intrinsic relationship between a door and a bed, there is a clearly demonstrable connection between the opposing keys of a sonata movement.

If you strike a lowish note on the piano very loudly, and hold it down, with your ear fairly close to the strings, you may hear that vibrating within it is another, higher note. In point of acoustical fact, there are *many* different pitches set into vibration by that first, fundamental note – by any note. The fact is that every note we hear is actually a kind of harmonic rainbow. But there is one of these secondary, auxiliary, varyingly audible tones which is stronger and more clearly distinguishable than all the others. It hovers over the main note rather as the moon, in its orbit, hovers over the earth: a clearly observable, individual entity which is nevertheless subsidiary to a more powerful, more central entity, the earth, or as we say in music, the tonic – that fundamental tone whose most strongly discernible 'moon' we call the dominant. The analogy can be stretched further to embrace a whole solar system, in the shape of a scale. Once again, no technical knowledge is necessary to hear the unique phenomenon of tonal gravity in action. Play or sing any incomplete scale, starting, say, from Middle-C (your ear will

tell you whether it is incomplete or not), and you will find that the last note you played leaves you unsatisfied, that it has about it a feeling of unrest, an apparent will to be something other than it is, a will to move; that it generates a feeling of energy. From here on, acoustics can tell us nothing. That energy, that sense of tonal magnetism, is the single most important ingredient of all sonatas, and it takes us beyond the scientifically objective into the psychologically subjective.

After the opposing of two main key-centres, and arising directly from it, the most essential contrast of the sonata idea is between stability and flux (or to put it more immediately, between confidence and doubt, inertia and movement,

Robert Delaunay's 'Circle Forms', in which form is broken up by light to create structurally organized coloured planes. In music sonata form is constructed out of an entire scale made up of keys that exist in a state of mutual tension.

all of these, so far, are in the nature of props and costumes. As yet we have the makings, the trappings of a drama, but no cast. This the composer delivers in the form of themes: self-contained melodies, or melodic figures, which are short enough and simple enough to develop further as the drama unfolds. In most cases the two opposing key-fields will have their own contrasting themes – contrasting not only in character but in form: if the first main theme is based on a rising broken chord, set out in a jagged, militaristic rhythm, the second may be based on a falling figure of evenly spaced, undifferentiated time-values. Very often the two main themes, whose interaction and/or conflict provides the basis of the drama, will be cut from the same cloth, as it were - the second being basically a variant of the first, turned upside down (the first movement of Beethoven's *Appassionata* Sonata is a good example). In the course of the drama, a sweetly serene tune in the major may reappear tragically altered, now cast in the minor mode and supported by different harmonies or rhythms, or both. Conversely a tragic, doom-laden theme may emerge transformed by a change into major and a subtly smoother rhythmic profile.

Techniques

The techniques used to achieve these various ends may be summarized as follows:

AGENTS OF STABILITY A clear sense of key, achieved by the juxtaposition of tonic and dominant, without the use of so-called 'accidentals' (any notes not found in the scale or principal chords of the home key). The opening theme will almost always be based on the definitive chord of the home key (in the case of C major, C-E-G), either spelling it out at the start (as in the opening of Mozart's so-called 'Easy' Sonata, K. 545), or filling it in, either scale-wise or through various ornamental figures.

Themes, however brief, will tend to be well-rounded and symmetrical.

The rhythmic emphasis will be on the main structural beats of the presiding metre (again, as in Mozart's K. 545).

AGENTS OF FLUX Use of 'alien' tones (accidentals) to weaken the sense of key and introduce an element of harmonic drift.

Weakening of metric stability by more ambiguous time-patterns, generally more flowing and less differentiated, sometimes stressing the 'weaker' beats at the expensive of the metrically definitive 'strong' ones (ie, beats 2 and 4 in a four-beat bar rather than the structurally stable 1 and 3).

Well-defined themes will give way to more fragmentary material.

knowledge and suspense, and so on). We now have a double duality of contrasts: of keys, and of conditions. A further contrast is of modes: of major and minor, which can exist within a given key as well as in contrasting ones. This leads on to a similarly dualistic opposition of different types of character: masculine/feminine, angry/happy, tragic/comic, active/passive, energetic/ quiet, etc. These, in turn, can be emphasized by the use of opposing textures: from the chordal, harmonic and hymn-like to the melodic, polyphonic and speech-like. And still more contrasts are marshalling: those of rhythm, from the regular, stable and metrical to the irregular, unpredictable and syncopated. But

57

The Sonata: Forms and Patterns

The term 'sonata' covers such a wide range of styles, techniques and forms that no single definition can possibly do it justice. Originally, it served simply to distinguish a piece that was played, or sounded (the term deriving from the Latin *sonare*, 'to sound') from one that was sung (a 'cantata', deriving from *cantare*, to sing). Today we tend to think of a sonata as being an instrumental work in several movements, each of which follows certain standards of character and form, and at least one of which, usually the first, conforms to a standard design, generally known as 'sonata' or 'first movement' form. But the sonatas of Domenico Scarlatti (see page 98), the earliest to have found a central place in the piano repertoire, are brief works of one movement only (relatively few exceed five minutes) and are designed along different, and simpler, principles, as the composer himself acknowledged:

"Do not seek ... profound intentions in these pieces, but rather an ingenious trifling with art, to extend your freedom at the keyboard."

The Classical period (c.1750–1825) was the golden age of what could be termed the sonata ideal, and the overwhelming majority of piano works written within it were sonatas (Mozart left 26, Haydn 62, Beethoven 32, Schubert 21). The piano sonata was no different in form and overall concept from the symphony, the string quartet and the concerto, which are simply sonatas for orchestra, sonatas for four strings, sonatas for soloist and orchestra, going on to embrace duos, trios, quintets, sextets, etc. One might legitimately include in any pianistic survey virtually all of the chamber and orchestral works in which the piano plays a prominent role.

Domenico Scarlatti. His sonatas are the earliest to have found a place in the piano repertoire.

Layout of Movements

A fully-fledged sonata will be a work of several movements (normally three or four, but Brahms's Third Sonata has five, and several of Beethoven's have only two). The standard pattern is fast-slow-fast, or in four-movement sonatas, fast-slow-medium-fast.

FIRST MOVEMENT Generally fast, but not extremely so, it may be preceded, as in many Classical symphonies, by a slow introduction (excellent examples are Beethoven's *Pathétique* and Op. 111). The movement as a whole will be in so-called 'sonata form' (also known as 'first-movement' or 'sonata-allegro' form), as outlined below.

SECOND MOVEMENT Slow or at least slow-ish, this movement too is often in "sonata form", but may also be a 'theme and variations'.

THIRD MOVEMENT A dance-based movement, usually a medium-paced minuet and trio (the trio being a secondary minuet in three voices, hence the name) or its quicker and more energetic offspring, a scherzo (in triple metre, like the minuet, but at a pace where the units of measurement are whole bars instead of individual beats within a bar).

FOURTH MOVEMENT Generally the fastest movement, this too is often in 'sonata form', or it may be a rondo (A-B-A-C-A), or a combination of both.

In most three-movement sonatas (all of Mozart's, most of Haydn's and many of Beethoven's), the minuet or scherzo is left out.

Layout of Sonata Form

Surprisingly few movements by great composers conform to the pattern taught in schools, academies and colleges for many decades. Nevertheless, that pattern does give an idea of the general principles at work.

A 'proper' sonata movement, then, is in three sections, of which the first and last are essentially the same, with one very important exception, while the second is substantially different.

Section 1: EXPOSITION

The first section begins with a theme in the home key of the movement as a whole. Sooner or later this runs into a

58

transitional passage, in which the home key is effectively dissolved, to be replaced by a second key and a new theme, which will contrast in style, mood and texture with the opening. The new key is then clearly established, and confirmed with a clear cadence. In almost every case, the composer will indicate at this point that the Exposition should be repeated. The result is a stark juxtaposition of its two rival keys – a sudden emphasizing of the distance travelled – and a second chance for the memory to absorb the outlines of the plot this far.

Section 2: DEVELOPMENT

After the (optional) repeat of the Exposition comes the central Development section. Here everything is much freer. Some of the materials of the Exposition may now reappear in a sequence of new guises (hence the term Development), or they may give way to musical ideas which seem entirely new (the difference generally being more apparent than real). The music is likely to be more fragmented, it may run through a whole sequence of different and often unexpected keys before returning to the home key. On its return we arrive at Section 3.

Section 3: RECAPITULATION

As its name implies, this section is basically a repetition of the Exposition. This time, however, the whole section will remain in the home key (tonic). The contrast or opposition of keys that generated the principal drama of the Exposition has been replaced by a newfound unity.

In many sonatas, there is a further section, added at the point where the Exposition ended. Called a 'coda' (literally, 'tail'), it may serve simply as a kind of epilogue (especially in slow movements), or it may, in fast movements, take on considerable dimensions, serving as a kind of second development and bringing the movement to a final (generally resounding) climax. There will often be a smaller coda (also known as 'codetta') at the end of the Exposition itself.

The Russian virtuoso Emil Gilels was a revelatory exponent of Beethoven's sonatas.

The Sonata: History and Repertoire

Although the first works ever composed specifically for the piano were sonatas (Giustini, 1732), it was to be another 30 years before the great stream of sonatas intended optionally or primarily for the instrument really got underway. Even then, the option 'harpsichord or pianoforte' became general only in the 1770s, and the reverse option of 'pianoforte or harpsichord' was still being used by publishers in the first decade of the 19th century, long after Mozart, Haydn, Clementi and Beethoven had forsworn the harpsichord and begun to compose highly idiomatic works for the piano.

Whereas in earlier duo sonatas, the keyboard was regularly cast in the role of accompanist to the violin or flute or cello, the Classical period saw an interesting case of role reversal. Keyboard sonatas were published 'with [strictly optional] violin accompaniment'. This description was even applied to most of the violin sonatas of Mozart and even the earlier ones of Beethoven. Such was the rage for 'accompanied' keyboard sonatas that publishers took the liberty of adding 'accompaniments' of their own to solo sonatas by such popular and admired composers as J.C. Bach. Gounod's controversial addition, in the 19th century, of a vocal *Ave Maria* to the First Prelude of J. S. Bach's 'Well-tempered Clavier' was, in fact, a grandiose throwback to a once popular tradition. So popular, indeed, that publishers had occasionally to specify on the title page that certain sonatas were 'for pianoforte only'.

The pianist Sigismond Thalberg contributed the three-hand technique to the 19th-century sonata.

The Classical Sonata Takes Shape

As the Classical sonata matured, the simplistic accompanied melodies of its earliest phases gave way to works of greater textural variety, and the assembly-line, Alberti-bass type of accompaniment was used to spin a harmonic web of increasing richness and power. Examples of its

transformation into an agent of drama, excitement and drive can be found in the first movement of Beethoven's well-known *Pathétique* Sonata, the last movement of the still more famous 'Moonlight', and in the slow movement of the so-called 'Emperor' Concerto, where it rises to the surface of the harmony to become a melodic figure of quite magical beauty.

Between Haydn's early examples and Beethoven's, the length of the average piano sonata more than doubled. Whereas Haydn's and Mozart's sonatas were typically three-movement forms, following the standard fast-slow-fast pattern, a significant number of Beethoven's (Nos.1–4, 7, 11, 12, 15, 18, 28, 29, 31) are in four movements.

Strange to say, it was not until the 1830s that the sonata became a featured item in piano recitals. Before that, it had been regarded as a solitary diversion, an instructive piece, and fit fare for private concerts and evenings in the salons of fashionable aristocrats. It was only in 1861, 34 years after the composer's death, that all of Beethoven's piano sonatas were played in public (by Charles Hallé, in London).

The Romantic Piano Sonata

The tide of Romanticism in the early 19th century caused the themes of the sonata to become more consistently lyrical and symmetrical. The two main themes of sonata-form movements came to be almost universally characterized as 'masculine' (bold, dramatic, vigorous, emphatically rhythmical) and 'feminine' (lyrical, reflective, dreamy, flowing). New kinds of keyboard figuration, increasingly lightweight and curvaceous, began to characterize dance-based movements such as the minuet, and the routine Alberti basses were generally replaced by the standard sort of oom-pah-pah accompaniments featured in marches and waltzes. Another feature was the three-handed effect whereby a melody was shared between the two thumbs and surrounded with swirling veils of arpeggios (a technique which was the stock-in-trade of the virtuoso Sigismond von Thalberg, but widely used, too, by Mendelssohn, Schumann and many others). A further feature of the great Romantic sonata is its sheer difficulty, in purely pianistic terms. No longer directed at the home, the salon, the accomplished amateur, the mainline Romantic sonata is aimed straight at the concert hall and the professional virtuoso. Its drama is more theatrical, its harmonic scenery more lavish, its form more self-generating.

The declining fortunes of the piano sonata in the 19th century are reflected in their relative abandonment by great composers after Beethoven. Chopin, Schumann and Brahms left only three apiece. From Liszt we have two at most (the so-called 'Dante' Sonata being a borderline case). Grieg wrote only one, and Tchaikovsky only one of lasting substance, while Wagner, Strauss, Mahler, Berlioz, Dvořák, Rossini, Sibelius, Verdi, Bruckner, Franck, Debussy, Borodin, Rimsky-Korsakov, Mussorgsky, Schoenberg, Elgar, Vaughan Williams and Gershwin left none at all (excepting one or two student works). More typical and far more numerous are the sonatas by now forgotten figures such as Draeseke, Gade, Heller, Hiller, Kalkbrenner, Kiel, Moscheles, Raff, Reubke, Ritter, Sterndale Bennett, Thalberg, and many others.

In the 20th century, the sonata revived somewhat, particularly among Russian composers. Scriabin, Prokofiev, Rachmaninov, Shostakovich and Stravinsky all left valuable examples, as did Berg, Bartók and Hindemith, but generally speaking, the term sonata has all but lost its meaning (beyond signifying, as in its earliest days, an instrumental rather than a vocal work). Of the above composers, only Scriabin, Prokofiev and Hindemith repeatedly returned to the medium. In the United States there have been significant contributions from Ives, Copland, Sessions and Carter, and in France the most considerable offerings have come from Boulez and Barraqué.

The German-born pianist and conductor Sir Charles Hallé was the first to play all of Beethoven's sonatas in public.

Sonatas were the first works specifically for the piano, the earliest by Lodovico Giustini in the 18th century.

The Central Repertoire

Far and away the greatest body of piano sonatas ever composed is Beethoven's epoch-making sequence of 32, written at various periods throughout his life and constituting the boldest, the most astonishingly imaginative and the most spiritually transcendent diary of the soul ever committed to musical notation. In their unprecedented demands, including the greatest violence ever depicted in music, these revolutionary works forced the pace of the piano's evolution. Beethoven was the first composer who deliberately wrote for the future.

Of the composers who came before him, only Haydn approached Beethoven in the sheer range and boldness of invention which he lavished on his own sonatas. Mozart's 26 are always impeccable works of art, but by general consensus they rarely come close to the greatness of his concertos. Exceptions are his only two minor-mode sonatas, K. 310 and 457, the F major, K. 533, with the astonishingly modern harmonies of its Andante, the Sonata in D for Two Pianos, and the last two of his six sonatas for piano duet.

Weber's four sonatas were once classed with Beethoven's, but posterity has not endorsed that judgement. Clementi's are impeccably crafted and far more prophetic of pianistic developments than Mozart's, but their emotional and spiritual range is far narrower and shallower.

With the death of Schubert in 1828, at the age of 31, the golden age of the piano sonata came to an end. Of his 21 sonatas for piano, seven or eight rank with the greatest ever written: the final trilogy, composed in a fever of invention in his last months, the sonatas in G and D major, the two great A minor sonatas, and the so-called 'Wanderer' Fantasy, whose cyclic form anticipates Liszt.

The Concerto

The basic principle behind any concerto is that of contrast: of the one with the few (as in Mozart's three concertos K. 413–415, which can be played, with the composer's sanction, by piano and string quartet); of the few with the many – as in all so-called *concerti grossi*, where a smaller group of instruments is contrasted with a larger group (Bach's 'Brandenburg' Concertos are probably the best-known example); or of one *kind* of instrument with a band of a differing kind (any kind of wind or keyboard instrument with string orchestra). From the point of view of contrast alone, the piano concerto is ideal, since the piano differs more from all the instruments of the orchestra than any of them do from each other (if we exclude the harp and percussion).

In the history of the concerto, the keyboard as soloist makes a very late entry. Until Bach promoted it to the rank of soloist in the Fifth 'Brandenburg' Concerto (where it shares the honours with flute and violin), the harpsichord was always regarded as a supplementry part of the orchestra, providing the continuo (see page 44). Thereafter, Bach used it repeatedly as the solo instrument in concertos, and these keyboard concertos (including ones for two, three and even four harpsichords and strings) are still occasionally played on the piano, despite the vogue for 'authenticity' that looked set to swamp the musical world in the last quarter of the 20th century.

The story of the authentic *piano* concerto really starts with Mozart, unless one includes the many agreeable concertos of his friend and mentor in childhood, J. C. Bach – the first man ever to play a piano solo in public. Most of these, however, work just as well on the harpsichord. Mozart's 'mature' piano concertos, on the other hand, were not only

composed specifically for the piano, but so idiomatically that they are hardly conceivable on any other instrument. They also bring the piano concerto to a peak of perfection. There were subsequent developments in the medium, of course – nobody is about to discount the concertos of Beethoven, Schumann or Brahms – but Mozart's, by common consent, remain unsurpassed and seldom equalled (surprisingly, Haydn's concertos show none of the inspiration that permeates his symphonies and string quartets).

The Structure of the Concerto

The concerto as Mozart first encountered it was an inheritance from the High Baroque, where it was unchallenged as the most popular form of instrumental music. During the first half of the 18th century, however, it ceded pride of place to the newly developing symphony, without absorbing much of its influences. Whereas the guiding principle of the symphony was that of thematic development, the concerto clung to the standardized and somewhat static nature of its Baroque forbears. Its straightforward structure and its scope for repetition, varied only or principally by contrasts of instrumental texture, made it a natural favourite with composers and listeners of limited imagination.

Of the standard three movements (fast-slow-fast), the first generally consisted of an opening orchestral section in the home key, followed by a solo discourse on the same material, also in the home key. The orchestra, in an abbreviated form of the opening, would then modulate to a closely related key, usually the dominant, in which the first large-scale section, the Exposition, would come to a close.

The central Development section was dominated by the soloist, the orchestra being reduced to little better than an accompanying lackey. Only after this was the orchestra allowed a return to the foreground for the beginning of the Recapitulation. By and large, this consisted of a slim-line version of the Exposition, giving way to a solo cadenza (traditionally improvised) before a final return to the opening material for a formal close.

The second movement often followed a similar procedure, though in contrasting mood, key and tempo: slow, but not too slow, essentially lyrical, though with greater harmonic and structural freedom than in the first movement, and still weighted heavily in favour of the soloist.

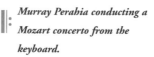

Murray Perahia conducting a Mozart concerto from the keyboard.

The finale, by contrast, was generally virtuosic and quick, though some composers were happy to close with a graceful dance in the style of an extended minuet. The guiding principle, a clear offshoot from the operatic aria, was that of melody (solo) and accompaniment (orchestra). This, then, was the concerto as Mozart inherited it: essentially a lightweight vehicle for instrumental virtuosity in which foppish good manners and an unassuming tunefulness prevailed over emotional depth or meaningful dialogue.

Anatomy of a Mozart Concerto

From K.271 onwards, every Mozart piano concerto, with the one possible exception of the so-called 'Coronation' Concerto, is a work of the highest art. And while no two are quite alike in design, they do, of course, have many features in common. Among these is an opening orchestral exposition of the main themes, which unlike the normal exposition in an instrumental sonata remains in the home key (tonic). The piano then enters, either with the first main theme or with an entirely new (but related) idea, as in Nos. 21 and 25, and both minor-key concertos (Nos. 20 and 24).

The principal material is then explored in generally conversational style by both soloist and orchestra. In this section the piano usually indulges in some purely pianistic figuration by way of establishing its own distinct individuality and introducing a clearly competitive element ("Just you try this!"). In this radically more varied approach to the material and shape of the opening, orchestral exposition, the tension of opposing keys and the alternation of stability and flux play a crucial part, as in the solo sonata, and the first big 'solo' section ends with a firm cadence in the secondary key (the 'dominant' in the case of major-key concertos, the 'relative major' in minor-key concertos).

The central Development tends to follow the usual procedure, drifting through several keys, and exploring new aspects of the relationship between solo and orchestra. Before the end of the third main section, the Recapitulation, the orchestra always comes to a dramatically inconclusive stop (technically a 6/4 chord) and the piano then leaps into the breach and plays around with the various themes in a highly brilliant and improvisatory way (in Mozart's time this cadenza was indeed improvised on the spot) before welcoming the orchestra back with a long trill, after which a (generally brief) coda – shared, in the case of No. 24 – brings the first movement to a close.

As in solo sonatas, the slow middle movement (often not so slow, in Mozart's case) is likely to be cast either as a 'sonata form' or as a 'theme and variations' (Nos.15 and 18); and the finale is usually a rondo, but may also be another 'sonata form' movement or a set of variations.

It fell to Mozart to win for the concerto the same degree of structural and emotional mastery that Haydn had won for

Before J. S. Bach raised its status in the first half of the 18th century the keyboard had, at best, to share the honours with other instruments.

The Romantic concerto establi- shed the piano's heroic credentials as surely as did Napoleon's defeat of the Austrian army establish his own.

the symphony. The concerto as he left it, and the piano concerto in particular, was transformed almost beyond recognition. In place of the stereotyped virtuoso vehicle and the facile conversation piece cultivated by even the best composers of his youth, Mozart left a form in which the subtlest tonal variety played a prime part in the formal, colouristic and expressive cohesion of large-scale structures; a miraculous and paradoxical tapestry of interweaving strands in which unity was achieved through continuous diversity; an instrumental drama as eloquent and various as any opera – and above all, a Utopian vision of a world without victors and vanquished, a "republic of equals", to borrow a phrase from Schumann, in which altruism and self-interest are so intimately linked that they become indistinguishable.

The Romantic Concerto

The Classical concerto reached its climax with Beethoven, who also forged the key to the Romantic concerto of the

19th century. The first two of his seven concertos with piano are clearly inspired by Mozartian models, but already one can sense the developments to come. Among Beethoven's innovations were the increased importance of the orchestra, to the extent that his last two, despite their three-movement layout, can be conceived almost as symphonies with piano obbligato. Beethoven was the first to link movements together, without a break (specifically, the middle and last movements of his Fourth and Fifth Concertos) – an idea borrowed by Mendelssohn and Schumann and further developed by Liszt.

In his Fourth Concerto Beethoven goes one better than the Mozart of K. 271 by beginning the work with a short piano solo, which the orchestra then answers with one of the most magical key-changes ever conceived. And in the Fifth (known in English-speaking countries as the 'Emperor') he allows the orchestra a single introductory chord before the soloist grandiloquently enters with a long, brilliant and resplendent cadenza, enhanced by two widely separated chords of support from the orchestra. With the piano's heroic credentials firmly established, the orchestra then takes over with an Exposition of extraordinary grandeur. Another innovation, is the built-in cadenza, with the specific instruction "do not make a cadenza here but go on at once to the following". And this, in turn, breaks new ground by allowing the orchestra to accompany the soloist from Bar 19 of the cadenza onwards. A further development of this idea occurs in the cadenza of Beethoven's curiously slapdash arrangement for piano and orchestra of his great Violin Concerto in D. In the piano version the soloist is accompanied through much of the cadenza by the timpani, whose four unaccompanied strokes introduce the first movement and provide much of the basis for its subsequent development. This is one of Beethoven's most tightly 'organic' works. With Beethoven, the extemporized cadenza became largely a thing of the past. Among those who followed his example, incorporating the cadenza into the main body of the movement, were Mendelssohn, Schumann, Brahms and Tchaikovsky.

Taking his cue from Beethoven, Liszt, in his two concertos, further developed the idea of connecting movements. He went beyond simply composing links, modifying in rhythm, tempo and mood the shared thematic material running through the whole work in order to suit the prevailing character of each movement. As he was to do still more ingeniously in his great B minor Sonata some years later, he created what was in effect a single, unified structure, whose apparently self-defined movements served, on a higher level of coherence, as Exposition, Development and modified Recapitulation.

However disciplined and inventive Liszt was in unifying large-scale structures, he remained in his concertos, as in his *Hungaria* Fantasy and *Totentanz* (Dance of Death), a gladiatorial virtuoso who was perhaps too ready to put bravura display before musical substance. This was, in fact, to become the principal hallmark of the Romantic concerto: a shamelessly rigged encounter between a heroic soloist and a severely wing-clipped orchestra, whose main function was to glorify the pianist through a lot of empty sabre-rattling. Among the long-forgotten Romantic concertos which have recently been staging a comeback are those by such once-household names as Dussek, Ries, Moscheles, Field, Scharwenka, Herz, Sauer, d'Albert, Paderewski, Henselt, Litolff, Anton Rubinstein, Bortkiewicz, Reinecke, Alkan, Lyapunov and Steibelt (who wrote a concerto for piano, two orchestras and triangle!). But it was not all dross and passing fancies. Of the serious Romantic concertos which have held their place in the repertoire, the best-known are by Schumann, Mendelssohn, Chopin, Weber (whose *Conzertstück* in F minor is written to a specific

'literary' programme), Liszt, Grieg, Tchaikovsky, Saint-Saëns and Rachmaninov, all of whom, with the sole exception of Liszt, fell back on the old Classical three-movement scheme, while retaining the standard Romantic concept of the soloist as hero. The piano concertos of Dvořák, Glazunov, Rimsky-Korsakov and Delius, despite the popularity of their composers in other respects, have never achieved more than curiosity status with the musical public at large.

The two piano concertos of Brahms are in a category of their own, both of them being of a size, length and seriousness unique at the time of their composition and unsurpassed since (except by Busoni's monstrosity of a concerto, complete with male chorus, which holds the record for sheer length and self-conscious grandiosity, clocking in at roughly an hour and twenty minutes). Both, too, hark back to Classical ideals, and especially to Beethoven. In neither is the soloist cast as gladiator, yet both, and particularly the Second, are of colossal difficulty. More than any other concertos of the Romantic era, these two great works engage the mind as much as the spirit. There is nothing, however, remotely arid or excessively cerebral in either. The canvas may be vast, but the paints are mixed by one of the greatest lyric song-writers in musical history. As a melodist, Brahms is at least the equal of his idol Beethoven, and his use of melodic ideas, his capacity to make them flower and develop, is hardly less wonderful. The Second, in B flat, is the only concerto of the Romantic era to be cast in four movements and is the most symphonic in scope and size of all the great concertos. The 'extra' movement is a powerful scherzo, which Brahms unusually places second.

The most successful piano concertos of the 20th century, apart from those of Rachmaninov, who continued to compose in a 19th-century idiom, are Bartók's three and Prokofiev's five (all of which emphasize the piano's percussive qualities and rely heavily for effect on their driving and exciting rhythms), two each from Ravel (one for the left hand alone) and Shostakovich (one for piano and trumpet), Falla's 'Nights in the Gardens of Spain' and Gershwin's Concerto in F (though this has never won the same popularity as *Rhapsody in Blue*). While much admired by many musicians, the concertos of Schoenberg, Stravinsky, Britten, Tippett, Barber, Carter, Bennett and a good number of others have failed to find lasting favour with audiences.

65

Rachmaninov in 1916. His four piano concertos are composed in a 19th-century Romantic style.

The Forms of Romanticism

The Romantic era in music, stretching from roughly 1820 to 1910, was an age in which 'subjectivity' and the mood of the moment increasingly ruled supreme. Where the piano is concerned this resulted in an abundance of works, especially in the realm of the miniature, which were as much studies in feeling as they were musical artefacts. This, together with their relative freedom and flexibility of form, caused a population explosion in printed music which weighed down the pianos of the world with more trifles than masterpieces. But masterpieces there certainly were, and each of the forms discussed here have survived because of them. Unlike the dominant concepts of the Classical era – sonata form, rondo, variations – their design, shape and length were so much generated from within (arising, improvisation-style, from the musical material itself rather than from any preconceived structures), that they can hardly be discussed in general terms. What follows now, therefore, is a survey of popular Romantic genres as exploited by the greatest composers.

Ballade

The term was first applied to piano music by Chopin, whose four works of that name (the earliest dating from 1831) are among his greatest and most famous works, though their titles are ambiguous, to say the least. While they stand today as a kind of family, they were never envisaged as a group, nor do they establish or develop any particular form, or conform to any sort of 'literary' programme (despite unfounded claims that they were inspired by the ballad poetry of Chopin's fellow Pole Adam Mickiewicz. Chopin's steadfast opposition to designedly programmatic music is just one of the many ways in which he was essentially out of step with the Romantic movement). Among the similarities which might very loosely be said to bind them together, and which might provide a clue to Chopin's choice of title, is an element of rhythmic ritual which is certainly one of the hallmarks of the folk ballad, whose claim on our memories is inseparable from its strongly metrical cast, and each of Chopin's ballades is characterized by an almost hypnotic grouping of beats in units of six.

Among works inspired by Chopin's example are two by Liszt, which also lack a 'literary' programme – surprisingly, given his heavily programmatic leanings. Also surprisingly, since he generally deplored such things, Brahms's Four

Ballades, Op.10, do have a literary tie-in, the first of them being headed "After the Scottish ballad 'Edward' in Herder's *Stimmung der Völker*". There is, however, a strong possibility that this particular work actually began life as a song and was only latterly confined to the piano. Other pianistic ballades are Grieg's in G minor, one of his most substantial works, cast in the form of 'theme and variations', and Fauré's for piano and orchestra.

Barcarolle

With their vivid imagery and sensual, vaguely exotic character, the traditional songs (*barcarolle*) of the Venetian gondoliers held a great appeal for the Romantic imagination, although they had been widely known in Europe since the middle of the 18th century. Barcarolles of whatever kind are characterized by their gently lilting rhythm, representing the steady, lulling movement of the boat through the water. The most famous of all is Chopin's, in F sharp (1845), widely considered to be his greatest achievement. Other examples include those of Mendelssohn (the *Gondollieder* from the 'Songs Without Words'), Anton Rubinstein, Balakirev, Glazunov, Novak and MacDowell, but the most important, after Chopin's,

Liszt's keyboard studies, or études, have secured a permanent place in the repertory.

are the thirteen composed by Fauré between 1885 and 1916. The most famous, however, is the Barcarolle from Offenbach's opera *The Tales of Hoffmann*, which has been the victim (and occasionally the beneficiary) of numerous piano arrangements.

Berceuse

Literally, a cradle song or lullaby. As with the ballade and the barcarolle, it was Chopin who provided the model for the pianistic Berceuse in one of his most bewitching and ingenious miniatures. His Berceuse in D flat, is a sequence of variations on a simple, two-chord harmonic progression, with the D flat present in the bass of every two bar phrase, yet there is never a hint of tedium as the right-hand elaborations proceed from one sparkling miracle of pianistic tracery to another. Liszt's Berceuse, also in D flat, is clearly derived from Chopin's but ranges further afield in harmony and dynamics. Other piano berceuses are by Balakirev, Benjamin Godard, and Debussy.

Etude

The keyboard 'study', in one form or another, has been around as long as keyboard instruments, and is distinguished from the mere 'exercise' by its musical intent. In the 18th century, even that distinction was blurred, to say the least. Scarlatti's first 30 sonatas are in quite the same category as his other 525-odd sonatas but were published in 1738 as *essercizi*, and the equivalent German term *Ubung* graces some of Bach's greatest keyboard music, including the six Partitas, the famous Italian Concerto and the monumental 'Goldberg' Variations, all firmly established in the central piano repertoire. In the 19th century, the term 'exercise' denoted a short figure or passage to be repeated many times over, often in a sequence of keys, with the sole intent of developing one or another aspect of keyboard technique.

In the 19th century, the enormous popularity of the piano in almost every class of Western society spawned a profusion of studies for every level of amateur and aspiring

The barcarolle owes its name to the songs of the Venetian boatmen.

professional, some of which are still in use today. Among the best were those by J. B. Cramer (much admired by Beethoven), Muzio Clementi (ditto) and Ignaz Moscheles (liked and greatly respected by Mendelssohn and Chopin). Less appealing, but with astonishing staying power, are the innumerable studies by Beethoven's pupil Carl Czerny which are still the bane of many a piano student's life. Towering over all comers, however, were two composers who raised the concept and the reality of the étude to previously unimagined heights. One was Liszt, the other was Chopin.

Chopin's 27 études mark the summit of all works composed with an overtly didactic purpose. Every one of them is first and foremost a work of art, no two are alike, and virtually all of the first set – the 12 of Op.10 – were completed before he even reached the age of official manhood. Many of them, and the underlying concept of them all, can be traced to his early immersion in Bach, the only composer who so consistently combined the requirements of art and instruction at the very highest level. Each of Chopin's études is predominantly focused on a single technical problem (the rapid expansion and contraction of the hand, quicksilver scales and trills in double thirds, the combination of two or more outwardly conflicting rhythms, etc.) and on a single musical idea. Most are studies in legato of one kind or another, aimed at making the piano 'sing'. To this end, they require the almost continuous use of the sustaining pedal as a primary source of colour. Where Liszt exploited the essentially percussive nature of the piano (it is, after all, an instrument in which strings are struck, and in which every note begins at its loudest and then rapidly diminishes in strength), Chopin does everything in his power

to transcend it. In many ways he seems to anticipate Debussy's ideal of the piano as "an instrument without hammers".

As in his playing, so in his music, Chopin lacked the range of Liszt, and contrary to widespread belief his études are by no means all-encompassing in their scope. Pianists wanting to shore up the cracks in their trills, tremolos, broken octaves, hand-crossing and chordal skips and the drum-like alternation of the hands will do better with Liszt, who really does deal with all the principal categories of a pre-20th-century technique.

Liszt's études, too, explore the extremes of emotion and mood, and contain some of the most technically challenging music ever written. His Paganini Etudes, the *Etudes de Concert* and the fearsome Transcendental Etudes, despite their formidable difficulty, have secured a permanent place in the modern piano repertoire. Other, similar works to have done likewise are Schumann's Symphonic Etudes, Brahms's 'Variations on a Theme of Paganini' (études in all but name), Debussy's astonishing set of twelve (1915) and Rachmaninov's *Etudes-tableaux*.

Impromptu

Although generally associated with Schubert and Chopin, the term was first used by the Czech composer Vorisek in 1822. While the term suggests improvisation and the spur of the moment, all the most notable works of the name are highly organized and meticulously calculated. Nor do they really add up to a form, as such, except in the loosest possible way. Most have a ternary structure (A-B-A), with a relatively fervent, even stormy middle part, sandwiched between sections of brilliant and graceful figuration, often of a relaxed, devil-may-care character. But then Chopin's famous Fantasy-Impromptu is quite the reverse (its languid middle section finding its greatest fame as a popular song of 1918, 'I'm Always Chasing Rainbows'), and Schubert's seventh Impromptu is a straightforward 'theme and variations'. Chopin's four and Schubert's eight are the most famous examples of the genre, such as it is, but there are also noteworthy examples by Schumann, Sterndale Bennett, Dvořák, Scriabin, Balakirev, Rimsky-Korsakov and Fauré.

Nocturne

The Irish composer-pianist John Field (1782–1837) is credited with 'inventing' the nocturne, though pieces answering to the description had certainly been around before Field coined the name. Basically a simple A-B-A form, its outer sections are generally, though not invariably, of a dreamy, languid, reflective character, a long-spun melody unfolding over a gently undulating harmonic accompaniment. The middle section is of contrasting character, usually consisting of new material and having a more agitated feel to it, as well as a different, often more percussive texture. Having muddied the peaceful waters of the opening section, it then generally subsides, to be followed by a return to the original reverie, usually in some slightly altered form. Field's nocturnes are among the first works to exploit the use of the sustaining pedal, allowing left-hand accompaniments to cover the whole lower register of the instrument in a beautiful harmonic 'wash', far removed from the old Alberti bass whose mechanistic compass had to lie within the span of a single hand position. The long-spanned, vocal-style melodies floating above this iridescent sea were directly inspired by the *bel canto* tradition of Italian opera.

Liszt, in his preface to the first collected edition of Field's nocturnes, went so far as to claim that they "opened the way for all the productions which have since appeared under the various titles of Songs Without Words, Impromptus, Ballades etc., and to him we may trace the origin of pieces designed to portray subjective and profound emotion."

Field's nocturnes had a direct influence on Chopin's, but Chopin's inhabit a world of inspiration and resourcefulness quite beyond the dreams of Field, whose own examples, for all their charm and grace, seem extraordinarily insipid by comparison. Like Field's, they cultivate a lyrical, non-virtuosic style (with one stupendous exception, in the stormy C minor), and conform to the taste for moodscapes which persists to this day

The term 'nocturne' may be given to any piece suggestive of the calm beauty of night; painting: **Moonlight by** *Joseph Wright.*

69

For his 'Hungarian Rhapsodies' Liszt drew strongly on the gipsy traditions of his native land.

tunes, arias and ensembles from well-known operas or other sources; alternative titles are Reminiscences, Fantasia and Variations. Liszt's are the best-known examples (most notably those based on Mozart's *Don Giovanni*, Verdi's *Aida* and *Rigoletto*, Bellini's *Norma* and the *Totentanz* for piano and orchestra, subtitled *Paraphrase über das Dies irae*), but there are many more, by such now relatively forgotten composers as Thalberg, Czerny, Hünten and Herz.

Prelude

One result of the Romantics' unprecedented interest in the past was the re-awakening of forms that had lain dormant for decades, among them the prelude and fugue, brought to its highest peak by Bach in the first half of the 18th century. In terms of form, the term 'prelude' is so loose as to be virtually meaningless. Originally it was merely a semi-improvisatory introduction to something else, and it was in this spirit that Mendelssohn wrote his six Preludes and Fugues, Liszt his Prelude and Fugue on B-A-C-H and César Franck wrote his well-known Prelude, Chorale and Fugue, and the less familiar Prelude, Aria and Finale. More common, however, are the many self-contained 'preludes' that precede nothing but each other, including all of those by Hummel, Alkan, Rachmaninov, Szymanowski, Debussy and Scriabin. Towering above them all, though, and providing the inspiration for most, is the amazing sequence of 24 that comprise Chopin's Op. 28. In their startling brevity of utterance (almost half of the préludes last less than a minute), their subversion of traditional harmony, their extraordinary range of tone colours and their spell-binding virtuosity, these pieces collectively could well be enshrined as a keyboard Romantic's manifesto. In several cases, Chopin's preludes are generically indistinguishable from his études, many of them being exclusively addressed to a single musical-cum-technical idea. Today, a vision of the Opus 28 Préludes as a single, inviolable cycle is widespread, even dominant, to the extent that few pianists venture to dismember it. Chopin, on the other hand, repeatedly played varying selections of preludes, mixed in with nocturnes, studies and waltzes.

but which then enjoyed a fashionable novelty. In the subtlety and power of their harmonies, the extraordinary flexibility of their rhythmic invention and the unprecedented suppleness and significance of their ornamental melody, Chopin's nocturnes are in a class of their own, and had far-reaching effects on composers as distinctive and distant as Scriabin, Debussy, Rachmaninov and Ravel. The form itself continued to be popular after Chopin's death. Fauré wrote thirteen, and there are also notable examples by Liszt, Schumann, Glinka, Balakirev, Tchaikovsky, Rimsky-Korsakov, Grieg, Scriabin, Satie, d'Indy and Poulenc.

Novelette

This term was used by Schumann as the title of his Op. 21 – several pieces, ostensibly of a 'narrative' character (as in the literary novel), and consisting of several contrasting sections, enivisaged as musical 'chapters'. No knowledge of the novel is necessary, however, to an appreciation of the music.

Paraphrase

Generally a free and virtuosic arrangement, medley-style, of

Rhapsody

The term dates from the days of Ancient Greece but was not applied to music before the early 19th century, when the Czech composer Tomazek issued six piano pieces of that name in 1803, closely followed by his pupil Dreyschock. Like so many terms beloved of the Romantics, it denotes no particular form but rather a certain, epic, expansive and generally unbuttoned character, often associated with various national styles, as in the nineteen Hungarian Rhapsodies of Liszt, Dvořák's Slavonic Rhapsodies, Gershwin's determinedly American *Rhapsody in Blue* and so on. Apart from the Gershwin and three Rhapsodies by Brahms (Opp. 79 and 119 No.4), Liszt's are far and away the best known, although they were rather frowned upon by some musicians in the mid-20th-century as 'cheap'. Liszt's models were the blatantly manipulative and theatrical *lassu* and *friss* of

70

the Hungarian gypsy bands and their featured violinists. With their combining of the deeply exotic and seductive with dazzling keyboard pyrotechnics of the most unabashed kind, they were among the most popular items in the whole of the 19th-century bravura repertoire, regularly whipping up audiences into a near-frenzy of excitement, especially when played by Liszt himself.

Scherzo

Before being appropriated for artistic purposes, 'scherzo' was simply the Italian word for 'joke'. In the second half of the 18th century, Haydn used the term to denote a much-accelerated minuet in the context of a sonata design, but it was Beethoven who gave it pride of place in the musical history books. In his hands the scherzo loses all but the most vestigial resemblance to the formal sobriety of the minuet. Its tempo is quickened to the point where the chief unit of measurement is not the triplet-metre grouping of beats within a bar, but the duple-metre grouping of bars within a

phrase. Beethoven's scherzos, like Haydn's, were conceived as parts of a larger design and contain, on the whole, enough good-humoured energy to justify their label on etymological grounds. Chopin's scherzos, on the other hand, are self-contained works, more notable for their alternating intensity and lyricism than for any spirit of playfulness – though an exception must be made for the intensity and lyricism than for any spirit of playfulness – and the dance element is largely submerged in favour of an epic 'narrative' style, drawing loosely and idiosyncratically on the basic principles of so-called sonata form (see pages 56–9). Other self-contained scherzos for the piano include two lilting examples by Schubert (more examples are to be found in his sonatas), one each by Mendelssohn and Brahms, and a couple of miniatures by Schumann and Alkan. There are also three noteworthy examples for piano and orchestra by Brahms (in his Second Concerto), Strauss (his *Burleske*) and Litolff (from his Fourth *Concerto-symphonique*).

Chopin's four scherzos are emotionally intense – far removed from the 'joke' of the word's meaning; painting: Turner's **Yacht Approaching the Coast.**

Romanticism and Literature

Anyone doubting the Romantics' obsession with literature need only look at some of the general titles used by 19th-century composers for purely instrumental, hence non-verbal works – for example, Novelette, Poem, Ballade, Sonnet, Romance, Legend – or at those derived from specific literary works or authors: from Goethe, for instance (*Faust, Tasso, Hermann und Dorothea*), Sir Walter Scott (*Rob Roy* and *Waverley*), Byron (*Manfred, Harold in Italy, The Corsair, Mazeppa*), Shakespeare (*Romeo and Juliet, Macbeth, A Midsummer Night's Dream, Julius Caesar, King Lear*), Lenau (another version of *Faust*), E.T.A. Hoffmann (*Kreisleriana, Coppelia, The Nutcracker, Tales of Hoffmann*), Petrarch (Liszt's *Sonneti del Petrarca*), Victor Hugo (Liszt's *Mazeppa* and *Ce qu'on entend sur le montagne*), Jean Paul (Schumann's *Papillons* and many other works), Dante (Liszt's *Dante* Symphony and the so-called *Dante* Sonata) and so on. Of the great Romantic composers, Chopin alone stood apart from the literary obsession. Yet it was he who initiated the purely instrumental 'ballade' (see The Forms of Romanticism, page 66), to be followed by Liszt, Gottschalk, Fauré, Glazunov, Grieg, Brahms and many others. One would look in vain through all these works, however, to find anything approaching a definitive form.

When it comes to piano composers, none exceeded the literary passions of Liszt and Schumann. But here, too, any search for definitive forms is doomed. Schumann's eight Novelettes (like those of Gade, Glazunov, Poulenc and Sibelius) make clear reference to the novel in their title, but in no obvious sense do they parallel the developing narrative of a literary plot, fictional or otherwise; nor in Schumann's case are they even spiced with programmatic allusions or specifically descriptive music.

The most obvious reflection of the literary model is the profusion of programme music that flooded 19th-century concert platforms and drawing rooms alike. Programme music as such was nothing new to the keyboard and had been around since Elizabethan times, but with the Romantics it reached epidemic proportions.

The inspirational Romantic writer and thinker Goethe, depicted in 1775/6.

A central feature of Romanticism was an idealized worshipping of nature, and it took no-one very long to discover that the piano was a tailor-made simulator of such natural phenomena as storms, the wilder the better. With its celebrated capacity to swoop from one extreme of volume to another, it was a natural for the representation of waves, both rippling and tidal, winds, from gentle zephyrs to cyclones, babbling brooks, twittering birds (first and foremost, of course, the time-worn cuckoo).

Another still more important part of the prevailing trend was the concept of the hero, and what better place to celebrate his exploits than on the pianistic battlefield. Keyboard thunderstorms paled into near-insignificance in the face of pianistic salvos from whole battalions at a time, urged on by the tub-thumping chauvinism of ten-fingered military bands, simulated cymbal-crashes and the satisfying thud of fallen foes. Pianos and battle pieces were made for each other. But lest the keyboard strategist lack sufficient skill or imagination to achieve an acceptable degree of authenticity, pianos began to be equipped with an impressive range of extras. Mostly operated by the feet (some pianos ran to as many as eight pedals), these clever devices simulated tambourines, triangles, drums, bells and other accoutrements of verisimilitude to thrilling (or at any rate deafening) effect. The market was flooded with battle pieces, whose similarity went largely unnoticed by those who enlisted in their cause, but one in particular achieved a popularity seldom exceeded in the history of music. *The Battle of Prague* raged for decades in parlours and drawing-rooms around the world, but its tenacity cut little ice with its composer, one Frantisek Kotswara, who had bidden farewell to earthly life by hanging himself before the Romantic Century had even dawned (see page 26).

Pictorial music, *imitative* music was only a start, however. Music is first and foremost a language of feelings, and here, of course, the Romantics fairly ran riot. Liszt's introduction to his symphonic poem *Tasso* is typical, even though it concerns an orchestral rather than a piano work:

"Tasso loved and suffered at Ferrara; he was avenged at Rome; his glory is yet living in the popular songs of Venice. ... To render this in music we have first conjured up the great shade of the hero, ... haunting the lagoons of Venice; we then catch sight of his haughty, saddened countenance as he glides through the fêtes of Ferrara ...; Finally, we have followed him to Rome, the Eternal City, which in crowning him glorified in him the martyr and the poet."

The pitfalls of programmatic music are nowhere better illustrated than in the sad case of Francesco Berger (1834–1933), who wrote a piano piece to a specific programme and then invited three colleagues to hear it and tell him what they thought it meant. The 'meanings', they suggested, apparently in all seriousness, were 'Daybreak as seen from the lowest gallery of a Welsh coal mine'; 'A boar hunt in Russia'; and 'An enamoured couple whispering vows'. Poor Mr. Berger. His intention had been to illustrate 'the discovering by Pharaoh's daughter of the infant Moses in the bullrushes'.

The most fruitful encounter between literature and the piano naturally took place in the world of song, and in particular, the German song or 'Lied'. Here, the finest verse of Goethe, Schiller, Heine, Rückert, Hans Christian Andersen, Byron, Shakespeare, Kerner, the Brothers Grimm and many more was set with unsurpassed poetry, resourcefulness and intimacy by Schubert, Schumann, Brahms, Wolf, and Mahler, with lesser but still considerable contributions from Mendelssohn, Liszt, Carl Gottfried Loewe (1796–1869) and Robert Franz (1815–1892). In all of this the piano played a role at least as important as that of the voice, not merely 'accompanying' the singer with a few well chosen chords or rippling arpeggios but amplifying and probing the meaning of the words, and providing a kind of psychological and emotional commentary on them, revealing layers of meaning beyond the scope of mere melody, however beautiful or dramatic. Interestingly, the Lieder of Mozart and Beethoven are of relatively little importance.

The most lavish manifestation of the Romantics' literary obsessions took place in the opera house, where words, music, plot and spectacle combined to sensational effect. In the operas themselves, the piano played little or no part. But how many people lived within reasonable reach of an opera house? And of those, how many could afford a ticket? To the great mass of music lovers, it was the piano, and the piano-arrangement, that gave them access (albeit vicarious) to the theatrical pleasures of the rich and mighty. These ranged from simple, undemanding medleys to virtuoso epics like the operatic 'paraphrases' of Liszt, Thalberg and Czerny.

Literary and musical figures of the Romantic age: (from left to right) Dumas or de Musset, Hugo, Sand, Paganini, Rossini, Liszt and Marie d'Agoult.

National Music

The Nationalist movement in music could loosely be said to have started in Russia, with Mikhail Glinka's opera A *Life for the Tsar* in 1836. It was in large part a reaction to the long-standing dominance of Germanic music, whose traditions are epitomized today by the staggering line-up of Bach, Handel, Haydn, Mozart, Beethoven, Schubert, Schumann, Mendelssohn, Wagner, Brahms, Bruckner, Mahler and Schoenberg. More fundamentally, it was a phenomenon cradled in those emergent nations on the periphery of Western Europe and across the Atlantic. Until late into the 19th century, nationalism played little or no part in the music of France, Germany, Britain or Italy, each of which had rich traditions of its own. It was in the following countries that the need for a national musical identity asserted itself most vigorously.

Bohemia

Although renowned for the musicality of its people, Bohemia (Slovakia and the Czech Republic) has produced no piano composers of the front rank. Dussek (1760–1812) was much admired in his day, but produced no 'national' music of any consequence; Dvořák (1841–1904) scored a tremendous and well-deserved hit with his Slavonic Dances for piano duet (best known today in orchestral dress), and his *Legends*, also for piano duet, have many lovely things, but his solo piano music is negligible. Only the G flat *Humoresque* ever found real popularity, and today that too has all but drifted into oblivion.

More considerable are the many delightful and often adventurous polkas by Bedřich Smetana (1824–84), a largely self-taught pianist who made his debut at the age of six and was later celebrated for his performances of Liszt, Thalberg and Henselt, among others. In their nationalistic intent, if not in range and subtlety, these works are comparable in Smetana's output to Chopin's mazurkas, and their almost total neglect by present-day pianists is hard to understand.

Of Bohemian composers for the piano, only Leoš Janáček (1854–1928) has found a place anywhere near the centre of the recitalist's repertoire. While Dvořák and Smetana were reared in the sophisticated European traditions of Bohemia's industrialized western flank, Janáček came from the east, and from a predominantly rural area, where he was influenced by Slovakian and East Moravian folk music, with its sometimes almost Arabic scales and its irregular rhythms. Perhaps the most significant influence on Janáček's musical style, however, was the rising and falling inflections and the ever-changing rhythmic contours of human speech. His best known piano works are two suites, 'From an Overgrown Path' and 'In the Mist'.

As with nationalistic music elsewhere, the most vivid of Bohemian styles are rooted in the world of folk dancing. The dominant forms are the dumka, the furiant and the polka; see pages 50—1.

Finland

The national music of Finland has played a minimal role in piano music. Most of Sibelius's pieces are of an anonymous, *salon* type, composed with no very deep sense of the instrument's character and possibilities. Still, the six Finnish Folksongs of 1903, and especially the three *Kyllikki* of 1904 (based, like so much of Sibelius, on the Finnish national epic *Kalevala*) are worth investigating.

France

The fact that Debussy and Ravel had any recent French tradition to build on was due very largely to the efforts of one man, Camille Saint-Saëns (best known for his Second Piano Concerto and the 'Carnival of the Animals'). Like every other French composer of his generation (he was born in 1835), his musical development was based almost entirely on foreign models: on Bach, Handel, Mozart, Beethoven, Mendelssohn and Schumann. It was in 1871 that Saint-Saëns decided to redress the balance by founding the Societé National de Musique, whose sworn intention it was to give new French music a hearing. Among those championed were Chabrier, Franck, Chausson, Dukas, Ravel and almost every other French composer of any consequence. One scholar

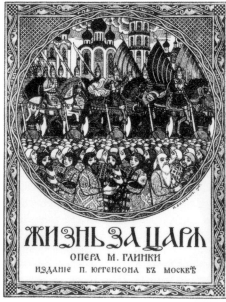

Title page of the opera A Life for the Tsar *by 'the father of Russian music', Glinka – see page 78.*

French music has a strong pictorial element. Debussy described it as "a fantasy of the senses". Painting: 'Peasants Gathering Flowers Beside a River', by Trouillebert.

rightly described the Society as "the cradle and sanctuary of French art, by way of which has come all that has been great in French music since 1870."

Unlike nationalist composers in such other countries as Hungary, Spain, Russia, Poland and the United States, the 'new' French composers had no very distinctive folk tradition on which to draw, simply because folk and 'art' music had rubbed shoulders in France so closely and for so long that there was relatively little to distinguish one from the other. There was no French equivalent of the vivid and exotic Spanish flamenco on which to build a conspicuously French style. For the foundation of anything that could fairly be described as a genuinely French tradition they had to go back to the days of Couperin and Rameau. And it was there that they rediscovered their heritage and put down new roots.

Even in the 17th and 18th centuries, the French were at ease with sensuality to an almost unique degree. But if their greatest pleasures were with the senses, their greatest pride was in the intellect. More than in any other country, and for longer, music has been understood in France as the art of arranging sounds in aesthetically seductive and intellectually satisfying patterns. The cardinal virtues have always been those of intelligence: logic, clarity, moderation and balance. The best way to get onto the same wavelength as most French composers, from Couperin to Boulez, is not to contrast their work with that of other composers, especially not Germanic ones, but with painters, sculptors and architects.

It is one of the hallmarks of the French tradition that a piece of music is regarded not primarily as an exercise in soul-stretching (a hallmark of Germanic music) but as an artefact – a thing of meticulously calculated shape, dimensions, colour and consistency. In the words of Debussy: "French music is all clearness, elegance; simple natural declamation. The aim of French music is, above all, to please ... The musical genius of France may be described as a fantasy of the senses."

The pictorial element, too, had pride of place in French musical thinking. Just look at the titles chosen by Debussy for various piano pieces: *Poissons d'or* (Goldfish), *La puerta del vino* (a specific doorway in the Moorish palace of the Alhambra at Granada in Spain), *Le cathèdrale engloutie* (The Engulfed Cathedral), *Reflets dans l'eau* (Reflections in the Water), *Feux d'artifice* (Fireworks), *Des pas sur la neige* (Footsteps in the Snow) and many more. Or by Ravel: *Jeux d'eau* (Fountains), *Oiseaux tristes* (The Mournful Birds), *Une barque sur l'ocean* (A Boat on the Ocean), *Le Gibet* (The Gallows).

If pictorialism and tone-painting were key elements of the new French style, so was a cultivation of the exotic and foreign, either nearby (Chabrier, Debussy and Ravel all had a fascination with Spain) or far distant (the oriental influence, particularly that of the Javanese *gamelan*, as heard at the great Paris Exposition of 1889, prompted the use of scales, harmonies and colours far removed from the Western

Bartók's fascination with the folk melodies of his homeland led him to collect them. They provided the inspiration for some of his greatest music, including the Fifteen Hungarian Peasant Songs.

Classical tradition). Turning to analogy, one might say that while Germanic, Hispanic and Italian music are based on consonants, French music is based on vowels (no-one but a Frenchman would have idealized the piano as "an instrument without hammers" – Debussy's phrase). If Germanic music is mountains, crags, forests and valleys, French music is rivers, lakes and the sea, in which are reflected the surrounding topography. The image of reflection is perhaps the single most striking feature of the so-called French Impressionists (a title, incidentally, which Debussy rejected).

In addition to Chabrier, Saint-Saëns, Debussy and Ravel, other consciously national piano composers include Vincent d'Indy, Paul Dukas, Ernest Chausson, Erik Satie and that 20th-century group known as Les Six: Milhaud, Poulenc, Honegger, Auric, Durey, Tailleferre, of whom only the first three achieved world fame.

Hungary

The most famous 'Hungarian' styles are those popularized by Liszt, in his Hungarian Rhapsodies and Brahms, in his Hungarian Dances (in two versions, one for solo piano, the other for piano duet). These were based, however, not on the authentic, indigenous folk music of the Hungarian peasantry but on the highly urbanized music of professional Hungarian gypsy bands. Derived from the traditional Hungarian *verbunkos* (associated with military recruiting rituals), the typical gypsy 'rhapsody' is divided into two main sections, a slow, exotic, often highly sensual introduction (the *lassu*) and an extravagantly lively, virtuosic fast section (the *friss*), often followed by a highly ornamented closing section (*figura*). Closely related to this is the popular *csardas*, deriving mainly from the *friss* of the *verbunkos*.

Grieg's source for his Slåtter *piano works was the music of Norwegian peasant fiddlers.*

In addition to the many examples from Brahms and Liszt, there are also 'Hungarian' pieces by Haydn and Schubert.

It was not until the trail-blazing field work of Bela Bartók and Zoltán Kodály that authentic Hungarian peasant music was effectively discovered. Virtually every composition from Bartók's maturity is based on it in one way or another. More than a quarter of Bartók's output was for the piano (he was a superb pianist himself) and much of it is among the most important music of the 20th century, most notably the Fifteen Hungarian Peasant Songs, the imposing three-movement Sonata of 1926, the *Mikrokosmos* (effectively a six-part course in piano technique, progressing from the very simple to the highly demanding and exploring almost every aspect of the piano's potential), the two books 'For Children' (whose sophistication, variety and poignancy are above most children's heads), the vividly evocative 'Out of Doors' suite, with its characteristically Bartókian 'night music' and, most importantly of all, the three concertos, the Music for Strings, Percussion and Celeste and the hair-raising Sonata for Two Pianos and Percussion. Outstanding among his output of chamber music is the set of 'Contrasts' for piano, violin and clarinet, commissioned by the great jazz clarinettist Benny Goodman. Bartók's style is usually highly dissonant, predominantly percussive and rhythmically fascinating, and his colouristic range is almost a match for Debussy's.

Kodály's piano music is not very extensive and remains far less well known than Bartók's. His best piano works include the Dances of Marrosszek, the Nine Pieces, Op. 3 and the Seven Pieces, Op. 11.

The music of Ernö Dohnányi (1877–1960) is the most immediately accessible of the output of Hungarian composers in the 20th century. He largely stood apart from contemporary developments and continued to compose in a basically 19th-century vein. Recommended are his Variations on a Hungarian Folksong, Op. 29, the suite *Ruralia Hungarica*. His best-known work by far, however, is the set of Variations on a Nursery Song ('Twinkle, twinkle, Little Star') for piano and orchestra.

Norway

Where the piano is concerned, Norwegian music is synonymous with the name of Edvard Grieg (1843–1907). As in much of Scandinavia at the start of the 19th century, Norway's culture was very largely imported – mostly from Germany, and from neighbouring Denmark (amazingly, middle and upper class Norwegians often spoke the Danish language in preference to their own). In 1864, when he was 21, Grieg met Rikard Nordraak, the 22-year-old musician at the head of the growing nationalist movement. From that moment on, he scarcely wrote a bar of music that was not

intended to enshrine the musical identity of his homeland. On the whole, he did it in the realm of the piano miniature (his ten books of Lyric Pieces serve as a kind of musical diary of his creative life), yet the piano work most famously associated with him is no miniature at all but the expansive Concerto in A minor – now long established as one of the most popular ever written. Its debt to Schumann's concerto in the same key is well known. Hardly realized at all outside Norway is that virtually everything in it is derived from the melodic patterns of Norwegian folk music. The connection is more obvious, indeed unavoidable, in the case of his most interesting piano music, the *Slåtter* (pronounced 'slaughter'), which are settings of dance tunes taken down by Grieg from an old peasant fiddler in Telemark. An interesting offshoot of Grieg's Norwegian researches is the resulting stylistic anticipation of French Impressionism. Debussy was more affected by Grieg's music than he liked to admit, and Ravel went so far as to state that he had never written anything that was not influenced by Grieg.

Liszt (seen here in Polish national costume) used the national dance forms of his country in his piano music; see overleaf.

Led by Balakirev, Russian nationalist composers shook free of German influence; painting: Kandinsky's 'Song of the Volga'.

Poland

Where the piano is concerned, Polish music simply is Chopin. It was he who put it on the international map, and no subsequent composer has come close to matching his achievement. With few exceptions, foremost among them the *Krakowiak* (which provides the basis for the finale of his Piano Concerto No.1), he did it within the confines of two national dances: the mazurka and the polonaise (see page 51). Of his followers, only Karol Szymanowski (1882–1937) wrote music of even vaguely comparable quality.

Russia

Mikhail Glinka, born in 1804, is widely known as the 'father of Russian music'. He was not the first Russian composer by any means, but he was the first consistently and deliberately to write specifically Russian music, drawing heavily, like other nationalists, on the great reservoir of indigenous folk music. His most important works are orchestral and operatic, but he also composed the first specifically Russian piano music, though most of it is little better than run-of-the-mill *salon* music. Following Glinka's death in 1857, the banner of musical nationalism passed into the hands of an unlikely band of amateur composers, among them a sometime railway administrator by the name of Mily Balakirev.

Born in 1837, he was a highly accomplished if not excessively refined pianist (claiming to have had a mere ten lessons in his life) and remains best known as the founder and guiding light of the so-called 'mighty handful' (comprising, in addition to himself, Borodin (a renowned chemist), Mussorgsky (a military man and civil servant), Rimsky-Korsakov (a naval officer) and Cesar Cui (an engineer). This impassioned band of nationalists was pledged to counter the Germanic influence of Anton Rubinstein, and even Tchaikovsky, with music of an unassailably Russian character.

In 1860, on a boat trip to the Caspian Sea, Balakirev set about collecting folksongs, including the now almost hackneyed 'Song of the Volga Boatmen'. He was not a prolific composer, but one piano work, *Islamey* (written in 1869 and subtitled 'an oriental fantasy'), has become a staple of the virtuoso repertoire, especially in Russia, and rivals in difficulty even the 'Transcendental Studies' of Liszt. Although Balakirev's influence on Russian music and musicians continued throughout his life, he himself forswore the profession in 1872 and took up a full-time job in the goods department of the Central Railway Company, on the

Warsaw line (thus maintaining at least a symbolic link with Chopin, whose services to Polish music had played a formative part in Balakirev's own nationalistic aspirations).

The greatest piano work to arise from the Russian nationalist movement, however, is Mussorgsky's famous 'Pictures from an Exhibition', still better known in the brilliant orchestration of it by Ravel. Inspired by the paintings and designs of his friend Hartmann, who had recently died at the age of 39, it depicts the composer's feelings and impressions as he considers ten dramatically varied paintings linked by a series of *promenades*, all of which are compressed variants of the splendidly stirring opening movement. The music displays the fantastic sense of colour and tonal imagination, as well as the brilliant virtuosity and the folk-like simplicity that characterize the Russian nationalist movement as a whole. The haunting *Vecchio Castello* (The Old Castle) is an almost eerie reminder of the extent to which the true Russian is both Western and Eastern. The vividness of the musical imagery is scarcely credible as it brings to life grotesque and sinister gnomes, terrifying witches, gossiping women in the marketplace, a confrontation between a rich and a poor jew, a ballet of unhatched chicks and so on. In its peculiar combination of the sophisticated and the primitive, of delicacy and wildness, of dazzle and shadow, it is uniquely Russian. So, too, is its basically episodic character, its intense concentration on the experience of the moment. Progressive thinking, the evolution of ideas through logical development, is not, on the whole, a characteristic of the Russian tradition. Other nationalistic piano composers include Sergei Lyapunov (1859–1924), whose Transcendental Etudes (directly inspired by Liszt) include the dazzlingly effective *Lezghinka*, and Anatol Lyadov (1855–1914). Hardly remembered at all today, Lyadov was a remarkable craftsman whose few piano works are of great charm and sophistication. His style is often reminiscent of Schumann, Mendelssohn and Chopin.

Spain

The nationalistic music of Spain is dominated by flamenco, the style of the Spanish gypsies, based mainly on the so-called *cante hondo* or 'deep song' of Andalusia in the south of Spain. Characterized by a wailing, highly emotional style of singing, it is also vividly rhythmic – a fact emphasized by the almost constant use of castanets, hand clapping (*palmada*) and stamping feet (*zapateado*). As with so much other folk music, it is rooted in the experience of oppression. Both the gypsies and the Spanish jews (*Sephardim*) have a long history of persecution, and it is said that much of the flamenco style was born in prisons, many of whose inmates were gypsies or jews. The words of the *cante hondo* are often extremely erotic, and that sense of raw sensuality is a key element in flamenco. The compass of *cante hondo* is relatively limited, rarely exceeding a sixth (C up to A on the piano). The singing is highly ornamented, non-metric and sometimes uses microtones (intervals smaller than the smallest Western interval, the semi-tone). Almost all Spanish music is accompanied by the guitar, and guitar-imitation has been the outstanding feature of all self-consciously 'Spanish' keyboard music, from Scarlatti and Soler in the 18th century to Rodrigo in the 20th. A notable characteristic is the use of fast repeated notes, and a primitive 'strumming' technique, often including highly dissonant 'tone clusters'. The flamenco style is deeply influenced by Arabic and even Indian music, from which it derives much of its exotic character, particularly the 'orientalism' of its melody. Like virtually all Spanish (and African) music, it is composed mostly of dance songs. (See also Popular and National Dance Forms, pages 50–3.)

United States

When the Czech composer Dvořák was invited to the United States it was in the hope that he could do for American music what he had so brilliantly done for that of his native Bohemia, namely to forge a distinct and recognizable national style. It was a naïve hope. For a start, a national musical identity of any substance has to be forged from within, not without; and in any case, a native American composer had already forged a distinctly American style and had made it for a time the talk of musical Europe. His name was Louis Moreau Gottschalk, a brilliant pianist and one of the first matinée idols of the international piano circuit. Born in Louisiana in 1829, he was fascinated from an early age by the music of the black slaves he heard on the plantations and in Congo Square. As a composer, he made his mark before he was even twenty with such exotic reminiscences of his native New Orleans as *Bamboula*, *La savane* and *La bananier* and was justifiably renowned as the first authentic musical spokesman of the New World. With these works and others – like the hugely enjoyable *Ojos Criollos* (Creole Eyes), which he once arranged for forty pianos (!), *Manchega*, *Le Mancenillier*, *The Banjo* (a really

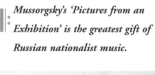

Mussorgsky's 'Pictures from an Exhibition' is the greatest gift of Russian nationalist music.

A truly national voice in American music grew out of the experience of post-Emancipation black communities.

splendid, characterful showpiece, fully deserving of revival), *La Gallina* and still more – he anticipated many later features of American music with extraordinary prescience. Ragtime, jazz, the Latin Americana of Gershwin, Copland and Bernstein, the populist allusiveness of Charles Ives and the American experimental tradition, all are prefigured in Gottschalk's piano music. Gottschalk did much to raise the standards of American musical life, and during the years of the Civil War (1861–65) he toured the country tirelessly,

covering more than 95,000 miles by train and giving more than 1100 recitals. He was dead by the time Dvořák was sent for, and it has to be admitted that his lead was not followed, except in the world of travelling minstrel shows and the growing urban communities of post-Emancipation blacks. There, and with the help of homegrown tunesmiths like Stephen Foster, a truly national voice was emerging and would eventually result in the birth of a new kind of 'art' music (ragtime – overwhelmingly a piano style) and a new kind of folk music (the world's last) that came to be loosely known as jazz. (See also page 52.)

During his stay in America, Dvořák had relatively little contact with this kind of music, and still less with the music of the American Indians. He paid lip service to both (in his 'New World' Symphony, his 'American' Quartet and in the words of advice he gave to native composers), but the hoped-for 'American' music – specifically, American 'classical' music – was not forthcoming. American popular music, on the other hand, was burgeoning, nourished by such diverse sources as bluegrass country fiddlers, southern banjo pickers, Christian hymns, military marching bands, patriotic songs and so on.

Meanwhile, the American pianist-composer Edward MacDowell was putting the finishing touches to his professional training in France and Germany. But while he became the first American composer whose works were widely taken up in Europe, he continued to compose in a basically European idiom. His many piano pieces were once quite popular, particularly *To a Wild Rose*, and have seen an attempted revival in recent years, but he advanced the cause of a distinctively American music hardly at all. Indeed, he openly scorned Dvořák's folkloric recipes for a national music.

America has always produced a rich crop of rugged individualists, not to say madcap eccentrics, and isolated figures like Anthony Philip Heinrich, William Henry Fry had already heaped dollops of native folkloriana on their basically European creations, over the span of more than half a century. But the piano composers who were really cleaning up were those now all-but-forgotten also-rans Charles Blake

(b.1847) and the hygienically named W. F. Sudds (1843–1920). The first composer to achieve a deeply, fundamentally and unmistakably American style, using indigenous ingredients as something more than stylistic seasoning, was Charles Ives, a cantankerous, reclusive insurance man whose work remained unknown for decades (see Great Composers). The second was George Gershwin, whose *Rhapsody in Blue* (1924) was famous even before he had finished writing it (again, see Great Composers) closely followed by Aaron Copland, whose own jazz-influenced Piano Concerto of 1927 was nothing like so well-received. Unlike Gershwin, Copland drew heavily as well on the folklore of white America and in his ballets *Billy the Kid*, *Appalachian Spring*, and *Rodeo* he achieved a uniquely 'nostalgic' strain of Americana, nourished by cowboy songs, hymn tunes, religious songs, country fiddling and other sources. With some exceptions, like the *4 Piano Blues*, his keyboard music is generally in a more difficult, 'intellectual' vein, using advanced twelve-tone techniques and considerable dissonance.

Other determinedly American composers for the piano are Leonard Bernstein, John Cage, Henry Cowell and Charles Tomlinson Griffes. Their fellow-Americans Elliott Carter and Samuel Barber are not, on the whole, specifically 'national' composers, but their best piano music (one sonata and one concerto each) is of major importance in the story of 20th-century music. Of contemporary American composers of music for the piano, John Adams, John Corigliano and Philip Glass are all highly regarded.

81

Louis Moreau Gottschalk was the first to forge a home-grown American musical style.

Blues, Boogie and the Birth of Jazz

One-leg Willy Joseph, Three-fingered Mamie Desdoumes, Cripple Clarence Lofton, James 'Stump' Johnson, One-arm Slim, One-leg Shadow, No-legs Cagey – what do they have in common (apart from physical abbreviation)? To a man – and one woman – they all played the blues, which could be a dangerous business in the bars and brothels of early 20th-century America. Whether they realized that they stood at the beginning of a tradition which was to permeate the entire world of popular music for at least a century is doubtful. Like most other American blacks at the time, it was all they could do to keep a roof over their heads, find enough food for their bellies and stay out of trouble. They were an underclass in a white man's world, and their music emphasized the gulf that lay between them and their erstwhile masters. It was a music that affirmed their sense of community in suffering, their indomitable resilience in the face of overwhelming odds and the universality of human experience, love and loss. It was the last great folk music of a rapidly industrializing world.

Blues

Arising from the rich cross-fertilization of revivalist hymns, spirituals, banjo and guitar 'rags', and above all from the work songs and plantation 'field hollers' of the American South, the original blues was primarily a vocal form whose origins can be traced back to the late 19th century. Like its vocal models, the piano blues is generally based on a 12-bar, unvarying harmonic sequence in duple time, with a melody favouring certain

'flattened' scale-steps which have come to be known for obvious reasons as 'blue' notes. They have no exact equivalent in the fixed pitches of the piano but they correspond to the lowering of the third and seventh degrees of the scale by a semitone (E flat and B flat in the white-key scale of C). The twelve bars of the basic framework are organized into three groups of four, the second of which is a generally varied duplication of the first. The resulting asymmetrical pattern (AAB) has a natural swing to it, and the blues, while not specifically a dance form, has often been used as an accompaniment to dancing – never more so than in the riotous 'rent-shouts' of New York's Harlem in the 1920s. The frequent use of echo-like repetition in the performance of each phrase has its origin in the call-and-response technique which is a hallmark of African music and a definitive element of jazz. The harmonic sequence of the blues, while giving rise to almost infinite elaboration, is based on the three most common chords of European music, the tonic (home key), dominant (a fifth above) and subdominant (a fourth above). In the key of C these are C-E-G, G-B-D and F-A-C. The most obvious feature of the blues, its expressive character, is the hardest to describe; originally one of deep sorrow, leavened by resilience, and often humour too, it now embraces so many different styles, and such a range of emotional conditions, that it defies easy or brief categorization.

The old blues forms – folk blues, country blues, prison blues, archaic blues – continue to flourish even today, and new variants keep appearing: urban blues, soul

Blues piano came out of the hard environment of bars, brothels and dance-halls.

82

Storyville Jazz Hall, New Orleans.

blues, rhythm and blues, most of them with clear geographical features. The folk blues of Texas and the Midwest spread further west to become the California 'big city' blues, the Mississippi folk blues shaped the Chicago blues, and so on. These, in their turn, have affected the development of white 'country' music, rockabilly, rock 'n' roll, heavy metal, and, where the piano is concerned, Elton John's early group, Bluesology. There is hardly an aspect of jazz piano that has not been affected in one way or another by the blues. Two early spin-offs emerged and matured between the turn of the century and the end of the First World War. One was called 'barrelhouse' style, the other was boogie-woogie.

Boogie and Barrelhouse

The term boogie-woogie, like the word jazz itself, is rife with extra-musical associations, most of them connected with sex. In the sub-culture of African-Americans during the first half of this century it was widely used to signify sexual activity in general and secondary syphilis in particular. Not until 1928, with the release of *Pinetop's Boogie-woogie* on the Vocalion label, did the term and the music become inextricably linked. Poundingly rhythmic and generally loud, boogie derived its most obvious characteristics from its sharply accented, continuously repeated walking bass, originally modelled on the banjo and guitar figures of the early blues singers, but later used to simulate the driving rhythms of the still-expanding steam railways which relied heavily on black labour. Unlike the closely related barrelhouse, it was a specifically urban style, which travelled both westwards to Texas and northwards to Chicago, where it reached its finest flowering before spreading southwards again, moving down the East Coast to Florida in the hands of players like 'Cat-Eye Harry', 'Jack the Bear', 'Tippling Tom', 'The Beetle', 'Speckled Red', 'The Toothpick' and many others. In the course of its travels, it developed a dozen or more regional styles and literally thousands of bass figures for the left hand. Its most famous exponents were Clarence 'Pinetop' Smith, Jimmy Yancey, Albert Ammons, Pete Johnson and Meade Lux Lewis. Among its relatively few

female champions was Mary Lou Williams, who brought to her playing a degree of refinement hardly even hinted at by her male colleagues.

It must be remembered that in the United States at the start of this century, the wave of pianomania which had engulfed the nation was only just beginning to decline. There were still more pianos than bathtubs in private ownership, and certainly no drinking establishment could afford to be without one. From the cocktail lounges of the best hotels to the saloons of the Wild West, where liquor flowed freely and human life was cheap, the alliance of pianos with the sale of alcohol was a long-established tradition. 'Barrelhouse' took its name from the ramshackle huts and converted railway wagons that stood in for saloons in the lumber camps of the Deep South. One of the least refined of all piano styles (the term itself became a synonym for 'rough' or 'crude'), it reflected the primitive and often dangerous environment in which it flourished. More than one barrelhouse pianist was shot dead on the spot if the customers or proprietor did not like his performance.

Unlike boogie-woogie, with its relatively quick tempo and eight beats in a bar, barrelhouse stuck to the slower, four-in-a-bar tempo of the blues and drew heavily on the standard ragtime bass and the heavy left-hand vamp known as stomping. Before long, aspects of barrelhouse were taken up by jazz musicians, who blended them with influences from New Orleans to create the hybrid style known as barrelhouse jazz. Many barrelhouse themes became popular standards and were used by blues pianists long after the original style died out. By the heyday of barrelhouse jazz in the late 1920s, however, the style had lost most of its pianistic associations.

83

Jimmy Yancey, a famous exponent of boogie, in 1939.

Modernism and Modernists

The definition of modernity has always been an elusive business. As commonly used today, the term 'modern', as applied to music, means something very much more than merely 'contemporary'. The latter refers only to time – 'now', as opposed to 'then'. But the madrigals of the 16th-century Gesualdo, the fugue of Beethoven's *Hammerklavier* Sonata and the finale of Chopin's B flat minor Sonata are still far more 'modern' to most ears than, say, the music of John Williams or Andrew Lloyd Webber. Modern music, then, is (or at any rate once was) progressive. While not necessarily turning its back on tradition, its primary concerns are with new frontiers, with discoveries and experiments, with challenges to convention, with forms of expression that reflect the here and now. At its best, it is music of marked and deliberate individuality. When Liszt said in reference to his later music that he was "hurling a lance into the indefinite reaches of the future" he was voicing what was then still a comparatively recent concept.

Igor Stravinsky's piano music shows complexity and violence of rhythm; illustration by Rudolf Grossmann.

Before Beethoven, arguably the first great composer consciously to address posterity, originality played a very minor role (if any role at all) in a composer's outlook. Only after Beethoven did it become enshrined as a virtue. With the Romantics it became almost a religion. In politics, in science, in religion and culture, the 19th-century was a time of unprecedented ferment. Values and assumptions that had sustained European society from the Renaissance to the French Revolution were progressively undermined. Science conferred on humanity a power previously attributed only to the Almighty. The publication in 1859 of Charles Darwin's *Origin of Species* marked one of the major watersheds in human history, as revolutionary in its way as any war. The omnipotency of God, even His existence, was called into question on a more systematic basis than ever before and there was scarcely any aspect of Western society that was unaffected as a consequence.

Harmony Subverted

In music, the revolutionary subversion of traditional harmony started by Chopin and Liszt was continued by Wagner, Mahler, Debussy and Schoenberg, to name only a few of the musical revolutionaries abroad. An essential part of this process was a steadily increasing use of dissonance (or 'discord'), and a decreasing incidence of its resolution. To this day, in the popular imagination, dissonance is the principal characteristic of 'modernism' in music. In varying degrees, it plays a key (or often a non-key) part in the piano music of almost every 20th-century composer.

Throughout the 19th-century, the system of key that had formed the bedrock of the Baroque and Classical eras had been progressively undermined by such revolutionary composers as Chopin, Liszt and Wagner, who had introduced so much chromaticism (the use of notes outside the scales that determine key – any black notes in the all-white key of C major, for instance) that the sense of key, of a self-determining order of notes, was weakened, sometimes to the point of so-called atonality (the total absence of a sense of key). The more 'alien' tones there were, the more dissonant (discordant) the music sounded. The Austrian composer Arnold Schoenberg completed the process of tonal disintegration by devising a system whereby every composition was based on a 'row', or series, of 'twelve notes related only to each other' (twelve being the number of notes – the collection of sharps and flats – that fall within the span of an octave). The result was a degree of dissonance (according to traditional ways of hearing) which was not only unprecedented in itself but all the more disturbing to the average music-lover for the lack of any single, tonal reference point. The procedure is widely known as serialism. Schoenberg's piano pieces are relatively few, mostly quite difficult to play, and still more difficult for most people to listen to with any sense of pleasure or understanding. His celebrated boast, "Someday milkmen will be whistling my tunes", looks increasingly unlikely to come true, but his influence on other 20th-century composers is incalculable.

Pianistic Aspects of Modernism

Dissonance, atonality and serialism, however, are aspects of tonal organization and therefore exist independently of instrumentation. If we want to seek out specifically pianistic aspects of 20th-century 'modernism', we must look first and foremost at rhythm.

Despite the near-miraculous sorcery of Chopin and Debussy, who almost succeed in persuading us otherwise, the piano is a percussion instrument. One hallmark of much 20th-century piano music is its refusal to connive in the great Romantic cover-up perpetrated by most composers in the 19th. Perhaps the most shocking aspect of works like Bartók's *Allegro Barbaro*, Prokofiev's First Piano Concerto, *Sarcasms* and *Suggestion diabolique*, Shostakovich's First Piano Sonata, Stravinsky's use of the piano in *Petrushka* and *Les Noces*, and other like-minded pieces from the early 20th century, was their sheer, unrelenting percussiveness. Closely allied to this, particularly in the works of Bartók and Stravinsky, was a complexity and violence of rhythm scarcely even hinted at by any but the most adventurous 19th-century composers.

Later composers, most notably, perhaps, the Frenchmen Olivier Messiaen and Pierre Boulez, the German Karlheinz Stockhausen and the American-Mexican Conlon Nancarrow, were to devise rhythmic complexities that made Bartók and Stravinsky look tame by comparison. But no composer, certainly no great composer, exists in a vacuum, and each of the above has powerful and vital links with the past. For all his percussiveness, Bartók was pianistically in a direct line of descent from Liszt and Debussy, with an impressionist's ear for colour and a late-

Although a major influence on 20th-century composers, Schoenberg's music looks as unlikely as ever to find favour with the public.

Dmitri Shostakovich – his 24 Preludes and Fugues were an act of homage to Bach.

Romantic's flare for poetical rhetoric. For his part, Messiaen was one of the supreme colourists of the century. His vision of music as a primarily decorative rather than a strictly developmental art was typically French, yet he derived sustenance not only from Debussy and Stravinsky but from such un-French composers as Mozart, Beethoven and Liszt.

Where the piano, in particular, is concerned, Messiaen has proved a greater influence than Bartók, Schoenberg, Stravinsky and Prokofiev put together. His pupils and long-term beneficiaries include Boulez and Stockhausen, whose dauntingly cerebral piano works are reckoned by connoisseurs to be the most important of the mid-20th century, the Hungarian Gyorgy Kurtag (b. 1926), whose

Paul Hindemith – one of the most neglected of 20th-century composers; see page 88.

piano music for the young also owes a debt to Bartók, and the far younger George Benjamin (b.1960) whose Piano Sonata of 1987/8 singled him out at once for special attention. The Japanese composer Toru Takemitsu (1930–96) was keenly influenced by Messiaen.

Standing largely apart from the dominant European trends were such all-American originals as Charles Ives (see page 136), John Cage, Henry Cowell and Lou Harrison, of whom the last three all owed a formative debt to the soundworlds of oriental music, whose use of tuned percussion fundamentally affected their use of the piano (most obviously in Cage's works for 'prepared piano', see page 43).

Total Serialism to Minimalism

In the middle third of the century, post-Schoenbergian serialism looked like being the single most dominant force in 20th-century music, although a number of significant 'modernist' composers such as Bartók, Shostakovich, Prokofiev, Stravinsky and Copland stood largely or entirely apart from it (20th-century composers such as Milhaud, Poulenc, Britten, Tippett and so on fall outside the scope of this discussion, never having assumed the 'modernist' mantle). With its apparently cold-blooded intellectualism, its fearsome complexities and its perceived abandonment of beauty and spiritual expressiveness, the school of 'total serialism', spearheaded by Stockhausen and Boulez, opened up the greatest rift between composer and audience in musical history. Many who could wholeheartedly enjoy the music of Bartók, Stravinsky and even Alban Berg (whose one-movement Piano Sonata came close to real popularity, among pianists at least) felt entirely excluded by the music of the mid-century avant garde, whose composers seemed to regard them with contempt.

In the last quarter of the century, however, a steadily increasing number of composers began to reject the serialists (who in any case had never stood much of a chance in the Soviet Union). The so-called 'minimalist' school, with its simplicity of material, its concern for euphony and its almost narcotic addiction to repetition, was pioneered, largely in the United States, by composers such as Terry Riley, Philip Glass and John Adams, all of whom have written for piano, though none of them extensively. Like the 'total serialists', the minimalists employ the most minute mathematical calculations, as subtle variations are introduced into the repetitions. While it can serve as a kind of generalized background music, establishing and maintaining a particular mood, it requires concentrated listening if its techniques are to be properly understood.

To judge from the output of composers in the final two decades of the 20th century, the piano would seem largely to have had its day. With the advent of electronic media, the

Karlheinz Stockhausen, the uncrowned king of the mid to late 20th-century avant garde, in Disneyland, 1966.

potentially infinite possibilities opened up by the computer, a widening interest in tone colour as a formative structural agent and a massive decline in domestic music-making, the piano, in terms of contemporary music, looks likely to suffer the same fate as the harpsichord at the beginning of the 19th century. But, to paraphrase Mark Twain, reports of its imminent death have been greatly exaggerated.

Major Modernist Voices

BELA BARTOK (1881–1945) Famous (though not entirely accurately) as the father of the modernist, percussive approach to the piano and for his crunching discords and complicated rhythms, Bartók was pianistically in a direct line of descent from Liszt and Debussy, with an impressionist's ear for colour and a late Romantic's flare for poetical rhetoric. What strikes one most in the recordings of him playing his own music is not its neo-barbarism but its simplicity, its clarity of contour, and perhaps above all, its essentially harmonic sonority. The dissonance is there, undeniably, but in his extraordinary balancing and 'voicing' of chords, however black and discordant they may look on the page, Bartók achieves a warmth of tone and a deployment of light and shade which most of his keyboard interpreters scarcely even suggest. Only when Bartók is recognized as one of the most refined and cultivated minds in musical history will the importance of his pianistic legacy be properly understood. (For an introduction to his most important piano works, see under National Music, page 77.)

IGOR STRAVINSKY (1882–1971) Stravinsky was a capable though not a virtuoso pianist, but he wrote surprisingly little for the instrument (surprising because much of his music is of a percussive, powerfully rhythmic character perfectly suited to the piano's elemental nature). Because his most popular music is so accessible, one easily forgets the degree to which Stravinsky was a revolutionary: not for nothing did the audience riot at the premiere of his ballet 'The Rite of Spring' in 1913. Here was a man who threw into question almost everything on which the Western musical tradition had been based since the Renaissance, be it in the realm of harmony, rhythm, metre, melody, even colour. His best known piano work, 'Three Dances from *Petrushka*', is drawn, as its name states, from his second most popular ballet (in which the piano plays a prominent part) and was made at the suggestion of the great pianist Artur Rubinstein. His two major original piano works are the highly attractive and engaging Sonata of 1924 and the Serenade of 1925, both from his fertile 'neo-classical' period. The Sonata looks back to Bach and is the more easily enjoyable of the two; the Serenade is a somewhat harder nut to crack. As with a number of Stravinsky's works it has an almost medieval feel to it, though the idiom is emphatically contemporary. Well down the line in importance, though thoroughly enjoyable and certainly noteworthy, are the Four Studies of 1908, still rooted in the 19th-century, the *Piano Rag Music* of 1919, as divertingly eccentric as the rest of his jazz-influenced music, and two enchanting little suites for piano duet, one part easy (this intended for his children) the other most definitely not. The piano also loomed large in a number of Stravinsky's more ambitious works, such as the Concerto for Piano and Wind Instruments, the Concerto for Two Solo Pianos, the Sonata for Two Pianos and the ballet-cantata *Les Noces*, scored for soloists, chorus, 4 pianos and 17 percussion instruments.

Prokofiev in 1934. His personal, modernistic style was rooted in tradition.

expressionistic kind to have achieved anything approaching popularity with sophisticated, 'intellectual' audiences.

SERGEI PROKOFIEV (1891–1953) Precocious both as pianist and composer (he wrote his first opera at the age of nine), Prokofiev developed a highly personal style, modernistic yet firmly rooted in tradition, extremely percussive yet full of lyricism, expansive yet tightly disciplined. His piano music is shot through with driving rhythms, abrasive discords, asymmetrical patterns and often a mechanistic type of excitement, but there are frequent passages of poignant simplicity and innocent charm. His pianistic style derived largely from Liszt, Mussorgsky and Rachmaninov and in turn influenced the piano-writing of many younger composers, including Kabalevsky, Shostakovich and the American Samuel Barber. His most important piano works include five dazzlingly effective piano concertos (the Fourth for the left hand alone) and nine piano sonatas, most of which look like having secured a permanent place in the repertoire, as well as the brief, epigrammatic *Visions fugitives* and the characteristically entitled 'Sarcasms'. As a pianist, Prokofiev was firmly in the anti-Romantic mould, sparing of pedal, steely-fingered, dry-toned and rhythmically explosive.

PAUL HINDEMITH (189--1963) Once among the most influential and frequently played of 20th-century composers, Hindemith has since become one of the most neglected. After a rebellious youth when his works were full of expressionistic dissonance, he became the foremost German neo-Classicist, although in fact he drew more nourishment from the Baroque than from the Classical era. Like his revered Bach, he was a highly contrapuntal composer (deriving his textures from the interplay of horizontal, melodic lines) and spurned the ivory tower inhabited by so many of his contemporaries. He deliberately set out to write 'useful' music, and contributed many pieces to what he hoped would be a revival in home music-making. He was a resourceful magpie (drawing on many styles, including jazz) and a brilliant craftsman. He wrote a considerable amount of piano music, and still more chamber music 'with' piano. For his time, he wrote in an approachable though never ingratiating style, and for the most part without the extreme discordancy cultivated by many of his colleagues. He was also an accomplished pianist and a viola-player of world class.

DMITRI SHOSTAKOVICH (1906–75) Widely regarded as the greatest composer to emerge from the former Soviet Union, Shostakovich was in many ways a tragic figure, a genius whose creative wings were clipped by totalitarian orthodoxy. Originally destined to become a concert pianist, he established himself as a brilliant *enfant terrible* with such boldly dissonant and experimental piano works as the First Piano Sonata (1926) and the 'Aphorisms' of 1927. At that time, Soviet musicians were being actively encouraged to perform and study the revolutionary works of

ANTON VON WEBERN (1883–1945) Like his fellow member of the Second Viennese School, Alban Berg, Webern's reputation as a major contributor to piano music rests with a single work, the three-movement Variations, Op. 27, composed in 1936. Requiring meticulous attention to detail and a technique of exceptional subtlety, it is not, however, a virtuoso work and its acutely cerebral idiom puts it generally beyond the reach of the average music-lover.

ALBAN BERG (1885–1935) The most accessible member of the so-called Second Viennese School (the others being Arnold Schoenberg and Anton Webern), Berg's contribution to the solo piano repertoire consists of a single, almost painfully personal and intense one-movement Sonata, whose prevailing dissonance belongs more to the 19th-century heritage of Wagner, Liszt and Mahler than to the revolutionary tactics of his teacher Schoenberg. The work, his Op.1, is firmly rooted in the classical framework of so-called 'sonata form' and is the only piano piece of its such then-firebrands as Schoenberg, Berg and Hindemith. It was a false spring. In 1932 the state assumed full control of all musical activity. By 1936 Shostakovich had fallen foul of the Soviet authorities and was condemned, among other things, for the unacceptable dissonance of his works. He drew back from the cultural barricades, and his music, while never as conservative as Rachmaninov's, took him down different paths, though his brushes with the state were far from over. His most important piano works include the two sonatas, two splendid and entertaining concertos, and perhaps above all, the remarkable (and thoroughly approachable) set of 24 Preludes and Fugues, an overt act of homage to Bach, and to Chopin, whose key scheme Shostakovich adopts. In character, form, length and emotional range, as in their quality, they are more remarkable for their variety than their similarity.

OLIVIER MESSIAEN (1908–92) In a direct line of succession from Chopin and Liszt through Debussy and Stravinsky, Messiaen was one of the supreme colourists of the century. His vision of music as a primarily decorative rather than a strictly developmental art was typically French. His style can be highly discordant and his rhythm dauntingly complex, and his music has so far proved more attractive to players than to listeners. Few musicians, however, would dispute either its importance or Messiaen's far-reaching influence as both composer and teacher (his pupils included both Stockhausen and Boulez). His most significant and compelling piano works are the two great cycles *Vingt regards sur l'Enfant Jésus* (his profound Roman Catholic faith informed virtually everything he did) and the *Catalogue d'oiseaux*, based on his meticulous annotations and transcriptions of birdsong.

CONLON NANCARROW (B.1912) This remarkable Mexican-American composer has specialized since 1950 in writing 'studies' for player piano, the only instrument capable of reproducing the extraordinary

rhythmic complexity of his music. His canons and other polyphonic compositions require 'voices' moving at subtly differing speeds, executing simultaneous speedings up and slowings down and attaining speeds beyond the capacity of human hand and brain. Among his many great admirers is the pianist Alfred Brendel.

PIERRE BOULEZ (B.1925) For the most part, Boulez's piano music is as difficult to describe as it is to play, nor does it constitute comfortable listening for the average music lover. Widely acclaimed as one of the most significant, influential and substantial composers of the mid-20th century, he has never courted popularity, and his piano music, some of it occupying the high ground of his musical thought, is characteristically uncompromising, and like most serious music of its time looks destined to remain a minority taste. Ruthlessly logical, intellectually forbidding and almost brutally sophisticated, it lies quite beyond the reach of all but the most accomplished professionals, and few have taken any of it into their repertoire.

KARLHEINZ STOCKHAUSEN (B.1928) By the middle 1950s, Stockhausen was established as the uncrowned king of the avant garde. His 11 Piano Pieces were all composed during this period of his life (1952–61) and are of such daunting complexity and technical difficulty that few pianists have been able or willing to master them. His music is so resistant to verbal elucidation that inquiring but inexperienced music-lovers can count themselves lucky if they encounter a single paragraph on the subject which is either comprehensible or enlightening, let alone both. For more useful illumination of this intractable subject, the intrepid investigator must seek out more specialist guides than this one. Suffice it to say, here, that to those who understand it Stockhausen's considerable body of piano works constitutes an important, even profound, chapter in the story of mid- and late- 20th-century music.

89

Olivier Messiaen was one of the supreme colourists of the 20th century.

The Piano in Chamber Music

Virtually all chamber music with piano can trace its ancestry to the trio sonatas of the Baroque, where the keyboard (usually the harpsichord, very occasionally the organ) served as a kind of blending agent, filling in the harmonies suggested by the bass line, adding emphasis to the bass line itself, and ornamenting the principal melody. As the contrapuntal weave of the Baroque gave way to the simpler texture of straightforward melody-and-accompaniment, the keyboard was moved closer to the foreground. By the last third of the 18th century, with the more vocally inflective piano ousting the inflexible harpsichord from public favour, the keyboard gained the upper hand and earlier roles were reversed, the violin now being cast in the reduced role of accompanist, to the point where it became little more than an optional extra. Meanwhile, the cello either dropped away altogether or continued, Baroque-style, to duplicate the bass line of the piano part.

And with few exceptions, the music itself shed much of its earlier, aristocratic sophistication and became increasingly simple, intimate and domestic in character. This conception was the direct result of the piano's status at the time as primarily a woman's instrument; it is a fact that while the majority of concert virtuosos are male, and always have been, the overwhelming majority of piano students, at any time in the instrument's history, have been female. Chamber music had always been essentially domestic, but in the High Baroque the homes it graced were mainly those of the ruling aristocracy. Only with the rise of the market-minded bourgeoisie did it become primarily a middle-class diversion.

The definition of chamber music has always been a little vague. Technically, it embraces all instrumental ensemble music to be played by no more than nine players, and with no more than one instrument to a part (excepting the cello, whose subservient nature has already been noted). The following survey is in ascending order of instrumental population, up to the number of seven, and is confined, on the whole, to the music of great composers.

A great duo: Rudolf Serkin (see also page 156) and violinist Adolf Busch in the 1920s.

Sonatas and Other Duos

The first important instrumental duos with piano come from Mozart, whose contributions fall into two categories, those for piano duet and those for violin. Of the former, three works stand out above all the others. The last two sonatas for four hands at one piano are among the greatest of all his keyboard works, comparable even with his great symphonies, and the Sonata in D for Two Pianos, K.448, is rivalled in quality only by Brahms's in F minor (an earlier version of his Quintet for Piano and Strings).

Of Mozart's violin sonatas, all of the earlier ones conform to the then prevailing style of the 'accompanied piano sonata', in which the violin is little more than an attendant lackey, sometimes doubling the melodies of the piano part, sometimes just contributing innocuous little accompanimental features. The first sonatas in which he treated the violin as an equal, so to speak (and incidentally, he was himself an excellent violinist), were written in Mannheim, Germany, in 1775, when his attitudes to instrumental drama were fundamentally affected by the dynamic style of orchestral playing being pioneered there. Thereafter, violin and piano met on equal terms – theoretically, at least. If only because of its nature, the piano still gets the lion's share of the material, though any sense of the violin being merely an 'accompanist' has now been removed.

It is generally agreed that Schubert's mature instrumental duos are less consistently fine than Mozart's. The three Violin Sonatas (often called Sonatinas) are certainly attractive; so is the Sonata for Arpeggione, now always played on the cello. (The arpeggione was a freak hybrid – a cross between a guitar and a cello – which fluttered briefly and then died.) The *Rondo brillant* for violin, on the other hand, is very much more than an effective showpiece, but it pales next to the great Fantasia in C, whose stature and difficulty place it among his very greatest chamber works. Among his duos its only rival is the magnificent and tragic Fantasia in F minor for piano duet.

With Beethoven's ten violin sonatas, the dramatic potential of the medium is brilliantly exploited, culminating in the glory and excitement of the so-called 'Kreutzer'

Sonata, which in Beethoven's own words is "just like a concerto". No duo sonata of such dimensions, such drama, such virtuosity had ever been written before, and few written since have matched it; those in the same class include Brahms's Third Sonata and Franck's only sonata. (Schumann's two sonatas have many virtues and deserve greater exposure, but they are not in the 'Kreutzer' class).

Beethoven's five cello sonatas are the greatest of the Classical period, but they have surprisingly little competition. Amazingly, Boccherini (a virtuoso cellist and a prolific composer of chamber music) wrote none, nor have we any from Haydn or Mozart, and even Schubert's lone example was not originally for the cello. Of Beethoven's five, the first two, though wonderful music, are almost like piano sonatas with cello accompaniment. The middle one, in A major, Op. 69, is understandably the most popular but the last two, both of them in Beethoven's 'advanced' late style, are great works by any standard, though the last, in D major, demands almost as much of the listener as of the player.

In the Romantic era we have two very fine cello sonatas by Mendelssohn, one rather problematical one by Chopin and two great examples by Brahms, but few others. Brahms's second, in F major, almost does for the cello what

Beethoven's 'Kreutzer' did for the violin. From its very opening bars this is unmistakably a big, bold, exciting work of tremendous stature, and both players have their hands full in almost every sense. The 'Third' Sonata offered on some recordings (and very occasionally in recital) is, in fact, an arrangement in D of the wonderful G major Violin Sonata. Long believed to have been done by Brahms himself, it now seems clear that the arrangement is the work of the German conductor and composer Paul Klengel. Other Romantic cello sonatas include one each from Saint-Saëns. Grieg and Rachmaninov. Brahms's last duo sonatas were for clarinet (Op. 120), although he sanctioned their performance on the viola and both versions remain equally popular.

Schumann's duos embrace two splendid sonatas for violin, 3 Fantasy Pieces for clarinet (often played on the violin or cello), a splendid Adagio and Allegro for horn (also played on violin or cello), three hauntingly poignant Romances or oboe (frequently appropriated by violin or clarinet), a splendid suite for cello (Five Pieces in Folk Style), and another for viola (*Märchenbilder*) and, most intriguingly,

Mozart's sonatas for four hands are among the greatest of his keyboard works. The composer is pictured here with his father, Leopold, and sister, Nännerl.

In the piano trio the instruments usually called for are, in addition to the piano itself, the cello and the violin.

a set of accompaniments to unaccompanied string sonatas and suites by Bach and Paganini. All these works reflect Schumann's warmth of personality and in some cases his capricious imagination. The lively, sometimes rapturous interchanges between instruments perfectly bear out the much-cited description of chamber music as 'the music of friends'.

Other duos of exceptional distinction include the magnificent and formidably taxing Violin Sonata by César Franck (already mentioned), which is occasionally appropriated by cellists; the three Violin Sonatas by Grieg; the two Violin and two Cello Sonatas by Fauré; the Violin and the Cello sonatas of Debussy; the lone Violin Sonata of Ravel; the cello sonatas of Rachmaninov, Shostakovich and Britten, and the two violin sonatas by Bartók.

The Piano Trio

Not, as it sounds, a trio of pianos, but of a single piano with two other instruments, most usually a violin and cello.

From the mid-18th century onwards (and with the sole possible exception of the violin sonata), the piano trio has proved the most popular keyboard medium in chamber

music, drawing no less than forty-five from Haydn, eight from Mozart, eight from Beethoven (plus two sets of variations), three from Schubert (if one includes the one movement *Notturno*), three from Schumann, two from Mendelssohn, five from Brahms (including one with horn, another with clarinet), four from Dvořák, two from Shostakovich and one each from Chopin, Tchaikovsky, Debussy, Ravel, Smetana and Chausson.

For most of the 18th century, chamber music was designed primarily as a form of enjoyable but not very demanding home entertainment. Its job was to be attractive, generally cheerful, full of good tunes and intellectually lightweight enough not to require much in the way of concentration on the part of the listener. On the whole, the piano trios of Mozart and Haydn fulfil this brief at the very highest level, but there are examples in the output of each that wilfully overstep the boundaries of this convention. Mozart's first transgression was his Trio in E flat for piano, viola and clarinet (often known as the *Kegelstatt* (or 'Bowling Alley') Trio, since Mozart is said to have composed it in just such a place). Of his later piano trios, two in particular follow suit in being both entrancing and intriguing: the B flat, K.502, and the E major, K.542, are as near perfection as the genre gets, yet neither is in the least difficult to listen to.

Beethoven's six mature piano trios give notice from the

beginning that their composer means to be taken seriously. Powerful and brimming over with self-confidence, they rule out simultaneous conversation as an acceptable option. Each is enormously enjoyable, and the last three – the two of Op. 70 and the famous 'Archduke' Trio that closes the series – are among the very greatest chamber works ever written. The D major Trio, Op. 70 No.1 is known as 'The Ghost' because of its weird and hauntingly atmospheric tremolandos, and the pervasive darkness of its slow movement. Its companion in E flat is a sunnier work, and almost insolently healthy, but it is the 'Archduke' (dedicated to Beethoven's friend and patron the Archduke Rudolf of Austria) that takes the medium of the piano trio to heights, and, indeed, in its spacious slow movement, to depths, that have remained unmatched in the entire history of the form. Among Beethoven's many achievements is the final liberation of the cello from its servile, bass-doubling role throughout most of the 18th century. His one trio for piano, clarinet and cello is a delight rather than a philosopher's stone, and is often played with violin instead of clarinet, in which form it loses some of its pungency of tonal character.

Schubert's two trios are among the most entrancing pieces ever written, looser in construction than some pedants like but overflowing with inspired melody and dance-like lilt and containing music as joyful, as playful, as teasing and as unutterably sad as anything in the repertoire, trio or otherwise. And here too, more even than in Beethoven, the cellist is rapturously emancipated.

Mendelssohn's two trios reflect their composer's fantastic facility at the keyboard. The piano parts in each are positively bespangled with notes, though the strings do get more of a look-in than in many trios composed by virtuoso pianists (Hummel's and Chopin's, for instance). They plumb no great depths, perhaps, but they sparkle delightfully and are worthy of any listener's attention.

Of Schumann's three piano trios, only the second gives us Schumann at anything like his best. The first is full of wonderful things but the strings are treated like second class citizens while the piano laps up the limelight. In the second, both mood and scoring are much happier, and the texture is altogether more airy. The third, alas, was composed when Schumann was already in the grip of the mental illness which was soon to find him incarcerated in the asylum where he died.

Brahms's trios, on the other hand, belong with his greatest achievements. The first, written in youth and radically overhauled many years later, is another of Brahms's 'veiled symphonies', to borrow Schumann's phrase. The scale is immense, the piano-writing massive, yet the strings play an indispensable part. The Third Trio, in C minor, is a masterpiece of compression and emotional concentration, and again the texture seems to exceed the limits of a mere three instruments. The most unusual of Brahms's trios is the E flat, Op. 40, where he substitutes the French horn for the cello, producing a unique and extraordinarily vibrant sonority (this scoring was later taken up by two 20th-century composers, Sir Lennox Berkeley and the Hungarian Gyorgy

Ligeti). One of the most exciting chamber works ever written, it traverses an emotional range from wistful lyricism and youthful high spirits through a very dark night of the soul and finally out into the open for a rollicking 'hunting' finale. A far more inward and autumnal mood dominates the late Clarinet Trio (the clarinet here replacing the violin), but again Brahms draws from his instruments some magical sonorities.

Crown Prince Rudolf, dedicatee of Beethoven's 'Archduke' Trio for piano, violin and cello.

No survey of chamber music should ignore the two best of Dvořák's four piano trios, the darkly lyrical F minor, rich in Brahmsian undertones, and the unique *Dumky* Trio, named after the peasant dance from which it derives its strange and compelling swings of mood. In both these works, Dvořák's melodies are worthy of Schubert and Brahms, his instrumental mastery is in no way inferior and his tenderness is as affecting as theirs.

Tchaikovsky's lone piano trio is a very virtuosic affair and is about as far removed from the trios of his beloved Mozart as it is possible to get. This is no longer domestic music. Its place is firmly in the concert hall and the recording studio. The same, though to a rather lesser degree, can be said of the once very popular trios of Tchaikovsky's compatriot, Arensky.

The fortunes of the piano trio took something of a nosedive in the 20th century, though with some major exceptions. Ravel's single offering, for instance, the Piano Trio in A minor of 1914 is a serious work of major proportions and brilliant skill, and solves the long-tussled-with problem of instrumental incompatibility with one masterstroke after another – Ravel had no superiors when it came to tone-painting. Debussy's only piano trio is a very early work and has today little more than curiosity value, but the trios of Fauré, Ives and Shostakovich are certainly worth seeking out.

A significant number of piano trios have explored the possibilities of different instrumental combinations. In addition to the 'horn' and 'clarinet' trios of Brahms and Beethoven, there are excellent examples with flute (Haydn and Weber), clarinet (Bartók's 'Contrasts', Stravinsky's trio arrangement of his own 'Soldier's Tale') and with various combinations of oboe, bassoon, flute and clarinet (Glinka and Poulenc).

There have also been instances, as in Beethoven's so-called Triple Concerto when the standard piano trio has been the 'soloist' in orchestral works.

The Piano Quartet

The standard Piano Quartet is scored for piano, violin, viola and cello (though there are exceptions: the piano quartets of the Swedish composer Berwald and the French Florent Schmitt are for piano and wind). It emerged in the last third of the 18th century as the natural offspring of the accompanied keyboard sonata and the increasingly popular keyboard concerto. The concerto influence, whereby the pianist alternates between the role of accompanist and soloist, is particularly evident in the early piano quartets of J. C. Bach, J. S. Schroeter and Joseph Haydn (where they go by the name of divertimento). Of 18th-century examples, Mozart's two, in E flat and G minor respectively, are in a class of their own. Beethoven's three original piano quartets, written when he was 15, are attractive but musically outclassed by the composer's arrangement for piano quartet of his Op.16 Quintet for Piano and Wind. Mendelssohn's three are likewise products of his early teens and demonstrate the newly brilliant style of piano writing. The greatest piano quartets of the 19th century are those of Schumann (a wonderful work, unfairly overshadowed by the admittedly still greater Quintet), Dvořák, and Brahms, whose three works in the medium are unsurpassed – especially so in the case of the last, in C minor. Other examples that repay acquaintance are the two by Fauré, and moving into the 20th century, the haunting *Quatuor pour le fin du temps* (Quartet for the End of Time) composed in a concentration camp in 1941 by Olivier Messiaen.

The Piano Quintet

The first great piano quintet was not written for what was to become the standard combination of piano and string quartet, but for piano and wind. After writing his E flat Quintet for Piano and Wind in 1784, Mozart expressed the belief that it was the finest piece he had ever written. Considering the sea of masterpieces that came before it, one can take the remark with a pinch of salt, but it would be impossible to cite anything more perfectly realized. Its beauty, poignancy, high spirits and magical scoring remain fresh after any number of hearings. Never was musical conversation more breathtakingly stage-managed, not even in Mozart's operas. Mozart was the greatest writer

Among the many works written by the Bohemian pianist-composer Johann Nepomuk Hummel are two highly accomplished piano septets; see also page 140.

for wind instruments who ever drew breath, and the colouristic miracles he works with them never stale. Beethoven's Quintet in the same key and for the same forces (piano, oboe, clarinet, bassoon and French horn) was directly inspired by Mozart's and generally accompanies it on disc. It too is a delightful work, but Beethoven himself would have been the first to agree that it is also a lesser one.

The first quintets for piano and string quartet (the now standard form) came from the Spanish-based Italian Luigi Boccherini in 1799, but for all their charm and often vivid atmosphere they hardly count as major works. The first 'great' work for this combination was undoubtedly Schumann's rhapsodic and invigorating E flat Quintet, Op. 44. Written in 1842, it served as a model for similar works by such diverse composers as Borodin, Franck, Granados, Bloch and Shostakovich, but has been matched in quality (if not surpassed) only by Brahms's F minor Quintet, which exists also as a Sonata for Two Pianos. Unlike the basically sunny and youthful Schumann, Brahms's quintet is often brooding, intensely dramatic and exciting, and conceived on a scale of sound beside which all other piano quintets seem almost puny. If Brahms's symphonies can be described as chamber works for full orchestra, so this Quintet

can be called a symphony for five players. Spiritually if not stylistically, the enchanting piano quintet by Dvořák is a kind of happy blend of Schubert and Brahms. With its wealth of melody, its captivating rhythms and its amazingly resourceful (though never obtrusive) scoring, it deserves its popularity every bar of the way.

There is arguably no higher form of pure entertainment in the world of so-called serious music than Schubert's ever-popular 'Trout' Quintet. Written for the unusual combination of piano, violin, viola, cello and double-bass (a scoring pioneered by Hummel in 1802) it was composed while Schubert was on a summer holiday with friends in the Austrian Alps, and it exudes high spirits from beginning to end. The title comes from Schubert's song of the same name (*Die Forelle*) that serves as the basis for the variation movement.

Piano sextets are rare. Nevertheless, the 15-year-old Mendelssohn's immensely lively and attractive example in D is well worth seeking out. Not a masterpiece like his amazing Octet, maybe, but a delight. Piano septets are rarer still, but Hummel's two can be warmly recommended.

The standard piano quartet is scored for piano, violin, viola and cello.

the
Great Composers

Since music is not something that can be objectively or definitively assessed, musical judgements are notoriously subjective. There exists no scale of measurements by which a composer can be 'rated'. According to Tchaikovsky, a well-equipped connoisseur if ever there was one, Brahms was no more than "a scoundrel", a "giftless bastard", a "self-inflated mediocrity, compared to whom Raff is a giant". Then, too, a composer may be great in one sphere but not in another. Few would deny that Wagner was a great composer, but as a writer of piano music he was negligible at best. Less contentious is a composer's importance and influence. Like them or not, every one of the composers discussed here played a significant role in the developing story of the piano, even if the first three we shall look at in this chronological overview were unaware of it.

Bach, Handel and Scarlatti

The most remarkable year in the history of music was undoubtedly 1685, which saw the birth of J.S. Bach, George Frederick Handel and Domenico Scarlatti, generally conceded to be the greatest composers of their age. While none of them wrote specifically for the piano, then still in its relative infancy, their extensive keyboard music has become the first great staple of the piano repertoire. In the two and a half centuries of its existence it has been played, and continues to be played, far more frequently on the piano than on the clavichords and harpsichords for which it was originally intended. The climax of these three composers' careers coincided with the rapid ascendancy of the piano in Western Europe and the equally rapid decline in the fortunes of its predecessors. Had they each lived for another decade they would undoubtedly have adopted the instrument wholeheartedly. All three men were renowned as unsurpassed virtuosos of the keyboard, a fact reflected both in the range and in the often formidable difficulty of their greatest keyboard works. Nor has the playing of their keyboard music been eased in any way by the increasingly heavy actions of the piano as it has evolved between their time and our own.

J. S. Bach

Johann Sebastian Bach was born on 21 March 1685 into the most distinguished and durable family of musicians in all Europe. To this day, the name Bach appears more than any other in musical dictionaries, and in his lifetime Johann Sebastian was exceeded in fame by two of his sons, Carl Philip Emmanuel and Johann Christian, both of them among the first pioneers of a specifically pianistic style. Orphaned at the age of ten, Bach grew up in the care of his brothers and received the same rigorous training as the rest of his family. He was not a child prodigy, however, and it was only in his late teens that his true potential began to be recognized. Musicians were then by definition servants, either of the nobility or of the church, and customarily wore a servant's livery. Johann Sebastian was headstrong, lusty and hot-tempered, and never suffered fools gladly, even if they were his employers. On one occasion he drew a sword against his opponent in a street brawl and on another was actually imprisoned by his employer, Duke Wilhelm Ernst of Weimar. Twice married, he fathered twenty children, of whom C. P. E was the fifth and J. C. the last.

Strange to say, this great genius, regarded by many people today as the greatest composer in history, lived a life almost perpetually hamstrung by frustrations. Although renowned in Germany as a keyboard player of unsurpassed distinction, he was little celebrated as a composer. When Bach was appointed Cantor of the St. Thomas School in Leipzig in 1723, a post which he held until his death 27 years later, one Abraham Platz of the Leipzig City Council felt constrained to explain that "since the best man could not be obtained, we were forced to fall back on mediocrities." But for that choice remark, Councillor Platz would today enjoy the complete obscurity he so richly deserved. "The best man" in question was Georg Philip Telemann, who still holds the record for being the most prolific serious composer in history, having more than 3,000 works to his credit.

Once installed at Leipzig, Bach was lumbered with an unending procession of indifferent students and inadequate facilities. In addition to his extensive teaching commitments, he was responsible for the music and its performance in all four of the city's churches. This involved, among many other things, the composition each week of a cantata for the Sunday service, as well as Passion music for Good Friday. In addition to this, he furnished music for weddings, funerals and municipal celebrations. In 1730 he outlined for the city council his minimum requirements regarding personnel. These included a choir of at least twelve singers, though sixteen would be preferable, and an orchestra of eighteen to twenty players. What he had was an orchestra of eight nondescript sawers and scrapers, of whom he wrote "Modesty forbids me to speak at all truthfully of their qualities and musical knowledge."

Most of Bach's keyboard music was written during his earlier and happier service at the court of Anhalt-Cöthen (1717–23) and was composed largely for the delight and education of his family and pupils. His most famous keyboard work, the so-called 'Well-tempered Clavier' ('clavier' then being a generic name for any keyboard instrument), is a monumental collection of forty-eight Preludes and Fugues, divided into two volumes containing one Prelude and Fugue in each of the twenty-four keys. This, together with his monumental 'Goldberg' Variations (which if all repeats are observed takes well over an hour to play), remains unchallenged as the greatest solo keyboard music of the entire 18th century, exploring almost every aspect of technique, style and emotion to a degree, and to a standard, matched only by Beethoven roughly half a century later.

Less imposing in stature but still part of the mainstream repertoire today are the six French and English Suites (which are not discernibly French or English in either style or reference), the six wonderful Partitas (basically just another term for Suite), the so-called 'Italian' Concerto (in which he imitates the alternation of soloist and orchestra), the adventurous Chromatic Fantasy and Fugue and the two- and three-part Inventions, which remain a standard part of the piano student's education as do many of his delightful 'Little Preludes'. In the fifth of his great 'Brandenburg' Concertos,

97

Bach broke new ground with a long cadenza for solo harpsichord, which gave rise to his seven full-blown concertos for harpsichord and strings – the first keyboard concertos ever written. Their joy is unconfined and they have been frequently recorded, both on the harpsichord and the piano. Bach's keyboard music reflects both his own increasingly unfashionable devotion to polyphony, in which the music results from interweaving strands of melody (his mastery of fugue remains unparalleled), and the trend towards the simpler textures of a single melody with chordal accompaniment.

The keyboard music of J. S. Bach was written largely for the delight and education of his family and pupils while he was in service at the court of Anhalt-Cöthen.

Handel

Considering the lifetime of fame accorded him (in which he was widely regarded as the greatest musician who ever lived), we know extraordinarily little about Georg Frideric Handel (1685–1759) the man. Few great composers have been so secretive, yet few have been more unbuttoned and extravagant in their daily conduct, and fewer still have even approached his prodigious, and prodigiously varied, output. Unlike the outwardly provincial Bach, who never once set foot outside Germany, Handel was one of the most cosmopolitan and sophisticated figures of his day. Well read, witty and gregarious, he was university educated, had a scholar's appreciation of fine art and numbered one or two Rembrandts in his private collection of paintings. Generous of spirit and philanthropic with his wealth, he had a temper of Krakatoan proportions, and once came within a hair's breadth of throwing a temperamental soprano out of the window. As a young man in Italy, he fought a good-natured musical duel with Domenico Scarlatti (on organ and harpsichord), but four years earlier had nearly lost his life in a swordfight with his fellow composer Johann Mattheson. He had a gargantuan appetite, a correspondingly Pavarottian girth, and a taste for the good life in general, though we know next to nothing of his sexual activity.

Despite being German born and raised, he became the greatest writer of Italian opera, before taking British citizenship and becoming the greatest English composer who ever lived.

He was astonishingly prolific, a fast worker and a keen businessman with a canny appreciation of the musical marketplace, yet today he is universally known for a single work, the oratorio *Messiah*. Except for the so-called *Water Music* and perhaps the *Music for the Royal Fireworks*, most casual listeners would be hard-pressed to name another Handel composition, though the confirmed music-lover will know at least something from one or two of his other oratorios, his beautiful *Concerti grossi*, or a couple of operatic arias. Most of his keyboard works, however, remain known only to connoisseurs, and even there, to a relatively small proportion.

By comparison with Bach's, Handel's keyboard music is very much slighter, both in bulk and stature, but it contains some of the grandest and most 'orchestral' writing ever conceived up to that time (especially the six Grand Fugues, which are only seldom played in public today, even by harpsichordists). His most famous keyboard piece by far is the enchanting but rather conventional set of variations known as 'The Harmonious Blacksmith' (1720) (the legend being that Handel, who for reasons never satisfactorily explained was a notorious thief of other men's music, pinched the main tune from a blacksmith he had heard singing at his anvil in Edgware). His eight large-scale Suites contain some outstanding movements, but few would claim them as great works.

Domenico Scarlatti

Unlike Bach and Handel, both prolific all-rounders, Domenico Scarlatti (1685–1757) is known almost exclusively by his 550-odd sonatas for solo keyboard, almost all of them written during the last 29 years of his life and most of them demonstrating a genius hardly to be glimpsed in his earlier output. As with Handel, however, we know remarkably little about the man, beyond such arid statistics as his wedding date and those of his various appointments.

Considering that Scarlatti was already in his fifty-fourth year when the first of his sonatas were published (in London, early in 1739), we are confronted here by one of the greatest late-developers in human history. The catalyst appears to have been his introduction to the ceremonial, folk and popular music of the Iberian peninsula, where he spent the last quarter of his life: first in Portugal, and later at the royal court of Spain. Strange to say, if he had remained in his native Italy, he might well be remembered today as a rather minor composer, the also-ran son of *the* Scarlatti, Alessandro, then the unchallenged king of Italian (and more specifically, of Neapolitan) opera. Occasionally one or two of his choral or vocal works will get an airing, but his sonatas alone constitute his claim to fame, and more importantly, to greatness. They are quite simply among the most dazzlingly individual, exotic and brilliantly resourceful instrumental works ever written.

Handel's works for keyboard are few in number but large in conception; this portrait is by his fellow-countryman, Hans Holbein.

Scarlatti's sonatas without the influence of the Spanish guitar, the distinctive songs and dances of Flamenco and the court music of Spain and Portugal would be inconceivable. Not until Chopin and Bartók would there be a great composer so steeped in the music of an authentic folk tradition. Like them, too, Scarlatti was one of the greatest originals in the history of music, and a keyboard virtuoso with an unsurpassed understanding of his instrument. Indeed, where the evolution of keyboard style is concerned, Scarlatti's sonatas are as significant as the trailblazing concert études of Chopin and Liszt in the 19th century. With their vigorous 'strummings', their crunching, unprecedented discords and their snappy, catchy rhythms, many of them are as exciting and daring as any keyboard music ever written. Among their most original technical features are the frequent crossing of the hands, fast runs in thirds and sixths, leaps beyond the span of an octave, broken chords in contrary motion and rapid repeated notes, effected by constant changes of finger (a straight imitation of the

guitar). Not that these sonatas are invariably virtuosic; they contain many slow, meditative, intimate and moving works that have an extraordinary poignancy about them.

Unlike the Classical sonatas of Haydn, Mozart and Beethoven, Scarlatti's are all relatively brief single-movement works in two parts, the second of which generally introduces new and contrasting material before returning to the opening idea. Most of them fall into one of two categories: the one conditioned by the breath, the other conceived in terms of the dance phrase, though of course the two are by no means mutually exclusive. In general, the fast ones are dominated by the dance (an omnipresent force in Spanish music generally), while the slower ones, especially those marked 'cantabile', derive their rhythmic character from the nature and span of human breath, and have much of their inspiration in song. Scarlatti described his sonatas as "an ingenious jesting with Art".

The reputation of Domenico Scarlatti (seated at keyboard) rests almost exclusively on his sonatas for keyboard.

Haydn

Joseph Haydn (1732–1809) brought to a glorious conclusion that long era in which musicians had been by definition either servants or vagrants. For most of his professional life he wore a servant's livery, just like the coachman, the cook and the scullery maid. Like any reasonably accomplished musician of his time, he played the harpsichord and the piano tolerably well but he was never in the virtuoso class. The piano, therefore, plays a less decisive role in his output than it does in the works of pianist-composers like Mozart, Clementi and Beethoven. Still, 62 sonatas and a sizeable volume of miscellaneous pieces is not bad going, especially when you consider that in quality and significance the best of them can take their rightful place next to his ground-breaking symphonies and string quartets. The sheer variety of his sonatas was unprecedented for a single composer, with the possible exception of C. P. E. Bach, who nevertheless failed to reach the heights scaled by Haydn at his greatest. The range of his keyboard styles covers pretty well everything from simple song-like movements, with surprisingly unimaginative accompaniments, to massive, almost orchestral sonorities, as in the great E flat Sonata that crowns the series, and his rhythms often have an extraordinary suppleness and variety. To a large extent, however, Haydn as a piano composer remains something of a musician's musician. Only a handful of his sonatas find their way with any regularity into recital programmes, in concert or on disc, and of these only the last, in E flat, has achieved real fame.

His early sonatas, the first nineteen, all written before 1767, were conceived for the harpsichord, and several suggest the influence of Scarlatti at his gentlest and most pastoral, though it is unlikely that Haydn knew any of Scarlatti's music at the time. The similarity arises from a generally Italianate style that permeated Viennese musical life and reached Haydn through the works of such then fashionable composers as Wagenseil and the brothers Georg and Johann Monn, among the earliest of the Viennese symphonists. These early,

Haydn, c. 1795. The best of his sonatas can stand comparison with his ground-breaking symphonies and string quartets.

lightweight works, with their easy charm and elegant sprinkling of poignancy, give little hint of what was to come, although there were certainly telltale signs. From 1767 onwards, however, Haydn's solo sonatas were written expressly for the piano, making him the first great composer for the instrument, unless you count C. P. E. Bach, whose influence on Haydn's piano sonatas was immense. The moody, introspective and emotionally volatile experiments of Bach combined with the decorative escapism of mid-century Vienna to produce a style, or rather a tightly knit family of styles, that was uniquely Haydn's. One of the most striking features of Haydn's sonatas, like those of his sometime pupil Beethoven, is their extreme individuality – a fact which makes it very hard to speak of them in generalities.

On the whole, Haydn's approach to keyboard textures is more rugged than Mozart's, dealing in chunkier blocks of sound, often favouring chordal textures and rhythmic momentum over the ultra-refined, vocal-style melodies so common in Mozart. Where Mozart was essentially an operatic composer, guided by the ideal of the human voice, Haydn, though he too wrote operas, was emphatically an instrumental composer. His sonatas contain many passages which are almost impossible to sing. The leaps may be too great, the lines too long and awkward for the average human breath, or the phrases too fragmentary. Where Mozart's inspiration is effortlessly melodic, Haydn's will often be primarily rhythmic or harmonic. While Mozart's sonatas fall naturally into vocal-style ensembles and conversational interchanges, his themes interacting like characters in a drama, Haydn will often take as his starting point the merest idea, a fragment of melody or a pregnant rhythmic figure, which he then builds up and develops, sometimes almost beyond recognition. Instead of pursuing the Classical ideal of contrasting themes, he may base a whole sonata movement on a single theme. His sonatas often work primarily on the principle of developing variation. The 'theme' may be more a rhythmic figure than a

melody, and the 'development' may derive not from a tune at all but from its harmonies, or even its accompaniment. No composer's music is fuller of surprises. His sonatas are not whodunits but whatnows. This may explain their relative lack of popularity in our own time: they demand too much concentration. Yet they are seldom solemn. Haydn's humour is pervasive, but sophisticated. His invention is prodigal, his melodies sometimes inspired, his expressive 'colouring' is extraordinarily resourceful, but he is first and foremost an 'ideas' man. Not a cold intellectual by any means: his warmth and deep humanity are reflected throughout his music, and in his day he was the most popular composer in the world.

Haydn's sonatas provide a fascinating record of the piano's ascent in the latter half of the 18th century, proceeding from harpsichord style, in which the rise and fall of tone and intensity is perhaps desirable but not essential to success in performance, through the middle-

period sonatas (1767–80) where suppleness of outline and variety of expression play an ever-greater role (it would be hard to imagine a really satisfying performance on the harpsichord of the slow movement of the beautiful A flat Sonata (L.31, H.46), for instance), and on to the last sonatas (1784–94) whose play of light and shade is conceived in entirely pianistic terms. Haydn was also, incidentally, the first great composer to indicate the use of the pedals. Indeed, in the grand, witty C major Sonata (No. 60 in the Landon catalogue), he seems even to anticipate the 'impressionistic' Beethoven of the 'Moonlight', 'Tempest' and 'Waldstein' Sonatas). Frustratingly, Haydn wrote nothing for the piano in the last decade of his creative life, during which span the piano's development steadily accelerated and Beethoven advanced as far as the titanic, epoch-making *Appassionata*.

Haydn leading a quartet in rehearsal. He was emphatically an instrumental composer.

Mozart

In common with every other genius, Wolfgang Amadeus Mozart was an avid learner. His extraordinary originality (which was never an end in itself) was largely the product of his discriminating eclecticism. Throughout his life, we find him encountering new stylistic influences, assimilating them with enormous enthusiasm, and then shedding all those elements which were not true to his artistic nature. Nowhere is this more intriguingly or more inspiringly true than in the case of his concertos, which run the gamut from innocent exploration in childhood to the incomparable mastery of his maturity.

It was in 1773, at the age of 17, that he composed his first purely original concerto (the D major, K.175), by which time he was already a veteran of the musical theatre, with three tours of Italy and six original operas behind him – and it showed (nowhere in Mozart's concertos are operatic principles, or operatic procedures, very far from the surface). From this point onwards Mozart was to lift the form to previously unimagined heights and give it equal status with the symphony. Unsurprisingly, this same period also saw the

birth of his two most original and arresting symphonies to date, the turbulent No. 25 in G minor, and the unfailingly fresh and delectable No. 29 in A. The D major Concerto marks the first of many occasions on which Mozart was well ahead of his audiences. The contrapuntal finale struck his contemporaries as excessively severe (a finale that demanded concentration was one innovation too many). Mozart therefore gave it an alternate finale, now best known as the self-contained Concert Rondo in D, K. 382 – a parade of unchallenging delights which guaranteed its immediate and overwhelming success.

The Break with Tradition

In the E flat Concerto of 1777, however, we move onto another plane altogether. With its breathtaking originality and its unprecedented emotional range, it marks perhaps the greatest watershed in the whole history of the concerto. Its second bar alone must have snapped its first audience to attention like an electric shock. Immediately after the opening six-note fanfare, the soloist enters, breaking with the practice of every concerto up to that time and completing the opening idea unaccompanied. After a brief, good-natured tug-of-war, the piano retreats while the orchestra gets on with the business of the 'real' exposition. When the piano re-enters the fray, it again parts company with tradition by coming in several bars early with a long tension-building trill. From the beginning, and for the first time in the history of the medium, soloist and orchestra appear as equal partners in a genuine dialogue which continues throughout the concerto.

The break with tradition is symbolic as well as musical. The old melody-and-accompaniment approach to concerto-writing, as in other spheres of music, was a perfect mirror of the stratified society in which a wealthy aristocracy held sway over the far more numerous populace of its subordinates. The rise of an affluent middle-class, however, rendered this scheme of things increasingly intolerable and notions of democracy soon conferred unprecedented rights on the individual within society at large. Absolutism gave way to social structures which could achieve equilibrium only through a measure of compromise and accommodation on all sides. And so it was in music.

It seems wonderfully appropriate that Mozart, the first great composer to exchange the shackles of patronage for the

Genius in waiting: the 12-year-old Mozart as depicted by Thaddeus Helbling, c. 1768.

102

life of the freelance, was the first to liberate orchestra and soloist alike to engage in continuous conversation at the highest level. Both the level and the nature of the dialogue in K.271 were without precedent. So was the promotion of the wind section to the front ranks of musical diplomacy. Here, for the first time, we find the soloist actually accompanying the orchestra (the dialogue between oboe and piano in the opening Allegro was the first of many such charming exchanges). From now on in his concertos, with only a few optional exceptions, Mozart gives the wind band a dual role: as a magical blending agent in his orchestral palette, and as a mediator between the soloist and the rest of the orchestra. The integration of the one among the many, the combining of parts into a greater whole, was one of Mozart's far-reaching achievements.

Nowhere is the close connection between opera and concerto more evident or more powerfully expressed than in the slow movement of this amazing work, complete with profound arioso passages and even recitatives. Nor had Mozart ever achieved a more subtle and telling use of tone colour; this would be one of the most consistent features of all his subsequent concertos. The final movement is both topical and prophetic. Like many of his other finales, it adheres, though sometimes only loosely, to the form of a rondo, then all the rage among continental music-lovers. The main theme, a duple-metre *presto* of tremendous energy, is among the most exciting and delightful Mozart ever wrote, but what singles out the movement for special attention is the interruption in its midst of an extended episode in triple-metre, marked 'Menuetto cantabile'. The abrupt change of mood, texture and metre retains its delicious shock value even today.

Mozart's promise as a composer of piano music flowered in his first great concerto.

The Sonatas

Curiously, for a man widely held to be the greatest pianist of his day, Mozart wrote little for solo piano that can stand up to comparison with his greatest works. Only rarely do his 15 sonatas for piano even approach the perfection of his concertos for the instrument, or the calibre of his chamber music with piano. Apart from the sonatas in A minor and C minor, the late D major, K.576, and maybe one or two others, his most significant works for solo piano are the haunting A minor Rondo, K. 511 (perhaps the most lavishly and revealingly marked of all his piano works), the great B minor Adagio, K. 540, and the extraordinary, pungently chromatic Minuet in D, K. 355. The wonderful Sonata in D for Two Pianos, K. 448, leaves most of the solo sonatas way behind, and the last two of his sonatas for piano duet are fit to stand beside his great symphonies. Unlike the works of Beethoven, Clementi, Liszt and Chopin, however, they could not really be said to have pushed forward the frontiers of piano music or piano making. What they did do was to set a new standard for the truly idiomatic use of the instrument as it had then evolved, bringing an unprecedented grandeur and an unsurpassed subtlety to the music written for and played on it.

Mozart as Performer

No great composer or pianist has ever left a more complete and illuminating record of his relations with the instrument

Wolfgang, Leopold and Nännerl Mozart, c. 1763, as depicted by Louis Carmontelle.

than Mozart. In the letters he wrote to his family one can practically hear it evolving. That the piano developed as it did is due in no small part to his influence, both through his acquaintance with some of its makers, to whom he made many pertinent suggestions and comments, and through the incomparable quality of his playing on it. At the time of his birth in 1756 and during the years of his exploitation as a child prodigy, the piano was still largely a sinister interloper in the kingdom of the harpsichord.

His early keyboard prowess was forged at the latter instrument, and to a lesser degree at the clavichord and organ. But his style at the piano, as it developed from his late teens onwards, probably owed as much to his almost equal expertise on the violin and viola, and to his intimate acquaintance with the human voice. From the age of twelve he had been an avid and prolific composer for the stage, and many of his keyboard works can profitably be approached as undercover operas. Although the standard practice of the day was to employ a relatively detached touch, giving notes, as a rule, rather less than their written value, Mozart's pet phrase when it came to piano-playing was that "it should flow like oil". In his playing as in his music, he was the very model of classical proportion: controlled, meticulous in his attention to detail – but no less so than in his integration of large-scale structures, supremely eloquent but outwardly undemonstrative (he ridiculed the grimacing, gyrating school of keyboard deportment), texturally translucent, rhythmically supple yet metrically exact, and immaculate in execution.

His recipe for ideal performance, as summarized in a letter to his sister, was a judicious blend of "expression, taste and fire – but always with complete precision." It seems unlikely that Mozart ever played a wrong note. The most contentious of his maxims for a properly tasteful performance ('taste' and 'feeling' were his two favourite words when discussing performance) is his insistence that any flexibility of rhythm be confined to the right hand, while the left plays exactly according to the prescribed metre. The closest he ever came to notating this approach is in the wonderful A minor Rondo, K. 511. A literal adherence to this principle, however, is next to impossible for most lesser mortals, but what is clear beyond doubt is that Mozart regarded rhythm as (to use his own phrase) "the chief requisite in music". In his letters he places the greatest stress on beauty of tone, and was therefore probably rather restricted in his dynamic range, particularly at the upper end of the scale. He was likewise sparing in his use of the sustaining pedal, though his letters leave us in no doubt that he did use it, and regarded it as an important resource. (Many music-lovers have been puzzled by the apparent absence of pedals in photographs of some period instruments. In these the raising and lowering of the dampers were effected by knee levers just below the casing.)

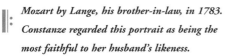

Mozart by Lange, his brother-in-law, in 1783. Constanze regarded this portrait as being the most faithful to her husband's likeness.

105

Beethoven

The man who was to leave perhaps the most lasting and profound influence on the history of music was born in December 1770 in the minor German city of Bonn. While he was certainly precocious by normal standards, he was never a boy-wonder like Mozart and none of the music by which we know him today was written before his entry to official manhood at the age of 21. At that age, however, he had been working as a professional musician for a decade, and from the age of 19, supporting a family put at severe financial risk by his alcoholic father, a musician of very modest gifts who according to the testimony of neighbours had forced the four- and five-year-old Ludwig to practise the clavier and violin, sometimes in the middle of the night, and used regularly to beat him mercilessly or lock him in the cellar as a punishment for 'disobedience' (this including Ludwig's keyboard improvisation, at which he was fabulously gifted from early childhood onwards). The child was also seen weeping at the keyboard and the survival of his love of music in these circumstances can only be put down to his innate genius and extraordinary strength of character. Early on, then, his experience of music, as of life, was deeply marked by a sense of inner conflict and a determination to transcend adversity, to "take Fate by the throat" (his own phrase, in reference to his Fifth Symphony – precisely because of its heroic and infinitely exciting victory over the powers of darkness).

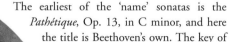

A miniature of Ludwig van Beethoven by Christian Hornemann, 1802.

The Sonatas

The core of Beethoven's keyboard output is his astonishing collection of 32 sonatas, in which one can follow his emotional, stylistic and instrumental development from the blazing self-confidence of his 'angry young man' phase, through the crisis of his middle years, when deafness almost robbed him of his sanity, to the transcendent spiritual and pianistic odyssey of his last six sonatas and the towering 'Diabelli' Variations. Unsurprisingly, perhaps, his most famous sonatas are those with nicknames – though these were virtually never his own and several gained currency only after his death.

The earliest of the 'name' sonatas is the *Pathétique*, Op. 13, in C minor, and here the title is Beethoven's own. The key of C minor was his favourite for expressing tumult and turmoil and each of his three sonatas in that key (Nos. 5, 8 and 32) is characterized by this atmosphere. However, the last movement of Sonata No. 32 is actually in C major and represents Beethoven at his purest and most exalted. At the time of its initial unleashing in 1799, only seven years after the death of Mozart and fully a decade before the death of Haydn, the *Pathétique* was a revolutionary shock to the system, unprecedented in the violence of its expression, the extremity of its contrasts and the audacity of its construction (though this last applies to the first movement only, with its recurrent interruptions by the doom-laden material of its opening section). Never before had music been punctuated with such frequent and jarring accents, nor had the frail fortepiano ever been asked to contain such passion, or such a range of emotions. Here, more clearly than in any previous work, Beethoven's use of the piano as a surrogate orchestra is dramatically revealed.

Probably the best known of all Beethoven's piano works is the so-called 'Moonlight' Sonata (the C-sharp minor, Op. 27 No.2), whose name derives from the critic Ludwig Rellstab's remark that the first movement resembles moonlight as reflected on the surface of Lake Lucerne. A less apt title for the galloping, demonic last movement it would be difficult to imagine. In structure this is another of Beethoven's experimental sonatas – a long, meditative, outwardly free-floating opening movement, followed by a charming if slightly heavy minuet, and ending with a demonic dance of death, the only movement to be cast in so-called 'first movement' sonata form. The whole work is one of his greatest and has an immediacy and urgency that can never grow stale.

Often combined with the *Pathétique* and 'Moonlight' sonatas on disc is the aptly named *Appassionata* (No. 23) of 1805. Written three years before the triumphant Fifth Symphony, this is perhaps the most anguished, the most violent and most exciting protest against fate ever set down in notes.

The so-called 'Waldstein' Sonata (No. 21), one of Beethoven's greatest hits, though it lacks the intensity and immediacy of the *Appassionata*, comes from the same period and derives its name from that of its dedicatee, Beethoven's friend and patron Count Ferdinand Waldstein, an accomplished pianist and a composer himself.

The earlier 'Tempest' Sonata (No. 17), composed in 1803 and still a favourite with recitalists and audiences alike, owes its title to one of Beethoven's most cryptic remarks. When asked about the 'meaning' of the work, he is reputed to have answered, "Read Shakespeare's *Tempest*". No more. No less. Again it finds him experimenting with form, most notably in the opening movement, with its alternating slow and fast sections, punctuated by operatic-style recitatives (a stylized speech-like form of singing used in conversational passages and to introduce extended songs or arias).

The so-called *Les Adieux* or *Lebewohl* ('Farewell') Sonata is one of the very few examples of 'programme music' in Beethoven's piano works, though its programme is so generalized as to be almost meaningless, simply depicting his feelings on the departure, absence and return of a beloved friend (the Archduke Rudolph).

Nowhere does Beethoven's 'symphonic' view of the piano sonata emerge more dramatically or at greater length than in the *Hammerklavier* Sonata (No. 29), which lasts for the best part of an hour in performance. The title is simply the German word for piano and derives from Beethoven's inscription at the head of the score, "Sonata für das Hammerklavier" (in a fleeting bout of nationalistic feeling, he used the same designation for both the preceding and the following sonatas). Here, more than in any other work to date, Beethoven pushes the frontiers of style so far in advance of his times that the gigantic, closing fugue still sounds almost impossibly modern and bewildering – and in 1818 it was far and away the most difficult piano piece ever conceived.

The last three sonatas have never acquired nicknames. They are generally conceded to be (with the possible exception of the *Hammerklavier*) the greatest piano sonatas ever written, taking music into realms of experience beyond the imagination of normal mortals, and driving pianos of the time beyond their capacity to deliver.

Beethoven directed people to Shakespeare's Tempest *when asked to explain the meaning of his 'Tempest' Sonata; painting by Joseph Wright of Derby.*

The Variations

No more sonatas were to follow, but Beethoven was not finished with the piano. Like most composers of his time, he wrote many sets of variations, including two based on *Rule, Britannia* and *God Save the King*. Most fall well short of genius but four stand apart from the rest. On the Thirty-two Variations on an Original Theme in C minor musicians and pianists are sharply divided. Some find greatness in them, others find them uncomfortably similar to the studies churned out in their hundreds by Beethoven's pupil Czerny. On the Variations in F major, Op. 34 (very few of which are actually in F major) there is more agreement, although performances are relatively infrequent. Very few would dispute the quality of the Variations on a Theme from *Prometheus* (usually known as the 'Eroica' Variations, though the work actually preceded the 'Eroica' Symphony which made the theme famous), but there is virtually universal agreement that the so-called 'Diabelli' Variations constitute the greatest set of variations ever written (its only rival being Bach's 'Goldberg' Variations). And thereby hangs a tale.

In 1819, Anton Diabelli, a Viennese music publisher and himself a very minor composer, sent a little waltz by himself to 50 different composers, asking each to contribute a variation on it. Among those who accepted were Schubert and the eight-year-old Liszt. Beethoven originally scoffed at the idea, dismissing Diabelli's waltz as "a cobbler's patch". He then thought better of it and proceeded to write not one but 33 variations (or "transformations" as he significantly and rightly called them). It was his longest and some believe his greatest work for piano, and its technical and intellectual demands are enormous. Like his 'Great Fugue' for string quartet and the finale of the *Hammerklavier*, the work demands almost as much of the listener as of the performer. Musically speaking, Beethoven was a bully, and poor Diabelli's theme gets the psychological drubbing of its life. From the first variation, which foreshadows Wagner's famous *Meistersinger* overture, he mocks the little waltz. "Take that!" he seems to say. "Here is a *real* composer" – and later in the work he dishes out similar treatment to various other composers whose work he alludes to.

Variation and Development

Variation was a central feature of Beethoven's piano writing in general. Five of his 32 sonatas contain a clear-cut set of variations on a theme, but more interesting still is the way he uses the *techniques* of variation to derive whole movements, and in some cases even whole sonatas, from a single, germinal idea. In its day, his music was uniquely organic. It would be wrong to say that he lacked melodic inspiration, but, whereas in Bach, Handel, Mozart or Schubert we may be entranced by the beauty of their melodies, in Beethoven the main interest lies not so much in his tunes as such but in what he does with them. The second main theme in the first movement of the *Appassionata*, for instance, is basically the opening theme turned upside down and reborn to a slightly different but clearly related rhythm.

Another typical Beethovenian device is to take fragments of a theme and subject them to a kind of obsessive rhythmic hammering (again the first movement of the *Appassionata* is an excellent example). In Beethoven as in no composer before him, rhythm, both as a unifying and a divisive agent, assumes an unprecedented importance, sometimes even taking precedence over melody and harmony. More themes by Beethoven can be recognized when tapped on a table-top than by any other composer. The dot-dot-dot dash of the Fifth Symphony may lead the pack, but close on its heels come not only the *Appassionata*, but the *Pathétique*, the *Hammerklavier*, the *Lebewohl* (or *Les Adieux*), and many other un-named sonatas whose opus numbers it would be tedious to list. His thematic acorns often give no hint of the mighty oaks they will become. Often they will be little more than melodic figures, more memorable for their rhythm than for their tunes (if any). The opening salvo of the *Hammerklavier*, or the ominous intro-duction of the *Pathétique*, or the virtually unsingable opening of the *Appassionata* could hardly be called tunes. Yet these are the very acorns from which their respective oaks develop.

Beethoven's approach to organic evolution is very rarely merely decorative. Unlike a fashion show in which the same model appears in a succession of different garments (and most sets of

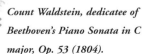

Count Waldstein, dedicatee of Beethoven's Piano Sonata in C major, Op. 53 (1804).

as a means to an end, and much of the difficulty of his music for performers lies in his refusal to be bound by its limitations. Such innovations as he did make can be described fairly briefly.

In reaction against the Classical era's general banishment of the left hand to the role of mere accompanist, Beethoven restores it to an importance that harks back, in degree if not in kind, to the formative bass lines that one finds so often in Bach. Indeed, he seldom uses the straightforward 'melody and accompaniment' textures so common in Mozart and so tedious in lesser composers of the period. His parts for the left hand are almost always interesting and frequently contribute to his distinctive sound-world; the contrasting articulation of detached notes against sustained, song-like melodies, for instance, in which the gaps serve to illuminate the melody above, giving the illusion that a sustained note can actually grow in intensity and volume after being struck. Another device, especially in the later sonatas, is the

A Romantic depiction of Beethoven as musical colossus.

109

Cover of a 19th-century edition of Beethoven's 'Moonlight' Sonata.

keyboard variations follow this pattern), Beethoven's variation technique is transfiguring. His music is intrinsically dramatic not only in its opposing poles but in its sense of consequence. In Beethoven, musical events are linked together in a continuous, ever-developing chain of cause and effect. And even when he does repeat material without external changes, its 'meaning', its expressive character, is often transformed by the experiences which precede it. Of no composer's music is it truer that context alters content.

Much of Beethoven's music is so great, so serious, even forbidding ('Diabelli' Variations, *Hammerklavier*, A major Sonata, Op. 101) that many pianists overlook the wit and the jokes which are also there. Humour, sometimes subtle, sometimes heavy-handed, was an integral part of his musical and psychological make-up, and no composer ever took greater delight in teasing his listeners, leading them to expect one thing and then doing another.

Beethoven's Keyboard Innovations

Ironically, Beethoven's writing for the piano was nothing like as revolutionary, in purely idiomatic terms, as his playing of it. He took the innovations of lesser composers like Clementi and Dussek and developed some of them to a level of unprecedented difficulty, but in very few senses did he expand the idiomatic vocabulary of the piano, as Liszt and Chopin were to do after him. In certain ways he was quite indifferent to the piano for its own sake. He saw it primarily

certainly are. Indeed, in its brevity alone, the A major, Op.119, No.10, anticipates the microscopic miniatures of Anton von Webern in the 20th century, lasting roughly seven seconds *with* the repeat. Trifles in duration these pieces may be, but some of them seem like the distillation of a lifetime's experience, in which spiritual suffering and the terrible isolation of deafness were matched by a sense of joy and a love of life without parallel in musical history.

Beethoven as Pianist

In 1792, the year after Mozart's death at 35, Beethoven moved from Bonn to Vienna, where he had lessons with Haydn and launched his career as a pianist. His debut was like a fireball exploding in the midst of the Viennese musical establishment. No piano player like this short, swarthy, uningratiating 22-year-old had ever been heard, in Vienna or anywhere else beyond his native Bonn. A young Titan fully aware of his powers, the youthful Beethoven fairly bristled with arrogance. Later, he was to declare "I acknowledge only one morality, and that is the morality of power." Power he had in apparently unlimited supply. As a pianist, Beethoven was the first to overwhelm the instrument with the force of his own personality. Compared to Mozart or Clementi, his playing, for all its brilliance, may often have been a trifle rough and elemental. Like Liszt after him, he was a chronic string-snapper – a far cry from Mozart's ideal of "flowing like oil". In his playing as in his music, Mozart had generally been content to work within the confines of 18th-century etiquette and 18th-century instruments. He, too, was a revolutionary in his way, but one who worked by stealth. He was a subversive rather than a guerilla. Beethoven, on the other hand, was prepared to shake any foundations, plumb any depths, and to challenge all-comers. Those who accepted quickly lived to regret it. Just as Mozart and Clementi had had their famous pianistic 'duel', so Beethoven took on the likes of Joseph Gelinek (a pianist-priest whose playing had been praised by Mozart himself), and the melodramatic Daniel Steibelt, famed for his *dramatic tremolandos* (a shiver-me-timbers device involving the rapid alternation of two or more notes that reached the peak of its popularity in the silent cinema). Gelinek remarked after his ordeal that Beethoven was not a man but the very devil who would "play me and all of us to death". Steibelt simply fled, never to return.

Beethoven was the first pianist who regularly overpowered his audiences, dragging them, effectively, into a world of unprecedented emotional intensity and spiritual daring. Particularly in his incomparable improvisations, he often moved his listeners not merely to tears but to convulsive sobbing. He drew back the curtains of reserve and laid bare the realities of life with a ruthless courage. Even before his Viennese debut, critics recognized the sheer danger in Beethoven's playing. As Carl Junker observed in 1791, "His playing differs greatly from the usual method of treating the piano. It seems as if he has struck out on an entirely new path for himself."

Beethoven's study in the Schwarzpanierhaus, Vienna, from a drawing made a few days after the composer's death in 1827.

wide separation of the hands, lending a unique kind of sonic bloom to the spaces in between, and often heightening the sense of drama by polarizing the complementary tensions of the two hands, as though each were straining to break free from the other. He was also the first composer (and the last) to elevate the trill from a simple form of embellishment into a virtuoso device at the highest level of art (the most striking examples being found in his late sonatas, Opp. 106, 109 and 111, and the slow movement of his Fourth Piano Concerto).

In terms of form, Beethoven was the first composer to bind several movements together as a single, uninterrupted entity, either instructing the player to proceed immediately to the next section without a break (*attaca*) or linking the movements together with through-composed material. Another technique was to bring back in one movement themes or ideas from another, as in the A major Sonata, Op.101, where the opening material of the whole piece reappears as a linking device between the third and last movements – a haunting reminder of the spiritual distance travelled since the work's innocent and tranquil beginning (in the 'wrong' key of E major).

In scope and structure, Beethoven's final music for the piano could hardly be more different from the towering heights scaled in the 'Diabelli' Variations and the last sonatas. Flanking the 'Diabelli' Variations are two sets of miniatures, characteristically entitled *Bagatelles* ('Trifles'). Brief they

Interestingly, Beethoven, like the equally original Chopin after him, had received the bulk of his musical instruction from non-pianists. Like Chopin, too, he was to expand the tonal palette of the piano into realms of beauty hitherto undreamt of. His late sonatas are as transcendently idiomatic as anything by Liszt, Chopin or Debussy, but at the same time he seems regularly to envisage the instrument as a kind of surrogate orchestra (which may explain in part why Liszt's wonderful piano arrangements of Beethoven's symphonies work quite as well as they do). And yet the mystical haze of his revolutionary pedal markings in such works as the 'Tempest' and 'Waldstein' sonatas could never be orchestrated with anything like the same effect. Nor can we assume that Beethoven himself used such pedalling only in those passages so marked by him. His pupil Czerny was not the only witness to suggest that such devices were an essential part of Beethoven's piano style. Other likely candidates for similar treatment are the opening movement of the famous 'Moonlight'

Beethoven in middle life. Habitual preoccupation with his own thoughts brought him the nickname 'raptus'.

Sonata and the slow movement of the Third Piano Concerto. At the same time, it seems clear that Beethoven was in no way reliant on the pedal for his legendary, soaring legatos. Like many great pianists (most of whom probably do it unconsciously), he would frequently allow notes to overlap, holding them down with his fingers well beyond their written values.

No pianist was ever more impatient with the instrument's inadequacies. He continually wrote beyond its capacities, and through the music he composed for it he forced the pace of its evolution. Alas, by the time John Broadwood sent him (in 1818) his most magnificent, most sonorous and most wide-ranging piano (over six octaves – a real novelty at the time), Beethoven's hearing was almost entirely gone. Nevertheless, he was transported by the instrument (which itself had been transported laboriously over the Alps like Hannibal's elephants), and though he soon reduced it to a ruin, it inspired him to some of his greatest achievements.

Schubert

Of all great composers, Franz Schubert was the most convivial and the most careless. Inspired melody, coloured by hardly less inspired harmony, flowed from his pen as naturally as rivers flow into the sea – and often with similar results. Having completed a piece, he frequently forgot all about it as his mind turned at once to something new. Indeed, he seems to have lost almost as much as he wrote.

Frustratingly for those who like to see music as a mirror of life, we know surprisingly little about this 'son of the muses', to quote the title of one of his most delightful songs (*Der Musensohn*). There is ample documentation of such relatively uninteresting details as his lodgings (or as was sometimes the case, his lack of them), his schooling, his employment (what little there was of it), his height (barely topping five feet) and other such vital statistics. But as to his thoughts, his attitudes (moral or political), his view of the universe, we remain largely in the dark. As a correspondent he was reticent, as a diarist he was a shambles. His unconcern with the practicalities of daily life was both breathtaking and serene: "The state should keep me," he once told a friend. "I have come into the world for no purpose but to compose."

God's Pupil

He arrived among us on 31 January 1797. Much has been made of the fact that among the great composers who made their home in Vienna (Mozart, Haydn, Beethoven and Brahms, to name only a few), Schubert was the only native. His music is not, in fact, any more permeated with local colour than that of most of the other great masters (it could be argued that musical greatness depends in part on its *transcendence* of locality) and musical geographers will search in vain for it in most of the works on which Schubert's reputation rests today.

Schubert's father, also called Franz, was a Moravian-born schoolmaster of peasant origins; his mother, a Silesian locksmith's daughter, was employed before her marriage as a cook. Both parents were musical, particularly the father. In 1808, when the eleven-year-old Franz left home to become a chorister at the Imperial Court Chapel, he had already begun to compose in earnest and had put behind him a number of songs and instrumental works, including some string quartets. The elder Schubert, however, entertained no thought of his son's becoming a professional musician. It was

Schubert aged 16. As a young man Schubert displayed a sweet and generous nature combined with an endearing capacity for friendship.

assumed that Franz and his two brothers would follow their father into the teaching profession (as indeed they did, though not in Franz's case for very long). The attraction of the Royal Seminary, which supplied the chapel choir, was that it combined a sound musical training with the best general education to be had in Vienna. Schubert was an able student in all subjects, but it was his principal music teacher who was driven to despair, albeit of the most seraphic kind: "I can teach this one nothing," he said. "He has already learned from God." Less daunted though no less impressed by the child's obvious genius was the court composer Antonio Salieri, who happily agreed to instruct him in composition. (Salieri's life had by this time been seriously blighted by the still persistent and wholly unsubstantiated suspicion that he had poisoned Mozart.)

At no time did this apparently Heaven-sent pupil betray the smallest grain of conceit. On the contrary, he was of an exceptionally sweet and generous nature and displayed a capacity for friendship which was almost as striking as his musical gifts. At the Seminary (known in German as the 'Konvikt', a name with misleading connotations for English-speaking readers), Schubert made a lifelong and useful friend in Josef von Spaun; and through playing in the orchestra (he was equally adept at the violin, viola and piano) came into contact with music by Cherubini, the now nearly-forgotten Méhul and, most importantly for his development as a composer, Haydn, Mozart and Beethoven. These three hover, not always from a great height, over much of his own music. An adolescent obsession with Mozart's Fortieth Symphony left a clear imprint on his own Fifth Symphony, and Schubert's public nods to Beethoven could form a catalogue all of their own.

Schubert's orchestral apprenticeship was interrupted a year after his entry to the Seminary by Napoleon, whose troops besieged and subsequently occupied Vienna in 1809. The composer's musical education was not confined to the school, however. On weekends and during holidays (to say nothing of invasions) he explored, and added to, the quartet repertoire with his two brothers and his father (a cellist whose enthusiasm often exceeded his skill).

To say that Schubert felt and was not afraid to show the influence of great masters is merely to assert his humanity. What separated him from most other mortals, even the most gifted, was his uncanny ability to combine eclecticism with apparently effortless originality. At an age when Mozart had yet to write an undisputed masterpiece, the 17-year-old Schubert produced in his setting of Goethe's *Gretchen am Spinnrade* something that was inimitably, uniquely and unmistakably his own; a work of genius rivalled in the crowded history of musical precocity only by Mendelssohn's Octet and *Midsummer Night's Dream* Overture. One year, 45 songs and 90-odd compositions later, he followed it with another Goethe setting, the terrifying and extraordinary *Erl King*.

After leaving the Seminary, he was drawn by the combined force of his father's hopes and a desire to avoid conscription into the thankless world (as he saw it) of the schoolmaster. Early in 1816 he saw a chance of escape: armed

with numerous testimonials, among them one from Salieri, he applied for the directorship of a music school in Laibach. Against all the odds, he was turned down.

Antonio Salieri, who taught composition to Beethoven, Schubert and Liszt.

Schubert was always a modest man, but he knew his own worth. He returned to the classrooms of his father's school with a bitter sense of disappointment (and it can only have added to the inner distress of this basically gentle youth that he took out his frustrations on his students. It makes sad reading to learn from his sister that "he kept his hands in practice on the children's ears."). Unsurprisingly, perhaps, it was following his rebuff at Laibach that Schubert took to keeping a diary. He abandoned it within months, but not before recording his first transaction as a professional musician. On 17 June 1816 he wrote: "Today I composed for money for the first time. Namely a cantata for the name day of Professor Watteroth. The fee is 100 florins." Not much, even then; but it was a beginning.

The Blending of Opposites

Before the year was out, Schubert was ready to throw in the towel as a schoolmaster and he moved in with a friend, the 18-year-old Franz von Schober. Schober has often been blamed for leading Schubert astray, yet it was due largely to him (and Spaun) that the composer was able to put schoolmastering behind him. With a circle of friends of which he was always the nucleus, he shared from around 1817 to the end of his life a largely bohemian existence. Lodging under the roof first of one friend then of another, sharing money, bedrooms, clothes and books, he gave himself up to composition from 9 in the morning till 2 in the afternoon, and to conviviality thereafter. Afternoons and evenings were spent either in cafés or at the homes of friends who housed a piano. (Schubert never had the money to rent, much less buy one of his own, and composed independently of it in any case.) Central to the free-wheeling and often intense lifestyle of this circle was the institution of the

Schubertiad – an evening (and there were many) given over entirely to Schubert's music, played by the composer and the friends for whom most of it was written. These parties were held indoors and out, in homes and in taverns; some even involved festive excursions into the Vienna Woods or to attractive semi-rural suburbs. A number of these affairs were openly propagandistic, arranged by his friends specifically to further Schubert's reputation.

It is a typically Schubertian paradox that the focal point of all this bubbling festivity was a man renowned for his shyness – an almost dwarfish figure whose adolescent beauty gave way in early manhood to bespectacled corpulence and the fond nickname 'Schwämmerl' ('Tubby'). As Beethoven's nephew Karl wrote in his uncle's conversation books, "They greatly praise Schubert, but it is said that he hides himself". From Beethoven, perhaps; though the two men inhabited the

Schubert (at keyboard), the centre of fun at a Schubertiad evening held at the home of Viennese friends.

same small city for many years and had a number of acquaintances in common, they remained virtual strangers.

Paradox was an essential part of Schubert's human and artistic make-up. We need not be surprised or shocked by his friend Kenner's assertion that "anyone who knew him knows how much Schubert was of two natures foreign to each other, and how powerfully the craving for pleasure dragged his soul down to the slough of moral degradation." And whether we understand or even believe it is finally irrelevant. The conflict of opposites is a common phenomenon in art; to a certain extent it may even be a precondition of it. But in the realm of music, no great composer (not even Mozart) so regularly, so poignantly so unnervingly *combines* opposites in the way that Schubert does. Extraordinarily few of his works are unambiguous in spirit. One is confronted again and again in his music by a kind of emotional synthesis in which innocence and wisdom, laughter and tears, serenity and emotional torment seem to appear not as alternating opposites but as simultaneous, almost indistinguishable aspects of whole experience. Schubert himself was well aware of this and had no need to contrive the effect for the sake of art. In a curious document dated 3 July 1822 and posthumously entitled 'My Dream', he writes: "For many and many a year I sang songs. Whenever I tried to sing of pain, it turned to love."

This blending of apparent opposites, the very essence of paradox, is increasingly evident in Schubert's music from 1820 onwards. Indeed the near-ubiquity of paradox extended to Schubert's creativity itself. In 1823 he suffered a serious illness, involving the loss of his hair and a prolonged period of depression in which, not for the last time, he fell "half in love with easeful death" – a combination of circumstances that would normally result, at the very least, in creative sterility. Yet this was the year in which he produced, among other things, the magical and far-from-depressing song cycle *Die schöne Müllerin*, the shorter of his two great sonatas in A minor, the delightful *Rosamunde* music and two operas.

The following year brought recovery and higher spirits, but surprisingly (and again paradoxically) rather little in the way of composition. What there is, though, is of rare quality. The richest fruits of 1824 (and what a study in contrasts they provide) are the D Minor and A minor quartets, the Grand Duo and the incomparable Octet.

The period immediately following the composition of the Octet was probably the happiest of Schubert's life. He was acquiring a celebrity which went far beyond the boundaries of Vienna (though not yet much beyond the German-speaking world), and after a stint in Hungary as music tutor to the Esterházy family (Haydn's former patrons), he savoured the company of his Viennese friends with extra relish. As reported by Moritz von Schwind, "Schubert is back, and divinely frivolous, rejuvenated by delight and a pleasant life." What with increasing publication and money from tutoring, he was also briefly solvent. Romantic images of the starving poet in his garret have tended to misrepresent Schubert's poverty. His problem, though he was too unworldly to see it as such, was not that he never *made* any money, but that he never kept it.

In the year or so following his return from Hungary, no fewer than 40 of his compositions were published. Those wedded to the idea of Schubert as a genius neglected in his time should ask themselves how many other composers could claim a similar rate of publication while still in their twenties. At the same age, Beethoven had yet to publish a single symphony, and more than two thirds of his piano sonatas were still unwritten, as were all of his string quartets; Bach had written scarcely any of the works by which we know him, and the same can be said of Haydn. Schubert was a notoriously bad businessman. If he failed to cultivate the patronage of the aristocracy as Beethoven did, it was not for want of opportunity but of inclination. He had no dependents, and his scale of priorities put music and friendship before material or monetary possessions. If he himself was not, so to speak, a sponger, the same could not be said for several of his friends, who regarded him, in Sir George Groves's phrase "as a Croesus". And after the one professionally mounted concert ever given of his works, he blew the proceeds on tickets to hear Paganini, whose presence in Vienna had kept every critic in the city away from his own concert.

Joseph von Spaun (from an oil painting by Kupelweiser) was one of Schubert's most loyal and supportive friends..

Schubert's Legacy

If Mozart's is the piano music of a largely Italianate opera composer, and Beethoven's that of a symphonist, Schubert's is self-evidently the work of an incomparable songwriter. Standing midway between Mozart and Liszt, and with more than a sideways nod to Beethoven, much of it set the tone for that sea of miniatures and self-contained character pieces that all but engulfed the domestic piano throughout the 19th century. Most of it was never conceived for the concert hall. Schubert was a fluent and infinitely subtle pianist but he was never a virtuoso. Nor, on the whole, did he write virtuoso music, though much of it is far from easy. Like Tchaikovsky and Ravel, he sometimes wrote beyond his own capacities as a performer – indeed he was probably the first great composer to do so. Halfway through the great fugue in his near-Lisztian 'Wanderer' Fantasy (a work, characteristically, with a song at its heart), he once threw up his hands in defeat, crying "Let the devil play this! *I* can't!"

While his great piano sonatas languished all but unknown for a hundred years, his smaller pieces – the two sets of Impromptus, the six *Moments Musicaux*, a cornucopia of waltzes, Ländler and écossaises, and a host of songs – were among the best-sellers of the 19th century. Like most of the great composer-pianists, Schubert was a marvellously inventive improviser, and his hundreds of dances for the piano probably give a reliable impression of the music that used to tumble out of his imagination whenever he sat at a keyboard. Not that he *required* a piano: legend has it that he began writing his superlative Octet on the tablecloth of a Viennese café.

Despite his fluency, Schubert was not a composer like Chopin, who often seemed to think through his fingers. His musical impulses sometimes paid scant heed to the practical realities of piano technique. There are numerous passages in his sonatas, for instance, which are actually harder to master than many a flashier, *saloniste* showpiece. Yet the music, for the most part, is compounded of grace, subtlety, refinement and elegance, even when plumbing the depths of sorrow, as in the slow movement of his last sonata – the great B flat, D. 960. Schubert's piano music requires the greatest suppleness of line to sustain his broad, arching melodies, and the keenest ear for the iridescent harmonies that support and often transform them. If the sonatas were neglected, the 'Wanderer' Fantasy certainly was not. Indeed Liszt, undoubtedly recognizing its affinity with his own music, arranged it as a concert piece for piano and orchestra, in which form it is still occasionally played today.

The Loneliness of Genius

In 1826 Schubert was persuaded once again to seek a salaried position. Once again he was passed over, and perhaps rightly. His career as a teacher had been anything but impressive, and as an administrator he would plainly have been hopeless. He suffered as well the disadvantage of being the first great composer who was neither a conductor nor a virtuoso instrumentalist. In any case, he lacked the temperament to champion his cause in the arena. By the end of the year he began to sense the dawning of a new kind of solitude. One by one, the friends who had formed his orbit drifted off, most of them into

An anonymous portrait of Schubert dating from the mid 1820s, the point at which he began his painful ascent to greatness.

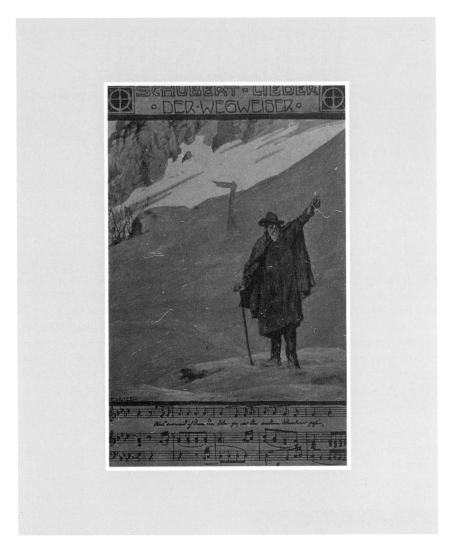

marriage, all but the youngest of them into the foothills of settled middle-age. But the greater solitude was the loneliness of genius.

In the major works of Schubert's last years one senses something more than steadily increasing mastery. There is the sense of an artist grappling head-on with the awesome, sometimes terrifying responsibilities which are the price of supreme talent. And one can hardly help the feeling that something in Schubert's creative unconscious was released, in 1827, with the death of Beethoven – that contemporary Colossus whose glowering presence in Vienna had been as intimidating as it was inspiring. Schubert was among the torch-bearers at Beethoven's funeral. Afterwards, at a tavern with friends, he proposed two toasts: one to the great man who had just been laid to rest, the other "to him that shall be next". Did he have any intimation that it would be himself? There seems little reason to believe that he did, but then reason is a poor guide to the mysteries of existence. In view of the astonishing quantity and incomparable quality of the music which poured out in the year that was left him, the suspicion that he *did* know is almost inescapable.

Ultimately, of course, it hardly matters. What matters is the music. The last three piano sonatas, the F minor Fantasy for piano duet, the two Piano Trios and the C major Quintet (to say nothing of the Impromptus, the jewels of the *Schwanengesang*, the final profusion of church music and The Shepherd on the Rock) would be remarkable enough as the work of a lifetime. That they should be the product of a single year, and several the work of a dying man, is little short of miraculous.

When Schubert died, on Wednesday 19 November, 1828 (almost certainly of syphilis), he had been on earth only a little more than three decades – though he once confessed to doubting that he was of this world at all. He left behind him some clothes, bedding, some printed scores (no books, no furniture, no money, no will) and a treasury of music comprising over 600 songs, 15 string quartets, 21 piano sonatas, 25 pieces of church music, 16 operas and other pieces totalling more than a thousand. The value of his possessions at the time of his death was fixed at 63 florins, roughly a fifth of his total debts, doctors' bills and funeral expenses. The value of his artistic bequest is beyond calculation.

'Der Wegweiser' (The Signpost) – from Schubert's song-cycle, Die Winterreise *(1827).*

Mendelssohn

Only during the last third of our century does Mendelssohn's reputation seem finally to have stabilized. A Jewish convert to Christianity who became the toast of European society, he was revered to excess in his lifetime (nowhere more so than in Britain, where Queen Victoria spoke fondly of "that nice Mr. Mendelssohn"), and paid the inevitable posthumous penalty of unjustified neglect. The best of his piano works have found stalwart champions in such artists as Ignaz Friedman, Rudolf Serkin, Murray Perahia, Daniel Barenboim and Andras Schiff, while even the once obligatory 'Songs Without Words' have staged a dramatic comeback after a century of patronizing abuse. Much of his chamber music, too, is now well established, more so indeed than in his lifetime. The evergreen Octet, composed in his mid-teens, is among the great masterpieces of the chamber repertoire. Of his chamber works with piano, the two trios are now often played, as are the cello sonatas, and even the youthful quartets get the occasional airing. Nor have singers neglected his songs (some of which are actually by his sister Fanny, whose gifts he rated more highly than his own).

Of all the great composers, none was as multi-faceted as Felix Mendelssohn-Bartholdy (1809–47) – an accomplished

Mendelssohn, a multi-talented artist whose popular piano works have only recently been accorded the respect they deserve.

water colourist, a fluent linguist of immense culture and breadth of knowledge, and one of the truly great letter-writers (at the age of 12 he was corresponding with Goethe). In the annals of musical precocity, he ranks with Mozart, and peaked sooner, writing his first authentic masterpiece (the Octet) at an age (16) when Mozart's still lay some years in the future. At the age of eight, he knew all the Beethoven symphonies (barring the Ninth, which had yet to be written) and could play them from memory at the piano. By the time he was 14 he had memorized all the keyboard works of Bach then known, including those for the organ. At 17, he composed the great *Midsummer Night's Dream* Overture, and by the time he was 20 he was already among the foremost pianists and conductors of his time, and a tireless champion of other composers – most notably Bach, whom he resurrected after seven decades of obscurity with his performance, mounted at the age of 20, of the *St. Matthew Passion*.

Like Chopin, Mendelssohn felt estranged from many of the tenets of Romanticism, though he enjoyed the friendship and esteem of many who were among its arch apostles. As in his output generally, his keyboard works are of extraordinarily mixed quality. Of his most outstanding piano compositions, those most clearly influenced by Bach are the six Preludes and Fugues, though each of them bears the very strong imprint of his own personality and belongs firmly to the 19th-century virtuoso tradition. Nowhere is Mendelssohn's ambivalent attitude to the Romantics more baldly stated than in the title of his once very well known *Variations serieuses*, a work in which he almost smugly distances himself from the froth and frivolity of the money-spinning variation merchants centred in Paris (hence the French title). Among his most substantial and unjustly neglected works are the dark-hued Fantasia in F sharp minor, with its brilliant and exciting finale, the Scherzo a Capriccio in the same key, and the captivating early Piano Sonata in E (for all its unapologetic debts to Beethoven).

The only substantial Mendelssohn piano work never to have suffered a moment's neglect is the deservedly popular *Andante and Rondo Capriccioso*, Op. 14. Combining his own very special brand of lyricism with his equally characteristic style of keyboard virtuosity, it reveals a composer who has discovered and developed his own individual 'voice' to perfection. That it was composed when he was 15 years of age is little short of miraculous.

If the *Rondo Capriccioso* and *Variations serieuses* are the Mendelssohn piano works best known to concert-goers, the famous 'Songs Without Words' are undoubtedly the most familiar to domestic music-makers. Written at various times, and published in eight modest books of five or six pieces each, most of them are clearly designed for the parlour or drawing-room. Partly because there are so many of them, covering a

Fanny Mendelssohn, as depicted in an anonymous portrait that appeared in Scribner's Magazine *in May 1888; see page 160.*

wide span of their composer's life, and partly because they were at least as much inspired by the market as by the Muse, they demonstrate more than any other body of his work the extraordinary inconsistency of Mendelssohn's output. Adored wholesale by the society for which they were written, and reviled no less comprehensively by that which succeeded it, they have only recently been accorded the balanced assessment they deserve. There is a pleasing irony in the fact that the best of these pieces, long regarded as piano fodder for the multitude, have held the attention and earned the respect of some of the most sophisticated musicians of modern times.

The term 'Song Without Words' is indelibly associated with Mendelssohn, but while he coined the phrase, he can not be credited with inventing the form, insofar as it is one. The idea of a piano piece in which a vocal-style melody is dovetailed with a flowing pianistic accompaniment is not in itself either particularly original or intrinsically interesting, and had been tried out, in any case, prior to Mendelssohn's example, by composers great and small. Among the great are Schubert, whose Impromptu in G flat is an exemplary song without words, and Beethoven, in the slow movements of several sonatas, one of which (that of Op. 79) might easily be mistaken for a Mendelssohn 'Gondola Song'.

Of Mendelssohn's large-scale piano works, the two concertos are the most brilliant and the most distinguished. Like all of his virtuoso works, they give the fingers a colossal amount to do (few composers have squeezed more notes into less space) and require stamina as well as poetry to do them justice. Of these, the G minor is the most popular, the difficult D minor being seldom played.

119

A drawing and notes taken from the record Mendelssohn kept of his journey to Scotland in 1829.

Schumann

Born in Zwickau, Germany, in 1810, Schumann was in some ways the most Romantic of all the Romantic composers. The quality of his work was uneven, but he enriched the piano literature with a profusion of works, mostly on a smallish scale, in which his fantastical imagination conjured up an aural dreamscape unlike anything else in music.

His music has seldom been rewarded with real popularity, and he remains something of a musician's musician. No-one would be less surprised by this than Schumann himself. Popularity was never his goal. Speaking of the Symphonic Etudes, now one of his best known works, he wrote in 1838 to Clara Wieck (his wife to be, and a superlative pianist): "You are wise not to perform them; they are not suitable for the public. And I should be foolish to complain if audiences failed to grasp something which was never intended for their approval but exists rather for its own sake" – the words of an uncompromising artist who was as pure as they come.

For all his obvious gentleness and diffidence, however, he was a genuine revolutionary. His music, designed to challenge the fashion for

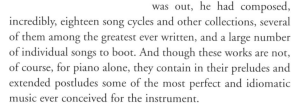
The Schumanns, c. 1850. Robert Schumann's works constitute a musical diary of his soul.

shallow note-spinning which flittered in the wake of Beethoven, was uniquely personal. The rapid shifts of mood and the sometimes extreme brevity of the pieces which make up his 'piano cycles' were genuinely bewildering to many of his contemporaries. Indeed they were often bewildering to *him*; but his mission was to write in music, as he also wrote in words, a kind of diary of the soul – a spiritual record whose fidelity to truth demanded that form be determined from within and not according to preconceived notions of musical etiquette. In principle his credo was simply stated: "The intellect may err, but feelings, never!" In practice, however, art, like life, was more complex.

The grace and apparent spontaneity that characterize so much of his music were often the fruits of intense labour. His Opus 2, the effervescent, touching and by no means lengthy *Papillons* was fully three years in the making, the final

outcome of countless sketches and arrangements. The amazing *Kreisleriana*, on the other hand, inspired by the writings of E. T. A. Hoffmann and taking almost half an hour to play, was composed from start to finish in the space of three days. There were some ways in which Schumann was a remarkably *unconscious* composer. "It is most extraordinary, " he once wrote, "how I write almost everything in canon, and then only detect the imitation afterwards, and often find inversions, rhythms in contrary motion, and so on." Schumann's output, like many of his individual works, went in cycles. Up until 1840 it consisted almost entirely of piano music. 1840 was his quite miraculous year of songs, during which he wrote nothing else. And so it went. He was a man of obsessions and lived for the moment with an intensity and rapture that have no parallel in art. In the spring of 1840, he wrote to Clara Wieck, "Oh my Clara, what bliss it is to write songs. ... I have already composed so much that it seems quite uncanny. But I can't help it. I should like to sing myself to death, like a nightingale!" Before the year was out, he had composed, incredibly, eighteen song cycles and other collections, several of them among the greatest ever written, and a large number of individual songs to boot. And though these works are not, of course, for piano alone, they contain in their preludes and extended postludes some of the most perfect and idiomatic music ever conceived for the instrument.

A prolific and imaginative writer as well as a great composer, Schumann was obsessed by codes and ciphers. His music and writings are full of things that are not what they seem. Behind most of his piano music were the twin influences of Clara and an author whose importance in Schumann's life was out of all proportion to his talent. The German Johann Richter, writing under the pseudonym Jean-Paul, was a pioneer in the cult of dual personality best exemplified by Stevenson's *Dr. Jekyll and Mr. Hyde*. In the same novel that inspired *Papillons* (*Die*

Flegeljahre or Adolescent Years), he created the characters of Vult and Walt, on whom Schumann modelled the subdivision of his own personality into the characters of Florestan, the passionate, impulsive extrovert, and the gentler, more reflective Eusebius. Together, in Schumann's imagination, they recruited an army of fanciful warriors against the latterday Philistines whom Schumann saw advancing all around him (well before madness overtook him). This so-called 'Band of David' makes its first appearance in Schumann's one indisputably popular work, *Carnaval*. They make their most sustained and high-spirited assault, however, in the wonderful though less familiar *Davidsbündlertänze* (The Dances of the Band of David) of 1837.

In addition to those already mentioned, the most significant of Schumann's works for solo piano are the early Toccata in C (an obsessive, exciting, étude-like sonata movement of formidable difficulty), the tender and intimate *Kinderscenen* (Scenes of Childhood), the eight Fantasy Pieces, Op.12 (a collection rather than a cycle,

containing some of the finest things he ever wrote), *Faschingsschwank aus Wien* (a five-movement suite of tremendous vitality, warmth and humour), and three large-scale sonatas, of which the second, in G minor, is the most often performed. Crowning them all, though, is the great Fantasy in C, a sonata in all but name and one of the supreme works in the entire piano repertoire.

In addition to his songs and solo piano music, Schumann wrote much beautiful chamber music with piano, most notably the Piano Quintet in E flat, the equally entrancing Piano Quartet in the same key, three Piano Trios and three Violin Sonatas. Nor should one overlook his works for piano and orchestra: the A minor Concerto, among the most popular ever written (though one critic at its unveiling opined that it was unlikely ever to have a second performance), and the two self-contained Concert Pieces, Opp. 92 and 134.

The writer Jean-Paul (Johann Richter), whose characters Vult and Walt corresponded to Schumann's subdivision of his own personality.

Chopin

A slight, almost suspiciously elegant man, barely topping five foot two and weighing little more than a hundred pounds, he spent more money on his clothes, his gloves and his coachman than he did on books or music. He relished his position at the very centre of Parisian high society, at a time when mere musicians entered the best houses only through the tradesmen's entrance. While still in his twenties he consorted on equal terms with princes, countesses and the greatest cultural personages of the day. His manners were immaculate, though his wit was quick, and his charm and modesty were as genuine as his quiet self-assurance. Yet behind this unruffled exterior lay one of the greatest revolutionaries in the history of music. An iconoclast who shunned academic orthodoxy in favour of a unique originality, Frédéric Chopin blazed trails which led straight to the 20th century. But he was more than this. And less. A facile, cosmopolitan craftsman, he contributed many sparkling additions to a sea of pianistic confectionery which was a truer reflection of 19th-century cultural life than all the music dramas of Wagner put together. His waltzes, écossaises, preludes and nocturnes could be found, well-thumbed, on almost every piano in the world. No great composer's music has ever enjoyed such lasting and continuous popularity with so large a range of people.

The Reluctant Romantic

Chopin gave to the Romantic movement much of its richest and subtlest vocabulary, musically speaking, yet for the most part it was a movement he deplored. He despised its posturings, its self-obsessions, its extramusical fetishes, its exhibitionism. In fact, he felt little sympathy for most of its music, despite his affection for many of its creators and his enjoyment of their company. He ridiculed Schumann's

The writer George Sand, who met Chopin in autumn 1836 and became his lover in 1838. In 1839 she wrote to a friend that "He [Chopin] does not really know on which planet he is living and has no precise notion of life as we others conceive it and live it". The couple's friendship ended a few years before Chopin's death from consumption in 1849.

literary inspirations, he was repelled by the noise and extravagance of Berlioz, and he deplored the musical affectations of Liszt, while acknowledging his wizardry as a pianist. Even Beethoven, in many ways the founding father of Romanticism, made him uneasy. He shrank from the violence of Beethoven's emotional eruptions, yet he himself composed some of the most strife-torn music ever written: the two C minor studies (the first of which, nicknamed the 'Revolutionary', is without doubt the most famous étude in the world), the B minor Scherzo, the First and Second Ballades ... the list goes on. There were only two composers for whom he felt unbounded veneration: Mozart, whose clarity and poise, whose perfection of form and economy of means moved him greatly and served him as a model all his life; and Bach, whose particular blend of exaltation and order inspired in him an almost religious sense of reverence.

To his posthumous misfortune, the externals of Chopin's life are a gift to the sentimental biographer. Who could resist the consumptive, wraith-like, handsome exile, dipping his pen in moonbeams and flooding the world with lovelorn melodies before expiring, poetically, at the age of 39? No one, certainly, more readily than Chopin himself. At almost every level, he was the very embodiment of paradox. As befits the chronic indecision which dogged him to the end, he had duality born into him from the moment of his conception. And that duality was decisive in his growth as an artist. For many decades even the date of his birth was disputed, some biographers following the evidence of the local parish register, which puts it as 22 February 1810, others relying on his own testimony (and that of his mother, who after all should have known) that it was 1 March. Nor was his nationality clear cut. His father was French, his mother Polish. It was in Poland that he spent the first half of his life, and in France that he spent the remainder. As a composer he was both uniquely Polish and the most significant link between the Baroque and Impressionist composers of the French tradition. Inspired above all by the human voice (from the beginning he was an avid opera lover), he never attempted an opera of his own but confined himself almost exclusively to the keyboard. A passionate lover with a prudish aversion to overt sexuality, he unveiled in the piano a realm of sensual possibilities never previously dreamt of. One of the greatest virtuoso pianists who ever lived – and a remarkable child prodigy – he gave no more than 30-odd concerts in his life. A man in whom feminine (as distinct from effeminate) characteristics abounded, his one consummated love affair was with a woman notorious for her adoptive masculinity – the cigar-smoking, cross-dressing novelist George Sand.

Chopin by Delacroix, painted in 1838, the year of some of his best keyboard works, including the Op. 28 Preludes.

Formative Influences

By the time he left Poland at the age of 20, Chopin's musical personality was essentially complete. For some years he had been writing music which was conspicuously individual and consistent in style, if somewhat uneven in quality. Of the main works by which we know him today, both of the concertos, most of the Op.10 Etudes, the great E minor Nocturne, several well-known waltzes and mazurkas and the remarkable B flat minor Nocturne, Op. 9 were completed before his twenty-first birthday. Of the rest of his so-called 'juvenilia', more than half are deliberately Polish in orientation.

From the moment of his birth, Chopin breathed the air of smouldering national pride and political upheaval. In 1810 it had been several centuries since Poland had been able to call itself its own. Three times over, in the lifetime of Chopin's father alone, the country had been partitioned, and by the onset of the 19th century it had all but disappeared from the map. Much of her culture, too, had been imposed, or willingly imported, from without. The opera was predominantly Italian, while instrumental, choral and orchestral traditions were largely derived from French and German influences. The young Chopin absorbed them all, gradually discarding those which did not fit in with his ripening needs and aspirations. The most crucial influence on his stylistic development, however, was homegrown. Unlike Liszt, who mistook the music of urban gypsies for the indigenous music of his native Hungary, Chopin experienced the folk tradition at first hand. Among the greatest delights of a happy childhood were his visits to the country villages surrounding Warsaw. Here he immersed himself in the traditional songs and dances of the Polish peasantry, relishing their very roughness and vitality and absorbing their characteristic subtleties of rhythm into his artistic bloodstream. By the time he had reached his middle teens his music began to reflect the rustic origins so carefully sanitized out of the mazurkas and other national dances to be heard in Warsaw. In its peculiar and highly original combination of the primitive and the sophisticated, it was already becoming unique. No composer before or since has achieved anything quite like it. This strand of his output is closest to the surface in his many mazurkas (a sort of rustic second-cousin to the Viennese waltz).

Chopin playing at Count Radziwill's Warsaw salon in November 1829.

His formal schooling drew heavily on the great Germanic classical tradition, exemplified by Bach, Haydn, Mozart and Beethoven (then very much a contemporary composer, his life overlapping Chopin's by seventeen years). Nor was it narrowly specialized. Chopin senior was determined that his son should have a fully rounded education and from 1823 to 1826 music necessarily took a back seat to Latin, Greek, mathematics and literature. Not that Chopin was musically idle during this period. Music flowed from his pen with apparent ease, much of it sophisticated, some already highly individual – the *Rondo à la Mazur*, for instance, bears the unmistakable imprint of Chopin's personality, both musically and pianistically.

But there was a another formative influence. The role of opera, and specifically Italian opera, in the shaping of his style was fundamental. Chopin had grasped early on that if melodies on the piano were to achieve the flexibility and expressivity of vocal lines they must 'breathe' according to similar principles. In putting this perception into practice, aided by his experiments with the pedals and the use of prophetic and illuminating harmonies, he created an entirely new kind of melody – based on vocal styles, yet uniquely and exclusively pianistic. Ironically, not one of Chopin's greatest melodies gains anything when entrusted to the voice, or to any other 'sustaining' instrument. The best examples of this unique style is to be found in his nineteen Nocturnes.

Three distinct traditions, then – German classicisim, Italian *bel canto* and Polish folk music, never brought together before – merged in Chopin's receptive imagination to nourish a wholly original approach to sonority and piano technique. From it, too, flowed a harmonic vocabulary of extraordinary freshness and piquancy. Chopin was the first great composer to mix sounds as a painter mixes colours, revealing in the process an astonishing kaleidoscope of aural possibilities. In the realm of technique, his 27 Etudes were the first works since Bach to demonstrate that an overtly didactic purpose could be combined with artistic perfection, though the variety of emotions, musical textures and technical challenges which they embrace dwarfs even Bach's accomplishments.

The crushing by the Russian Army of the Warsaw Uprising in 1830, while Chopin was on tour in Germany, unleashed in him an explosion of grief, rage, despair and fear (confided to his journal in an almost incoherent babble) that marked a turning point in both his life and his career. From now on he would live as an exile, championing the spirit of free and defiant Poland in his music (just listen to any of his polonaises from Op. 26 onwards) while carefully remaining on the fringes of political involvement. Never again, except through the piano, would he reveal the inner conflicts which fuelled the engines of his creativity. From now on, increasingly beset by illness, he would present to the world a façade of charming but impenetrable reserve, relaxing somewhat in the company of his fellow Poles (Paris in the 1830s became a kind of unofficial government in exile), but never again with the abandon, the gaiety, the genial and sometimes lacerating humour that had characterized his boyhood and early youth. His life at the centre of Parisian society, however, was far from tragic; he retained to the end his capacity for happiness, and was even able to regard his illness with shafts of humour. He retained, too, his capacity for friendship. And yet Liszt said of him, "He would give you almost anything, except himself." That he reserved, in all its richness and variety, for his music. (See also under The Performers, page 142.)

After the crushing of the Warsaw uprising in 1830, Chopin became a champion of the Polish cause.

Liszt

One of the most productive composers in history, Franz (Ferenc) Liszt left behind him at his death in 1886 more than 1,300 works, the great majority of them for the piano. These can broadly be divided into two main categories: original music and arrangements or transcriptions – and there has never been an arranger, including Bach, of greater skill, industry or imagination.

The Romantic movement of the 19th century was obsessed with literature and with a kind of glorification of ancient times and imperishable heroes. Almost all of Liszt's piano pieces have some sort of evocative title, and a great many are written to a specific programme. One result is the tremendous variety of 'sound effects' that Liszt draws from the piano – thunder and lightning, tolling bells, sparkling fountains, roaring torrents, priestly chanting, galloping horses and so on. Of all piano composers, Liszt is the most lavishly pictorial. Unlike Chopin, who revealed with extraordinary resource everything that the piano was, Liszt continually asks his piano to be what it *isn't*: a symphony orchestra, a gypsy band, a peasant's bagpipes, a shimmering fountain. Not all his effects succeed, but a remarkable number do. He is at his most picturesque and extravagant in the 19 Hungarian Rhapsodies, based on the music of the Hungarian gypsies, in which he uncannily recreates the sound of the traditional gypsy violin and the hammered dulcimer known as the cimbalom. The

standard is very variable but the best of them are among the most colourful, exotic and enjoyable picture postcards ever entrusted to the keyboard. The music, like the gypsies' own, is unashamedly manipulative, and to po-faced accusations of vulgarity Liszt would proudly plead guilty. He knew his audiences, and he knew exactly how to give them what they wanted. In his music as in his playing he was, in part, a kind of musical matador, with the difference that his adversaries usually survived him, though there were often three pianos on the stage just in case.

Inspired by the example of Niccolò Paganini, 'The Demon Fiddler', Liszt set out to do for the piano what the Italian magician had done for the violin – to reveal facets of the instrument that no-one had previously imagined. To that end, he composed a large number of concert 'studies' which raised the threshold of piano virtuosity to unprecedented heights. The most important, as a set, are the 12 Transcendental Etudes, most of which have picturesque titles and all of which combine pianistic virtuosity with serious, sometimes almost frighteningly concentrated musical intent. Like Chopin's, these are music first and studies second. Among the most popular individual studies from other sets are the famous *La Campanella*, based on a theme of Paganini's, the bewitchingly siren-like *La leggierezza*, the hauntingly yearning *Il Sospiro* and the goblinesque *Gnomenreigen.*

Less consistently taxing, on the whole, than the études, but no less beautifully coloured, is the four-volume collection entitled *Années de Pèlerinage* (Years of Pilgrimage), commemorating the sights, sounds and impressions experienced by him in Switzerland and Italy. The Swiss collection is predominantly concerned with nature, and is generally serene and pastoral, though *Orage* captures with extraordinary vividness the violence of a mountain storm, and *Vallée d'Obermann* achieves the stature of high drama. The matador, however, is nowhere in evidence. Throughout this collection we see only the nobler side of Liszt. The second, Italian, book pays tribute to the world of art, memorably and poetically paying homage to Rafael, Michelangelo, Salvator Rosa and Petrarch. Only with the last piece in the set, the demonic 'Dante' Sonata, do we glimpse the darker side of Liszt. A virtuoso work of disturbing intensity, its deliberately chaotic and violent recreation of Dante's *Inferno* is among Liszt's most spectacular soulscapes and is frequently played on its own. The third book, *Venezia e Napoli*, is a supplement to

Liszt, c. 1880. The vast majority of Liszt's 1,300 works were written for the piano.

126

As an arranger, Liszt made brilliant piano transcriptions of all the Beethoven symphonies, several organ works of Bach, the *Symphonie fantastique* of Berlioz and many other works, bringing them within reach of many who would never otherwise have had the chance to hear them. More controversial are his very free fantasies and paraphrases based on themes (mostly operatic) by other composers. In many of these he basically recomposes the material, using it as the substance for variations and transformations of extraordinary imagination and pianistic ingenuity. Had he simply called them 'Variations on a Theme of ......' he would have saved himself from a lot of intemperate abuse and denied hordes of upstanding critics the satisfaction of moralistic finger-wagging.
(See also entry in The Performers, page 142.)

Paganini. Liszt wanted to do for the piano what the Italian virtuoso had done for the violin.

The fountains of the Villa d'Este were the inspiration for Liszt's **Les jeux d'eaux la Villa d'Este.**

the second, and the final one again draws on Italian experiences, memories and reflections and includes one of Liszt's most prophetic pieces, *Les Jeux d'eaux la Villa d'Este*, whose impressionistic harmonies and vivid imagery had a decisive influence on Debussy and Ravel.

The greatest of Liszt's piano works, perhaps of all his works, is the revolutionary one-movement Sonata in B minor. In this, through the use of thematic transformation he succeeds in achieving three movements in one. The entire half-hour epic is based on four simple motives which are themselves closely related and continually reborn in different guises. In its uniquely organic development and its panoramic scope, as in its economy of means and its acute dramatic pacing, it represents Liszt's intellect at its peak but is in no way academic or austere. Like all great works, though perhaps rather more than most, it requires great concentration on the part of the listener if the true stature of its achievement is to be properly appreciated.

The piano music of the 1860s is predominantly religious in character. (Liszt himself took minor orders in the Roman Catholic Church, living for a time in the Vatican itself and acquiring the title of the Abbé Liszt.) The two best-known of Liszt's religious piano works are the two 'legends' 'Saint Francis of Assisi Preaching to the Birds' and 'Saint Francis of Paola Walking on the Water', both of which show his pianistic imagery at the height of inspiration and ingenuity alike.

At the end of his life, Liszt turned increasingly inward, experimenting with melodic patterns deriving from non-European scales and with harmonic combinations of unprecedented dissonance, anticipating the 20th-century 'innovations' of Schoenberg, Webern and Berg. It was his ambition, as he put it, "to hurl a lance into the indefinite reaches of the future". He succeeded beyond his wildest dreams.

Brahms

Born in the slums of Hamburg in May 1833, Johannes Brahms became one of the greatest figures in musical history, contributing equally to the realms of piano, vocal and orchestral music, though he never wrote an opera. From the beginning, his writing for the keyboard developed the 'orchestral' style pioneered by Beethoven and reflected in his own particular brand of keyboard virtuosity. His three epic piano sonatas (Opp. 1, 2 and 5), all written before he had reached the age of 21, were perceptively hailed by Schumann as "veiled symphonies" – a reference both to their size and scope and to the character of their keyboard style. Like Beethoven, only more so, Brahms often used densely chordal textures and exceptionally wide spacings between the hands, frequently requiring the player to leap with tiger-like agility from the centre to the extremities of the keyboard. As with his orchestral music, Brahms's piano-writing has been criticized for being too heavy and thick. The root of this illusory problem lies in his lifelong love of Baroque and Renaissance polyphony, in which loosely parallel melodies or melodic strands combine and intertwine. Heard 'horizontally' rather than in chunky harmonic blocks, the 'thickness' rapidly disappears.

Brahms wrote piano music from adolescence to old age. As with his revered Beethoven, it falls into three periods. In the first, with the influence of Beethoven glowering above him, Brahms was the epic architect, building on Classical ideals of form that were then widely regarded as outmoded but reviving them in a style reflecting subsequent musical developments – hence those "veiled symphonies". In the middle period, with the notable exception of the four beautiful but elusive Ballades, Op. 10, he concentrated mainly on variation forms, sharpening his polyphonic, contrapuntal skills (Bach now joining Beethoven in that personal pantheon that often intimidated as much as it inspired him). To this period belong the great sets on themes by Handel, Haydn and Paganini (see below). Brahms's third period is manifested in the sometimes dramatic and heroic but more often lyrical and introspective collections of short (or at least relatively short) pieces which

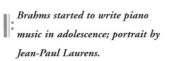

Brahms started to write piano music in adolescence; portrait by Jean-Paul Laurens.

often give us the composer at his most intimate and vulnerable. Some of these pieces Brahms poignantly described as "the cradle songs of my sorrows". There are others, however, which bow to none in their intensity, grandeur and drama. Artur Schnabel offered a key to the understanding of these pieces, in pianistic terms at least, when he dubbed Brahms "the first Impressionist".

Brahms was perhaps the most compulsively perfectionist composer who ever lived. An acute form of performance anxiety, which was by no means confined to his musical life, led to a symbolic self-immolation unique in the history of music: he consigned to the flames many more pages than he ever spared. His published work, therefore, represents only a fraction of his actual output. But then he was a man compounded of paradox. Cautious to a fault, he was possessed of a titanic self-confidence. A sense of destiny was with him long before Robert Schumann hailed him as a musical Messiah, yet he was genuinely modest and disliked being made a fuss of. Tactless, lonely and curmudgeonly, especially in later life, he nevertheless attracted and reciprocated the devoted friendship of men and women alike throughout his life, and was capable of the most unstinting generosity (it was largely he who put Dvořák on the international musical map).

No aspect of Brahms's character is more intriguing, more poignant or more pervasive than his deep-seated and often tragic ambivalence towards women. While idealizing femininity as a concept, he abhorred all forms of incipient or outright feminism and regarded the generality of women with ill-disguised contempt. And, within himself, the struggle to integrate masculine and feminine elements of his personality fuelled much of his creative fire, nourishing an intimacy of musical expression comparable only with Schubert's.

Apart from his mother, seventeen years her husband's senior, the greatest and most abiding love of his life was Clara Schumann, fourteen years his senior and herself the mother of seven. His many other attachments to women of his own class were almost certainly unconsummated, and most were free, through circumstance, from the threat of matrimony. Abused in childhood by the whores of Hamburg (where he was employed as the pianist in a brothel), he seems never to have reconciled the twin experiences of love and sex. For the latter he relied, perhaps entirely, on the services of prostitutes, thereby extending to himself, at least in part, the contempt which he had always felt for them. Late to mature physically, he retained a feminine and strikingly beautiful appearance well into his twenties and spoke throughout his life with a high-pitched voice which greatly embarrassed him. Interestingly, most of the women with whom he fell in love were not only singers but specifically contraltos – a fact reflected in his copious output of songs. Similarly notable, and not coincidental, was his lifelong predilection for low-pitched, dark-toned instruments.

That integration of the physical and spiritual which eluded him in life found unique expression in his art. There, sensuality, which runs like a tributary through his music, is combined with logic and proportion to a degree and on a scale

The last portrait of Brahms, taken on 15 June 1896, a few weeks after the death of his old friend, Clara Schumann.

which were then unprecedented and which have never been surpassed. In Brahms, the conflicting impulses of Classical discipline and Romanticism,

One of a series of sketches of Brahms made by Willy von Beckerath.

of form and feeling, reason and sensuality, find a perfect equilibrium. In his greatest music, be it epic or miniature, those fundamental tensions (which underpin the whole of 19th-century aesthetics) are synthesized through a lifelong exercise of will comparable only – in music – with the accomplishments of Beethoven and Wagner.

Brahms's greatest piano works are often formidably difficult, as in the Variations and Fugue on a Theme of Handel (1861), the two books of Variations on a Theme of Paganini (1862–3) and the two great concertos, No.1 in D minor (1854–8) and No.2 in B flat (1881). He also wrote five sets of miscellaneous short pieces for solo piano (Opp. 76, 79, 116, 117, 118 and 119), many songs with piano accompaniment, and a number of works for two pianos or piano 4-hands, including the famous Variations on a Theme of Haydn, better known in their orchestral form, the Waltzes, Op. 39 (in two versions, one for solo pianist) and the four runaway-bestselling books of Hungarian Dances. His chamber works with piano – the 5 trios, 3 piano quartets, the F minor Quintet, and the duo sonatas with clarinet, cello and violin – are among the greatest ever written.

A Trio of Russians

Russian composers, where the piano is concerned, fall broadly into three categories: those, like Balakirev, Mussorgsky and Rimsky-Korsakov, with a consciously nationalistic purpose, those, like Stravinsky, Prokofiev and the young Shostakovich, who identified themselves with the cutting edge of modernism, and those, like Tchaikovsky and Scriabin, who have steered a middle course, drawing primarily on the traditions of Western Europe but without losing their sense of Russian identity. Those in the first category are discussed in 'National Music', those in the middle, under 'Modernism and Modernists'. Among the most notable figures in the last group are the following:

Piotr Ilyich Tchaikovsky (1840–93)

Tchaikovsky was never better than a competent pianist, and his works for the instrument seldom even hint at his true stature. His one great 'hit' was the famous B flat minor Concerto (witness its near-universal identification, even by pianists, as 'the Tchaikovsky Concerto', though, in fact, he wrote three, of which 'the' is the first). Interestingly, it was initially pronounced 'unplayable' by none other than Nikolai Rubinstein, brother of the more famous Anton and an exceptionally fine pianist himself. Today there are few concert pianists who have not played it. Tchaikovsky's only really substantial piece for solo piano is the Grand Sonata in G major, which, despite the advocacy of several great pianists, has never found favour with audiences. For the most part, Tchaikovsky the pianist was a salon composer who churned out pretty little sweetmeats on demand, but he was not a bad confectioner and some of his pieces have authentic charm and style. His collection 'The Seasons' contains a goodly proportion of modest gems, and pianists should try not to bypass the *Dumka*, Op. 59, an inspired piece of nature-painting and one of the relatively few compositions by Tchaikovsky with a distinctly nationalistic character.

A portrait of Tchaikovsky by Kusnetsov in 1893, the year of the composer's death.

Sergei Rachmaninov (1873–1943)

Although two of his piano concertos, the 'Paganini' Rhapsody and a generous handful of solo works (including the Preludes and *Etudes tableaux*) have achieved popularity, most of Rachmaninov's large output remains little known. Perhaps the most conservative great composer of the 20th century, he composed, to the end, in a resolutely 19th-century style, strongly influenced by Liszt and Tchaikovsky yet strikingly individual. One of the greatest pianists who ever lived, he wrote for the keyboard with an unerring knowledge of its innermost secrets. Most of his music is extremely difficult to play, however, and is notable, among other things, for the liberation of the left hand from two centuries' worth of accompanimental clichés. The fluidity and elegance of his left-hand parts, combined with a predominantly Lisztian view of the piano in general (full of massive chords, orchestral textures and blazing octave passages), helped to bring the great Romantic piano tradition to a belated and final climax. Although he was Russian to the core (evidenced in his particular brand of melancholic grandeur and his fondness for long, sweeping melodies, both heroic and doom-laden), he was never a self-consciously nationalistic composer. In addition to the works already mentioned, his most important piano pieces are the *Moments Musicaux*, Op. 16, Variations on a Theme of Corelli, Sonata in B flat minor and the two suites for two pianos. Rachmaninov was also a brilliant arranger, and his piano version of the scherzo from Mendelssohn's *Midsummer Night's Dream* is one of the classics of the genre.

131

‖: *Above: Scriabin found his true voice in his later compositions, notably in the Op. 68 sonatas.*

‖: *Below right: Rachmaninov's expertise as a pianist enriched his keyboard compositions.*

Alexander Scriabin (1872–1915)

Few composers have travelled so far in style as Scriabin, who began his composing career as an ingratiatingly brilliant, seductively romantic neo-Chopin and ended it as something akin to a revolutionary anarchist. No composer was more open in paying his artistic debts. The forms and titles of his early works come straight from Chopin: mazurkas, nocturnes, preludes, waltzes, studies. So does his imaginative and resourceful use of the pedals. Later he moved on to larger works: ten remarkable, and remarkably different, sonatas, in which his increasing modernism took shape, as he moved through Lisztian and Wagnerian phases before abandoning them and moving into uncharted waters, where conventional notions of rhythm, key and colour dissolve in a style of extraordinary originality, blending the mystical and the sensual in a manner quite impossible to describe without recourse to jargon.

Debussy

Claude Achille Debussy was only ten when he entered the Paris Conservatoire, in 1872. Two years later, when he played Chopin's demanding Second Piano Concerto, it was clear that he was a pianist of exceptional quality. What was not yet quite clear was the formative effect Chopin's music was to have on Debussy the composer. "Chopin was the greatest of them all," he was later to say, "for through the piano alone he discovered everything." Another though more remote influence was Liszt, whom Debussy heard play when he was 23. Debussy's ideal was to get away as far as possible from the percussive nature of the piano, to make it sound, in his own words "like an instrument without hammers". To do this he had, like Liszt and Chopin before him, to rely heavily on the colouristic properties of the pedals, yet he seldom wrote any specific pedalling instructions into his music. The fact is that truly musical pedalling is too subtle and various to be notated in any but the crudest way. Far from being a simple on/off mechanism with a straightforward alternation of up and down, the pedals have many degrees and infinite possibilities of combination. It would be only a slight exaggeration to say that not so much as a single bar of Debussy's music can be adequately played *without* the pedals.

Debussy's first formal employment, at the age of eighteen, was with Tchaikovsky's patroness, Mme Nadezhda von Meck, whom he served as household pianist and tutor to her children. It was during this period that he came into prolonged contact with modern Russian music: of Borodin, Rimsky-Korsakov and, most importantly, Mussorgsky whose bold originality and often simple means greatly affected him. Debussy's own compositions of this period, however (the rippling *Arabesques*, for instance), give little hint of the revolutionary he was soon to become. Only with the enchanting *Suite bergamasque*, composed between 1890 and 1905 and containing the famous *Clair de lune*, does he

The sound-world created by Claude Debussy paved the way for 20th-century 'radicals' like Stravinsky and Stockhausen.

emerge as a strikingly original composer, whose highly individual dreamscapes, with their widely spaced *pianissimos* and harmonic mists take us into a world entirely of their own. It was a world already unveiled orchestrally, however, in the bewitching and mould-breaking *Prélude à l'Après-midi d'un faune* of 1894.

Although he later disliked to be identified as an 'impressionist', he quite consciously set out to reproduce in music the effects of his favourite Impressionist painters, and it is above all the instrumental 'colours' of Debussy's music that first strike the ear. The composer himself was well aware of his own importance and he wrote of his *Images* of 1905, "I believe that these three pieces will live and will take their place either to the left of Schumann or to the right of Chopin." Among the most creatively subversive qualities in his music was its liberation from the directional, gravity-like pull that had governed Western music for the best part of three centuries and which had its origins in the shifting tensions of the major and minor scales. Much of Debussy's music gives the impression of free-floating. By the early years of the 20th century, Debussy had created a style and a world of sound which more than the work of any other composer broke the traditions of 19th-century rhetoric and paved the way, by their own admission, for composers as diverse as Bartók, Stravinsky and Stockhausen. That style, that sound-world, derived from many influences, including such exotic sources as the *gamelan* music of Bali. The most pervasive, however, came from that most unpianistic of composers, Richard Wagner.

As a young man in the 1880s, Debussy, along with many other French musicians, fell passionately in love with Wagner's music, but unlike the majority of his fellow-enthusiasts he realized that it could have a corrupting as well as an enriching influence. His deep awareness of being French was intensified by Wagner's Germanness. Like most French composers he treasured lyrical clarity and was worried by Wagner's increasingly inflated orchestral textures, but at the

same time he shared with Wagner a sensuousness, an almost principled hedonism which was a source of much of his originality. When as a student he was asked by what law he could justify his unparalleled flouting of harmonic etiquette, he replied, to the point as always, "By one alone – that of my own pleasure."

It was a law by which he abided in life as well as in art. He used women like disposable handkerchiefs, drove first a mistress and then his wife to shoot themselves, fathered an illegitimate child and indulged himself to the hilt, mostly with other people's money. He surrounded himself with cats, both porcelain and Siamese, and savoured delicacy in all things other than his own behaviour. His taste for pleasure was both Gargantuan and refined. Indeed, there was an element of dandyism in him that extended to his superstitions: he would never go to bed at night without ritually blowing his nose and then fastidiously placing his slippers so that the toes pointed outwards. But though he was unabashedly a sensualist, he was too reserved to be labelled a voluptuary. As an artist, he was more concerned with the experience of the moment than with making statements about experience. Though his music often has about it an almost Classical clarity and delicacy of sound, he had little or none of the true Classical musician's preoccupation with form and development. He was interested (as his spectral mentor Schumann had been) in capturing as perfectly as possible a fleeting mood, in pinning down the essence of a

thought with the maximum economy. In this, as in his belief in the expressive properties of silence, he foreshadowed the intellectualized modernism of Webern. It is some measure of the revolutionary qualities of Debussy's music that it remained banned in the former Soviet Union several decades after his death.

As Debussy grew older, he acknowledged his musical debts as little as his monetary ones. "I am more and more convinced," he wrote, "that it is not in music's nature to be cast into fixed and traditional forms. It is made up of colours and of rhythms. The rest is a lot of humbug, invented by frigid imbeciles riding on the backs of the masters." Accordingly, he repudiated many who had once been his models. Massenet, for instance, was dismissed as "a master only in the art of pandering to stupid ideas and amateur standards." And he dispatched far greater masters with no more charity: "I heartily detest the piano concertos of Mozart – but less so than those of Beethoven."

There was one model, however, whom he could not knock down, one whose elemental power continually forced him to sharpen his own identity, and one with whom in the end he largely shared the responsibility for undermining the formal and harmonic structures on which the music of four centuries had rested. It could be said, with only a little poetic licence, that while Wagner may have forged the key to the 20th century, he left it to Debussy to unlock the door.

As an artist Debussy was concerned with the experience of the moment.

Ravel

While Debussy's music traces a consistent line of development, Maurice Ravel's often seems to have sprung fully grown from his meticulously honed imagination. The title and character of his first published piano work, the charming *Menuet antique* (1895), immediately identify three central strands of his creative outlook: a love of the dance, a reverence for the distant past and an open acknowledgement of his debts to earlier composers. Among the many dance-inspired works that followed are another minuet ('sur le nom d'Haydn'), the entrancingly beautiful *Pavane pour une Infante défunte* (Pavane for a Dead Princess), *La Valse* (an open tribute to the Viennese waltz), the notoriously

repetitious and ever-popular *Boléro* (though this one was not for the piano), the *Valses nobles et sentimentales* (even the title, in this case, taken straight from Schubert), and a 'Forlane', 'Rigaudon' and another 'Menuet' (all then archaic) from his best-known solo piano suite *Le Tombeau de Couperin*. And even in this brief list we have two composers of the past honoured by name (Haydn and Couperin, from opposite ends of the 18th century). Other composers honoured both in name and (loosely) in style include Borodin, Chabrier and Fauré.

Ravel is often thought of as a quintessentially French composer, and in many ways he certainly was. But an important part of his own identity lay outside France. His father was Swiss and his mother was from the Basque region of Spain, and Spain looms large in Ravel's output. The famous and finger-bleedingly virtuosic *Alborada del Gracioso* from his *Miroirs* (Mirrors) is based on a Spanish form, so in one way or another are the *Habañera*, the famous *Pavane* just mentioned, the orchestral *Rapsodie espagnole*, the opera *L'Heure Espagnole* and the songs based on Cervantes' *Don Quixote* (these last mentioned Ravel's final compositions before he succumbed to illness).

The fact that all these works involve a kind of musical dressing-up reveals another essential aspect of Ravel's make-up: his near-obsession with childhood. In very many of his works, Ravel seems to hide himself behind some glittering costume. And in many cases, too, he takes a piano original and turns it into a dazzling orchestral showpiece, in effect exchanging one costume for another still more brilliant. Among the works double-cloaked in this way are the *Alborada*, the *Valses nobles et sentimentales*, *Le Tombeau de Couperin*, *Une barque sur l'ocean*, and the suite for piano duet, *Ma mère l'Oye* (Mother Goose), another throwback to childhood. Stravinsky's description of Ravel as "the most perfect of Swiss watchmakers" gives an excellent idea of his painstaking craftsmanship and precision, and Martin Cooper's amendment to "the most perfect of French chefs" highlights aspects of his aural imagination and the way in which he balances and blends the materials before him to create "aural delight and aesthetic euphoria", but one might also add a third title and call him "the most perfect of fairytale toymakers". He himself scorned the term 'genius' or even 'artist' whenever it was applied to him, as of course it often was, and liked to think of himself simply as an artisan.

Ravel in 1911, in a portrait by Achille Ouvre. In his compositions Ravel often used the percussive aspects of the piano to emphasize rhythms.

The hallmarks of Ravel's style include an impressionistic use of all three pedals (there are certain passages which are unplayable on a piano with only two), a tendency to explore simultaneously the extreme registers of the keyboard, a strong identification of tone colour and expression, the frequent and often virtuosic use of repeated notes as an agent of atmosphere, a vaguely 'oriental' exoticism and a relatively sparing use of dissonance. His forms, on the whole, are more clearly drawn than Debussy's, and often etched by simpler means, and his melodies more self-contained and singable (surely one of the reasons for the huge popularity of the *Pavane*). Just as Debussy is often seen in a direct line of succession from Chopin, Ravel is seen as owing more to Liszt. For the most part, Debussy's ideal of an instrument without hammers is far removed from Ravel's, who often uses the percussive aspects of the piano to emphasize his rhythms, which in themselves are generally more clear-cut than Debussy's.

Ravel's works for piano include two very different concertos, one for the left hand alone (commissioned by the one-armed pianist Paul Wittgenstein, elder brother of the philosopher, Ludwig Wittgenstein), in which his mastery of orchestration and highly individual writing for keyboard are fascinatingly combined. The Concerto in G (1929–31), like his Sonata for Piano and Violin (1897), clearly shows the influence of jazz. Of his works for solo piano, the summit, by general consent, is the three-movement *Gaspard de la Nuit* (Shadows in the Night), written in 1908 and based on prose poems by Aloysius Bertrand. Here the listener meets Ravel at his darkest and most virtuosic. Close on its heels, however, in terms of quality must be counted the bewitching *Miroirs*, the less demanding but no less colourful *Valse nobles et sentimentales* and the suite *Tombeau de Couperin*.

Ravel and the great Russian dancer Nijinsky, photographed by Stravinsky in 1912, playing through the score of the ballet **Daphnis and Chloë,** *a commission by Serge Diaghilev for his Ballets Russes.*

Two Americans: Ives and Gershwin

Charles Ives (1874–1954)

Ives's most important piano work is the formidably difficult *Concord Sonata*, inspired by the writings of Ralph Waldo Emerson, Nathaniel Hawthorne, the Alcotts and Henry David Thoreau. Although published in 1919, the work was so ferociously complex in its physical and intellectual demands that it remained unperformed for 20 years. In Ives's case this was not unusual. His orchestral suite *Three Places in New England* likewise suffered a gap of two decades between completion and performance. His Third Symphony belatedly won a Pulitzer Prize in 1947, fully 36 years after it was written, and his Fourth Symphony, now widely considered a masterpiece, was completed in 1916 but not performed in its entirety until 1965, eleven years after the composer's death. In all this, Ives himself was at least partly to blame.

Known, insofar as he was known at all, as a shrewd New England businessman (the firm of Ives & Myrick was a prosperous insurance agency), Ives was a craggy, eccentric, cantankerous recluse who kept himself as far apart as he could manage from the mainstream of musical life. He seldom went out, never attended concerts and owned neither a radio nor a record-player. Although he was well versed in the great classics, especially those of Beethoven, Schumann and Brahms, and had composed in early manhood two highly accomplished symphonies, entirely traditional in style, he showed no interest in the musical life of his own time, and lived largely in ignorance of it. Yet closeted away in the small town of Danbury, Connecticut, he anticipated many of the major compositional processes of the 20th century, including polytonality (writing in two or more keys at once), atonality (the complete avoidance of key), serialism (the system, pioneered by the Austrian composer Arnold Schoenberg, in which a composition is based on a keyless sequence of the twelve tones of the chromatic scale), polymetres (writing in several metres at once) and complex polyrhythms (the combining of two or more outwardly incompatible rhythmic schemes), and microtonality (the use of quarter-tones rather than the chromatic semi-tones whose combination governs the scales on which Western music had always been based). In the second movement of the *Concord* Sonata, he specified the use of a strip of wood on the white and the black keys to produce 'echo-like' clusters, thus anticipating the 'prepared' pianos of Henry Cowell and John Cage. In the final movement, 'Thoreau', there is an optional flute part.

Other piano works by Ives are the Piano Sonata No. 1 of 1909, the slightly earlier *Three-Page* Sonata, the *4 Studies* of 1908–9 and a number of other short pieces, including three prophetic *Quarter-tone Pieces* for two pianos and *The Anti-Abolitionist Riots* of 1908. Among the hallmarks of his uniquely original and passionately American style is the combination of simple phrases taken from American church hymns, popular ballads, band music, minstrel songs, piano rags and so on with a complex and highly discordant fabric of intersecting musical lines serving as a kind of accompaniment. Among those whose 'innovations' he anticipated, Stravinsky and Schoenberg both publicly acknowledged his importance. By the time of his centenary in 1974, Ives was widely celebrated as one of the most original composers of the century.

Gershwin at an orchestral rehearsal, c.1935. He liked to play piano just for the fun of it.

George Gershwin (1898–1937)

Even as a child Gershwin knew he wanted to be a writer of popular songs. He took up the piano when he was around 10, published his first song at 18 and scored his first big hit with *Swanee* when he was 20. By that time he was a brilliant piano player with a dazzling, natural technique and a style all his own. Refinement, beauty of tone and subtlety of line were not for him, certainly not then. Used to pounding out songs from Tin Pan Alley, his own as well as many well-established numbers, he was a player of tremendous energy, stamina and drive whose powerhouse rhythms, swinging beat and love of showing off guaranteed the success of any party he attended. In one of the first of his solo piano pieces, *Rialto Ripples*, the influence of ragtime on his style is plain to hear, just as his more romantic numbers (*The Man I Love, Someone to Watch over Me*, for example) are deeply rooted in the blues tradition, while not being blues themselves. His gift for melody was second to none, his rhythm unsurpassed and rarely equalled, and his style was unique.

Gershwin was only 25 when he composed his most famous work, the evergreen *Rhapsody in Blue* for piano and orchestra (or as originally intended, for piano and jazz band). This was the first major work to blend the styles of jazz with the idioms of the concert-hall tradition and it occupies today a place very near to the centre of the concerto repertoire. It might be called the first example of so-called 'cross-over' music. At the time it was written, 1924, Gershwin had no experience of orchestration and that task was handed over to Ferdé Grofé, composer of the popular *Grand Canyon* Suite. While churning out one inspired popular song after another, often to the equally inspired lyrics of his brother Ira, Gershwin advanced further down the concert road with his Concerto in F, still the most-played of all American concertos. Both the Rhapsody and the Concerto combine jazzy material with a style of piano-writing clearly rooted in the world of Liszt, Chopin and Tchaikovsky and both are virtuoso works of considerable difficulty. Still more intricate for the pianist are the *Variations on 'I Got Rhythm'* of 1934. Of Gershwin's works for solo piano, pride of place is shared by the Three Piano Preludes and the eighteen song transcriptions (by the composer himself) published as *The Gershwin Songbook* in 1932. In bridging the gap between popular and 'classical' music, Gershwin came far closer than such jazz-influenced 'serious' composers as Ravel and Stravinsky.

A rare photograph of the reclusive Charles Ives, who shunned the musical limelight.

The Performers

THE PIANISTS PORTRAYED HERE HAVE BEEN CHOSEN ACCORDING TO THE FOLLOWING CRITERIA. WITHOUT EXCEPTION THEY ALL NOW BELONG TO THE PAST (ENABLING THEIR CAREERS TO BE ASSESSED IN THEIR ENTIRETY); THE IMPORTANCE OF EACH HAS BEEN GENERALLY ACKNOWLEDGED BY MUSICIANS AND AUDIENCES ALIKE; AND WITH ONLY A HANDFUL OF EXCEPTIONS, EACH OF THOSE WHOSE PLAYING HAS BEEN CAPTURED BY THE MICROPHONE HAS BEEN REGARDED AT ONE TIME OR ANOTHER, AND BY A SIGNIFICANT NUMBER OF PEOPLE, AS 'THE GREATEST LIVING PIANIST'. MORE BROADLY, THEY FALL INTO THREE MAIN CATEGORIES: COMPOSER-PIANISTS, RENOWNED EQUALLY AS CREATORS AND VIRTUOSOS; INTERPRETERS, WHO CONFINED THEMSELVES (IN PUBLIC, ANYWAY) TO THE MUSIC OF OTHERS; AND THOSE WHOSE CAREERS WERE FORGED IN THE FACE OF A DEEPLY ENTRENCHED PREJUDICE WHICH EACH DID MUCH TO DIMINISH: WOMEN — WHOM ONLY HISTORY HAS FORCED INTO A CATEGORY OF THEIR OWN.

Jan Ladislav Dussek

Born in Bohemia, Dussek (1760–1812) was the first of the great travelling virtuosos, although some of his travels were enforced either by political upheavals, such as the French Revolution, or by an urgent need to escape his creditors. Celebrated alike for his talent and his handsome appearance, he is said to have been the first pianist to play with his profile to the audience (a move generally attributed to his vanity), and was one of the most important pioneers of the new 'singing' style of piano playing which reached its height with Chopin in the 19th century. His writing for the instrument is often brilliantly virtuosic and in many ways anticipates both the styles and the techniques of such later composers as Schubert, Beethoven, Weber, Mendelssohn, Rossini, Chopin and Schumann. Celebrated in his prime as 'le beau Dussek' (he might be described as the first of music's matinée idols), he became immensely fat in later life, drank too much and spent most of his time in bed. A sad end, but in his day he had paved the way for a steady procession of virtuosos whose fame would eclipse his own. Among them was one whose rags-to-riches career might almost have been conceived for Hollywood –

Muzio Clementi

Clementi was born into a musical but impoverished Italian family in 1752. In 1766, now a brilliant performer on the harpsichord and organ, he was almost literally purchased from his parents by one Peter Beckford, an English aristocrat who removed the boy to his country seat in Dorset and undertook to oversee his education. In 1770 Clementi made a sensational London debut as a pianist, and three years later published his Op. 2, a trilogy of works dedicated to Haydn, much admired by C. P. E. Bach, and claimed by some scholars to have definitively established the form of the piano sonata. From that time onwards he was widely regarded as a musician of international significance. More important than his compositions, however, was his discreetly revolutionary approach to the piano. The earlier Classicists had cultivated a relatively detached touch at the keyboard (the treatises of the time leave no doubt that the vocal-style, legato, that "flowing like oil" so beloved of Mozart and so characteristic of the coming Romantics, was the exception rather than the rule). Nor, on the whole, did they indulge in very great contrasts of volume. If Czerny is to be believed, Beethoven, two years before his death in 1827, recalled even Mozart's playing as being "neat and clean, but rather flat and antiquated". Clementi was the first really influential pianist who openly rejected these conventions, pursuing a more wide-ranging, heroic, dramatically poetic ideal.

In his concentration on rapid double-notes and octaves, his unashamed bravura, his thundering chords and arpeggios and his unprecedented stamina, Clementi paved the way for Beethoven, Liszt, Brahms, even Ravel.

Jan Ladislav Dussek – the first of the great travelling virtuosos.

His epoch-making book of studies, *Gradus ad Parnassum* (1817), was the first of its kind and is still in use today. Through his teaching he shaped a generation. Among his many distinguished pupils were J. B. Cramer (much admired by Beethoven), Ignaz Moscheles, and Giacomo Meyerbeer. Nor did his influence stop there. He became in turn a music publisher and a successful piano manufacturer, and ended his days as a wealthy English squire, dying in 1832.

History is famously said to repeat itself, and in his treatment of one pupil in particular, Clementi must have seen an interesting counterpoint to his own early life. The

Muzio Clementi – the first influential pianist to pursue a dramatically poetic ideal.

pupil in question was a slovenly, surly-looking youth who would find his most lasting fame as the inventor of the keyboard nocturne, John Field.

John Field

Field (1782–1837) was both the son and the grandson of professional musicians, and it was from his grandfather that he had his first lessons in piano-playing. He took easily to the piano and was playing in public by the time he was six. By 1794 he had basically outgrown the musical and pianistic resources of his native Dublin and moved to London, where he made a highly successful debut and became apprenticed to Clementi, whose piano manufacturing business was now in full swing. Just as Beckford had taken the boy Clementi under his wing, so Clementi now undertook to supervise Field's musical development, although in this case the financial arrangements were reversed. It was Field's parents who paid through the nose to procure their son's apprenticeship, little dreaming of the extent to which he was to be exploited by his guardian. Clementi undoubtedly enriched the musicianship and pianism of his sallow and charmless ward, but he exacted a heavy price, forcing the boy to serve as an animated shop-window mannequin, demonstrating Clementi's wares at his London showroom. Louis Spohr, one of the most eminent composers of his time, visited the premises and was shocked at Clementi's treatment of the boy.

"Field had to play for hours to display the instruments to the best advantages of the purchasers. I still recall the figure of this pale, overgrown youth. ... When Field, who had long outgrown his clothes, placed himself at the piano and stretched out his arms over the keyboard so that the sleeves shrunk up nearly to his elbows, his whole figure appeared awkward and stiff in the highest degree."

Nor was Clementi much more attentive to the boy's nutrition. Exploited he may have been, but under Clementi's guidance Field became a keyboard virtuoso of exceptional distinction. When Clementi took him to Paris in 1802, he followed his debut with a number of other concerts and made a deep impression on audiences and critics alike. In the words of one reviewer, he played the instrument "with such precision and inimitable taste as to call forth from a Parisian audience the most enthusiastic applause." Having conquered Paris, the odd couple moved on, first to Vienna, then to Russia, where Field finally managed to free himself of Clementi's company. Four years later, Clementi returned to St. Petersburg to find his erstwhile charge transformed into a teacher, performer and composer of great celebrity. It was in Russia that Field composed the first of his nocturnes, whose dreamy, melancholy tunes floated above a deeply pedalled rolling bass, revealing a whole new sound-world that was to influence the piano styles of such vastly superior musicians as Mendelssohn, Chopin and Liszt.

As a performer, Field appears to have been entirely lacking in charisma. As Liszt remarked, "His inexpressive look aroused no curiosity whatever. ... His calmness bordered on apathy. Nothing could trouble him less than the impression he might produce upon his audience." That impression, nevertheless, was generally remarkable, and the English pianist Charles Salaman proclaimed Field "a really great player ... romantic and poetic, as if interpreting some beautiful dream, while in the singing quality of his touch, the infinite grace and delicacy of his execution, and his emotional expression, he was unrivalled in his day." Mikhail Glinka, celebrated as 'the father of Russian music', confirms the impression, describing Field's fingers as being "like great drops of rain, poured over the keys like pearls on velvet."

In both character and importance, Field was in many ways similar to Dussek, whose heavy drinking and dissolute lifestyle were mirrored in his own. Both may be spoken of in the same breath as the first great poets of the keyboard, and of both it can be said that their influence far outstripped their talents. In this they differed from their most celebrated contemporary, at least in the German-speaking world: a man who had the extraordinary distinction of having had lessons with Mozart, Haydn, Clementi and Beethoven.

Johann Hummel

Strange though it may seem to us today, Johann Nepomuk Hummel (1778–1837) was considered by many in his lifetime to be the equal of Beethoven as both pianist and composer. Yet he went into almost immediate eclipse after his death. His musicological resuscitation in the later 20th century has demonstrated how unjust posterity can be. A great composer he was not; a masterly and inventive one he was, and his works, while often extremely difficult to play, contain many delights. His greatest renown as a pianist was for the quality of his improvisations, which were never forgotten by those who heard them. Here, perhaps, the equation with Beethoven was just. In many ways he represents the culmination of the Classical tradition passed on to him through his teachers, but he had a formative influence on the young Chopin, as is revealed when his piano concertos, particularly the one in A minor, are contrasted with Chopin's own.

For many years Hummel was among the most influential and expensive teachers in Europe. His teaching methods are enshrined in his three-volume treatise on the piano, said to have sold thousands of copies within days of its publication in 1828, and reveal him as a curious blend of visionary and pedant. Like his own teachers, Hummel advocated only the most sparing use of the pedals, which too easily "cloak an impure and indistinct method of playing." On the whole he confined his own pedalling to broad, lyrical slow movements "where the harmony changes at distant intervals. All other pedal effects are of no value, either to the performer or the instrument." His finger control was evidently remarkable, and impressed no less exacting a witness than that indefatigable pedagogue Carl Czerny, who wrote "Never before had I heard such novel and dazzling difficulties, such clarity and elegance in performance, such intimate and tender expression or such excellent taste in improvisation." But Czerny's admiration did not blind him to Hummel's liabilities as an idol. "He was a very striking young man, with an unpleasant, common-looking face that constantly twitched. ... His

clothing was wholly without taste, and he wore valuable diamond rings on almost all his fingers." Contemporary portraits support this account. Like Dussek, he became enormously fat in his later years, so much so that a special semi-circular aperture was cut into his dining room table to accommodate his Falstaffian girth. In this, as in much else, he was the polar opposite of one quite extraordinary pianist-composer, who was as forward-looking and innovative as Hummel was conservative.

Carl Maria von Weber

Between 1810 and 1820 the most radical and far-reaching ideas about the piano, both writing for it and playing on it, came from a man who seldom if ever performed in public. It may seem inconceivable today, but there was a time when the piano sonatas of Weber (1786–1826) were ranked with or even above Beethoven's. An ex-prodigy, Weber was a keyboard virtuoso no less remarkable than Hummel. But

while Hummel belonged essentially to the elegant, Classically oriented school of pianism pioneered by J. C. Bach and Mozart, Weber belonged to that parallel line of descent originating with C. P. E. Bach and Clementi. In Weber, it might be argued, we encounter the first of the great Romantics. His keyboard music was orchestral in scope but supremely pianistic in style. The teenage Liszt, already an incomparable virtuoso, is said to have declared that Weber's music was to other music "as the gigantic nature of the New World and the Virgin forests of America are to the belted, box-treed, enclosed gardens of Europe." Much of it sounds like the sheerest dross today, but the best of it retains its appeal, and its challenges. In the 19th century there was hardly a pianist to be found whose repertoire did not include the A flat Sonata, the famous 'Invitation to the Dance', the *Polacca brillante* and the still splendidly effective *Concertstück* in F minor for piano and orchestra, all of which have survived the test of time.

Weber – the virtuosity of his piano music pointed the way to Chopin and Liszt.

Frédéric Chopin

By the time Chopin settled in Paris in 1831, aged 21, he was probably one of the two greatest pianists in the world (the other being his almost exact contemporary Liszt). And as in his music, he was almost certainly the most original. No-one had ever written for the piano as he did, nor had they played it as he did. In the flexibility of his hands, the carefree looseness of his wrists and the almost balletic suppleness of his arms, he brought something entirely new to the technique of piano playing. In many ways he was the first of the pianistic painters. His control over tone colour, like the extraordinary variety of his tonal palette, was unequalled. Despite his fabled physical weakness he could play for hours without showing the slightest fatigue. Stiffness and muscular tension were unknown to him. "Souplesse!" he would say to his students, "souplesse avant tout" ("Suppleness! suppleness before everything"). And though he wrote some of the most hair-raisingly difficult music ever composed, the most well-exercised adverb in his teaching vocabulary was 'facilement'

('easily'). Unlike Liszt, who practised like a man possessed, Chopin played the piano as naturally as he breathed, and in later life a good deal more easily. According to his father, he hardly every practised. In whatever he played there was always a sense of improvisation, of freshness, of music being minted on the spot. No man ever more magically transcended the mechanical nature of the piano than Chopin. His beautiful, arching, continuous unfolding of melody was comparable only with the greatest opera singers, who influenced him far more than any pianist.

In many ways, Chopin was the most reluctant virtuoso of all the great composer-pianists. He hated giving concerts, and by his own admission would be sick with nerves for three days in anticipation of the ordeal. His reputation as one of the greatest pianists who ever lived rests with little more than a couple of dozen public appearances.

One criticism only was made repeatedly of his major performances, and that was that he played too softly. For generations it has been mindlessly put about that Chopin played softly because he was too frail and weak to play any louder. The truth is more significant. The fact is that a five-year-old girl can get some very loud sounds indeed out of a grand piano, and a modern grand at that, incomparably heavier than anything Chopin ever played on. If Chopin played softly, it was not because he could not play louder but because he did not want to. And why not? Because he could not abide ugliness in any form, and there was a point beyond which the pianos of his time could not be pushed without taking on a certain harshness, without occasioning a certain loss of control, and that was anathema to Chopin. His playing, however, was by no means undramatic. His uncanny control of the quietest regions of the piano enabled him to build the same pattern of contrasts and relationships as might be achieved by a more 'powerful' player, and his rhythmic instinct was second to none. Indeed, it was unique.

In virtually every account of his playing, throughout his life, it was Chopin's entirely original way with rhythm that most forcibly struck discerning listeners. He himself put it down to his childhood immersion in Polish folk music. He took unprecedented 'liberties' with his inflection of right-hand melodies while never deviating from a strict observance of the underlying metrical pulse. In this, as in many other respects, he was remarkably close to the expressed ideal of his revered Mozart, though Chopin cannot possibly have known the now-famous letter in which Mozart spells it out.

Franz Liszt

It is a curious irony that the man who exerted the most formative influence on the piano music of the mid-19th century was not himself a pianist at all, but a violinist. If the accounts of Schubert, Liszt, Chopin, Schumann, Rossini and

Chopin – the reluctant virtuoso among the composer-pianists – in 1849, shortly before his death.

Berlioz are to be believed, he was probably the greatest violinist who ever lived. Indeed, so prodigious were the accomplishments of Niccoló Paganini that he was widely said to have made a pact with the Devil (some believed he was the Devil himself). On two performer-composers in particular, Paganini had a decisive influence, and neither played the violin at all. Both men resolved that they would do for the piano what Paganini had done for the violin: to reveal its very soul, discovering in it hitherto untapped resources and achieving heights of virtuosity never previously imagined. One was Chopin, the other was Liszt, and neither had yet achieved the age of 20. Of the two, Liszt alone was the wholehearted Romantic, steeped in literature, obsessed with mysticism and the concept of the Hero, drenched in a generalized worship of the distant past which was unsullied by scholarship, and obsessed, to a degree unimaginable today, with the piano itself. As he confided to a friend in 1832:

> "For a whole fortnight my mind and my fingers have been working like two lost souls. Homer, the Bible, Plato, Locke, Byron, Hugo, Lamartine, Chateaubriand, Beethoven, Bach, Hummel, Mozart, Weber are all around me. I study them, meditate on them, devour them with fury; besides this, I practise four to five hours of exercises (thirds, sixths, octaves, tremolos, repeated notes, cadenzas etc.) Ah! Provided I don't go mad, you will find in me an artist!"

His artistry was never in question, of course, and he did not go mad. Nor did those four or five hours account for even half of his daily practice time. Fourteen hours a day became his standard regimen. Despite this, he thought of himself, even then, primarily as a composer, and during most of his twenties he made relatively few public appearances. Having established himself as probably the greatest pianist who ever lived or ever would live, Liszt gave his last public concert in September 1847 and then astonished the musical world by announcing his retirement from the concert platform. He was thirty-five years old and at the very peak of his powers. From that time until his death just under forty years later, he devoted himself to composing, conducting and teaching. He did, in fact, play in public again, but never for money – nor did he ever accept a penny from his many pupils, who included several of the greatest pianists of the century, among them Hans von Bülow, Ferruccio Busoni, Eugen d'Albert, Moritz Rosenthal, Isaac Albeniz, Emil von Sauer and Karl Tausig.

It was Liszt more than anyone else who established the model on which the life of the concert pianist is based to this day. It was he who pioneered the solo recital (as he also invented its curious name: "How," people asked at the time, "can one 'recite' on the piano?"). He was the first to play whole programmes from memory, the first to embrace the entire keyboard literature, as then known, the first consistently to place the piano at right angles to the platform, so that its opened lid projected the sound outward towards the audience, and the first to play for gatherings of three

thousand and more. He was also the first (and, with the possible exception of Paderewski, the last) regularly to induce near-hysteria in his audiences.

Liszt in 1839, at the outset of his spectacular career as a travelling virtuoso.

Women threw their jewellery on to the stage, they shrieked in ecstasy (long before the bobby-soxers, teeny-boppers and groupies of the 20th century), they fought, they scratched and kicked each other over the gloves he contrived to leave on the piano or the snuff-boxes that he just happened to have mislaid. One lady, no longer in the first flush of youth, retrieved the butt of a cigar Liszt had smoked and sequestered it in her bosom to her dying day.

Even when he was a wen-covered, white-haired old man in a cassock, Liszt's effect on women was mesmeric, and more. But his power over people – as a performer, as a musician, as a man – far transcended matters of sex. Such reactions were by no means confined to women, youths and sycophants. Highly respected critics, too, lost all restraint. It is a matter of historical fact: Liszt's power as a performer was unprecedented, and remains unique in musical history.

144

Thalberg – renowned for a
suppleness of line that belied the
piano's percussive nature.

Sigismond Thalberg

Despite his fanciful claim to being the illicit offspring of Count Moritz von Dietrichstein and the Baroness von Wetzlar), Thalberg's birth certificate establishes him as the son of Joseph Thalberg and Fortunée Stein of Frankfurt. Widely regarded in his day as the greatest virtuoso pianist of the century, Thalberg (1812–71) is remembered today almost exclusively for his very public rivalry with Liszt, culminating in a pianistic 'duel' mounted by the Princess Belgiojoso at her Paris salon in 1837.

Apart from their virtuosity and cult status (especially among women), the two were in many ways polar opposites.

Schumann once suggested that "if anyone were to criticize Thalberg, all the girls in Germany, France and the other European countries would rise up in arms." Where Liszt was flamboyant and extravagantly athletic at the keyboard, Thalberg was the picture of sphinx-like passivity. While Liszt exuded animal vitality and a powerfully sexual aura, Thalberg was the ultimate gentleman, courteous but detached, charming but not ingratiating, confident but serene, and like Chopin, always immaculately groomed and elegantly dressed. There was something Zen-like in his manner. He told Ignaz Moscheles "that he had acquired his posture and self-control by smoking a Turkish pipe while practising his exercises; the length of the tube being so calculated as to keep him erect and motionless."

Unlike Liszt, Thalberg had a trademark, with the unfortunate effect that posterity remembers him for little else: a trick of dividing a melody between the two hands (mainly the two thumbs), surrounding it with sweeping arpeggios and lavish dollops of assorted pianistic confectionery, thus giving the impression of three independent hands. It was an idea briefly adopted by Mendelssohn and Schumann and seems to have been modelled originally on the playing of the harpist Parish Alvars. For all his bravura, Thalberg was in many ways a classicist, prizing a cool head and great clarity of texture, offset by a sensuous harmonic wash achieved almost entirely by the pedals, of which he was an acknowledged master. Like most pianists of his day, he seldom performed any music but his own. On the rare occasions when he did, he was restrained and respectful of the printed text. (Liszt, by comparison, was known virtually to recompose the music on the spot, embroidering it with all manner of embellishments, pedal effects, contrapuntal variations and so on.)

Among Thalberg's greatest accomplishments as a pianist was a suppleness of line which belied the essentially percussive nature of the piano. His particular manner of unfurling long, sumptuous melodies was something never heard before, and drew praise even from his adversary Liszt: "Thalberg," he wrote, "is the only man who can play the violin on the piano". Unsurprisingly, when Thalberg came, as was the custom of the time, to write his own 'mèthode', he entitled it *The Art of Singing Applied to the Piano*. With such witnesses as Mendelssohn, Berlioz, both Robert and Clara Schumann, and the scholar-critic Fétis, it seems fair to say that he was widely regarded, at the very highest level, as the equal of Liszt. He was the most expensive piano soloist of his day, but he gave unstintingly of his energies. In the season following his New York debut in 1856, he played 56 concerts in New York alone, often squeezing three appearances into a single day.

Thalberg retired, a rich man, in 1863, and thereafter pursued the life of a leisured Italian wine-grower, turning his back on music to such an extent that he did not even have a piano in the house. If he survives in history as little more than a footnote, it must be put down to the relative poverty of his music, although even here he attracted some very distinguished admirers, improbably including Schumann who was in general implacably opposed to everything Thalberg stood for. The few efforts made in the 20th century to revive interest in his music have largely failed and are unlikely to be renewed.

Charles Alkan

Born in Paris in 1813, Charles Henry Valentin Alkan (whose real name was Morhange) was among the most extraordinary musicians of his age. One of five brothers, all of them musicians, he was astonishingly precocious and won admission to the Paris Conservatoire at the age of six.

Like his friend and close contemporary Chopin, he was a pianist of fabulous accomplishment (indeed he was said to have been the only pianist before whom Liszt was nervous of performing) yet he rarely played in public, he wrote almost exclusively for the piano and composed two sets of études whose transcendent difficulty has ensured that they are seldom played, and still more seldom played well. Like Chopin, he wrote two piano concertos, an imposing cycle of Préludes, a piano trio and a cello sonata, but he remains unique in being the first composer ever to memorialize the railroad (in the onomatopaeic *Chemin de fer*, Op. 27). For more than a century his work was first largely ignored and then forgotten until such pianists as Ronald Smith and Raymond Lewenthal took up his cause in the 1960s and 1970s and revealed to new generations his remarkable originality and resourcefulness as a pianistic thinker. In sharp contrast to Chopin, he brought to bear on piano music the gargantuan perspectives of a Berlioz, as in his epic Symphony for Solo Piano, whose first movement alone exceeds half an hour in performance, or the equally colossal Concerto, again for piano alone. Sad to say, the well-aired story of his accidental death (1888) – that he was crushed beneath a bookcase which fell on him as he removed a copy of the Talmud from the top shelf – turns out to be entirely untrue.

Louis Gottschalk

Refused an audition for the Paris Conservatoire on the then-fashionable grounds that he was an American, Louis Moreau Gottschalk is said at the age of 16 to have been proclaimed by Chopin as the future 'king of pianists'. As a composer he became justifiably renowned as the first authentic musical spokesman of the New World. He became, too, the musical idol of Spain, memorialized in such delightful and taxing numbers as *Souvenir d'Andalousie* – the first piano pieces to popularize the pungent styles of flamenco. Like many Americans after him, he found it difficult to establish the fame in his own country that he had achieved in Europe.

After his father's death in 1853, the 24-year-old Gottshalk became the breadwinner for his six younger brothers and sisters, touring extensively throughout the Americas and hitting the jackpot with a whole series of sentimental, semi-programmatic 'weepies', most notably *The Dying Poet* and *The Last Hope*, both tailor-made for the genteel lachrymosity that was then the height of fashion. The most travelled pianist of his time, he covered hundreds of thousands of miles, giving thousands of recitals. He was one of the first of the piano's real matinée idols, and his love affairs and seductions became legendary. In 1865 he was forced to flee from his native land in the murk of a sexual scandal that titilated newspaper readers from coast to coast. With the vigilantes close on his heels, he set sail for South America, where after feverish activity (including the mounting of 'monster concerts' involving as many as 650 performers) he collapsed on stage while playing his own *Morte!*, dying shortly thereafter, on 18 December 1869.

145

Anton Rubinstein

Widely rumoured to be the illegitimate son of Beethoven (though the dates hardly tally), Rubinstein (1829–94) was one of those larger-than-life characters to whom legends cling like the proverbial limpets. Although he is remembered today (if only by connoisseurs) as an incomparable virtuoso, and by one or two piano pieces which crop up very occasionally in piano anthologies, there was a time when his music ranked with the most popular ever written. He was Russian-born but Western-trained, and as the nationalist school never tired of pointing out, much of what he brought to Russian music and musicians was imported from Europe. Nevertheless, he was the first Russian who achieved equal status as pianist and composer, and with his almost equally accomplished and influential brother Nikolai he did much to raise the standard of professionalism in Russian musical life, albeit by applying European methods of education and extolling the virtues of the great Germanic tradition (he was an especially renowned interpreter of Beethoven, but was unusual for his time in detesting Wagner). Among his many compositions

for piano the most popular were the Melody in F, *Kammenoi-Ostrov* (The Rocky Island) and the Piano Concerto No. 4.

As a performer he was phenomenal. His technique was colossal, if occasionally a little slapdash, his tonal palette was immense, his memory infallible, up to his 50th year, and his stamina unique. Even before undertaking his legendary 'historical recitals' (a seven-concert cycle, given in many cities and covering the entire history of piano music), his programmes regularly exceeded three hours and embraced as many as 20 works (not merely miniatures, either, but a generous handful of major sonatas, such as Schumann's F sharp minor, Beethoven's 'Tempest' and A major Sonata, Op.101, as well), and would offer encores by the dozen, including such imposing and lengthy works as Chopin's B flat minor Sonata in its entirety. Regarded by many as the near-equal of Liszt, he attracted an almost fanatical following. In the 1872–3 season he toured the United States, where he gave 215 concerts in 239 days, sometimes giving as many as three in a single day, each one in a different city.

Anton Rubinstein – the first Russian to achieve equal status as composer and pianist.

Hans von Bülow

Von Bülow (1830–94) was the first and for some considerable time the greatest of a new breed: the purely interpretative musician. As both pianist and conductor, he gave his life entirely to the music of others. No pianist of his time possessed a greater intellect, a more formidable grasp of the keyboard and its possibilities – or a more studiously abrasive personality. As a young man, he once wrote to his mother, "my unpopularity is unbounded – and I rejoice in it!". As he made his way to and from the piano at his historic recitals he regarded his spellbound audiences with undisguised contempt. Nor did he spare them his scorn during the performance. As one observer wrote, "his expression is proud and supercilious to the last degree, and he looks all around at his audience when he is playing. His face seems to say 'you are all cats and dogs' and I don't care what you think of my playing.' "A rabid anti-Semite, like his idol Wagner (who later stole his wife, Liszt's daughter Cosima), he believed utterly in the unassailable supremacy of German music and did more than any other musician to establish it as the very bedrock of the Western concert repertoire. Considering the cast, it can not have been all that difficult. What national tradition can match a line-up including Bach, Handel, Haydn, Mozart, Beethoven, Schubert, Weber, Schumann, Mendelssohn, Wagner, Liszt (Germanic in all but origin), Bruckner, Brahms, Strauss and Mahler?

A child prodigy, like most of the great pianists, he worked hard at the piano, but unlike most great pianists elected to go to university, where he studied law, wrote lengthy and scholarly political tracts, copious musical criticism of a largely polemical nature, and immersed himself in musical scores of every kind. He then became Liszt's pupil, whereupon he redoubled his pianistic endeavours with fanatical zeal. "I devote the greater part of my time," he wrote, "four or five hours daily, exclusively to the cultivation of technique. I make martyrs of the eventual founders of my material prosperity; I crucify, like a good Christ, the flesh of my fingers, in order to make them obedient, submissive machines to the mind, as a pianist must."

With those martyred fingers he did indeed found his material prosperity, and a reputation which would long outlast him. In alliance with his penetrating intellect and a depth of musicianship rarely encountered, they saw him enthroned as the king of the high priests of music. His authority was awe-inspiring. His repertoire encompassed almost everything, but he became most famous as a Beethoven interpreter, and was known to play all of the last five sonatas, including the near hour-long *Hammerklavier*, in a single programme. His performances were revelations, leaving his audiences thunderstruck. As one prominent critic put it, "Those who wish to add intellectual enjoyment to the pleasures of the imagination derive a happiness from Bülow's playing which no other pianist can give to the same degree." Nor did any other pianist come onto the platform fully decked out with silk hat, cane and gloves, which he would ostentatiously remove before attending to the business of the evening. None thought less of lecturing his audiences, or as the soloist in a concerto of audibly disparaging conductor and orchestra alike.

Bülow – king of the high priests of music. His reputation was founded on a penetrating intellect and formidable musicianship.

Paderewski – the most popular and highest paid pianist in history; seen here at New York City Hall in April 1918.

Carl Tausig

It may be that the greatest of all Liszt's pupils was one of the earliest, the Polish-born Carl Tausig (1841–71). His technique was second to none, including Liszt's, and he carried in his memory virtually the whole of the keyboard repertoire then known. He was also an accomplished composer, and his many piano arrangements include whole Wagner operas and, most famously of all, Bach's celebrated Toccata and Fugue in D minor for organ – once a staple of the piano repertoire, now seldom played. Like Thalberg, he abhorred 'athletic' pianists (he was too young to have heard Liszt in his heyday) and cultivated an impassivity at the keyboard that only added to the aura of sorcery surrounding him. Short, and short-tempered, with gleaming, fanatical eyes and a contemptuous curl to his lips, he was recalled by his pupil Amy Fay as "a perfect misanthrope ... an uneasy, tormented, capricious spirit, at enmity with the world." A cruel and irascible teacher, he would accompany his pupils' efforts with a continuous torrent of abuse ("Dreadful! Terrible! Shocking! Oh God, oh God!"). He would then sit down and demonstrate, which was hardly any better: as Amy Fay put it, "I always used to feel as if someone wished me to copy a streak of forked lightning with the end of a wetted match." He died in 1871 at the age of 29.

148

Tausig – possessed a technique second to none, even that of his teacher, Liszt.

Ignace Paderewski

Ignace Jan Paderewski (virtuoso, composer and statesman, who served for a time as the first Prime Minister of modern Poland) made his debut in Paris in 1888. Within two years there was not a musical city in Europe where Paderewski (1860–1941) was not a household name. By the time he made his American debut in 1891, his fabulous reputation had preceded him, prompting the quip by one critic present, "He's good – but he's no Paderewski." What he was, was the highest paid and most popular pianist in history: in 1914 he netted the equivalent of $2,000,000-plus for a tour of ninety concerts.

Paderewski's repertoire was wide-ranging but his name will always be linked first and foremost with the music of his compatriot, Chopin. The legacy of his recordings, many of which were made when he was well past his prime, and most of which have been transferred to CD, presents a confusing picture ranging from the sublime to the mannered and mundane, even when allowances are made for the vast differences in style between his era and our own, principally the apparently stilted rubato and the intentional de-synchronization of the hands. These may seem distracting to us today, but they were not peculiar to Paderewski. Behind them lie a deep-rooted artistry and aristocratic poise perfectly suited to Chopin's music. In his 1911 recording of the F sharp major Nocturne, Op.15 No. 2, and his 1912 version of its F major companion, as in the 1925 account of the A flat Mazurka, Op. 59 No. 2, music and musician become one. There has been no more naturally persuasive Chopin playing from anyone, and his recording of his own Nocturne in B flat (not to be confused with his rather pedestrian piano roll of the same piece) is one of the most humbling and ennobling performances ever captured on disc.

Leopold Godowsky

The ultimate 'pianist's pianist' of the 20th century was the Polish-born Leopold Godowsky (1870–1938), whose astounding technique (particularly in the left hand) and compositional ingenuity won the unstinting admiration, and the abiding disbelief, of virtually the entire piano-playing fraternity. Unfortunately, he very seldom played at anything like his best in public or in the recording studio, and consequently cut relatively little ice with the musical public at large. In the manifold beauties of his tone, the astonishing independence of his fingers, and his near-miraculous pedalling he was conceded by his colleagues to be unique. On leaving Godowsky's home one evening, Josef Hofmann turned to fellow-pianist Abram Chasins, and said, "Never ever forget what you have heard tonight; never lose the memory of that sound. There is nothing like it in this world. It is a tragedy that the public has never heard [Godowsky] as only he can play." None of Godowsky's recordings do him justice. His most celebrated legacy is a series of 53 studies in which he effectively recomposed 26 of Chopin's already fearsome études, raising them to a level of virtuosity undreamt of even by Liszt and demonstrating a uniquely individual pianistic ingenuity.

Sergei Rachmaninov

The term pianists' pianist is often used to describe artists whose true worth has been evident to their colleagues but not to the public. On that basis, Sergei Rachmaninov (1873–1943) – also Josef Hofmann (see below) – must be reckoned borderline cases. Rachmaninov's greatness as a pianist was widely acknowledged, and his concerts were sell-outs, yet he was never in any normal sense of the word a 'popular' pianist. His relations with the public were of the strictest formality. Tall, lean, unsmiling and ascetic in appearance, he came, he conquered and he went. His greatness was as obvious to people as his command of the keyboard was all-embracing, but behind it were subtleties and achievements appreciable only to the connoisseur. His fellow pianists stood in awe of him, not only for his technical wizardry, which he never displayed for its own sake, but for his Olympian vision, his structural grasp at every level, his penetrating interpretative insights, and his comprehensive professionalism. Unlike his friend Josef Hofmann (each, incidentally, regarded the other as the greatest living pianist), he was not a spontaneous, chance-taking, improvisatory performer. His interpretations could be almost unsettlingly consistent, and they were based on a detached, meticulous, almost mechanistic analytical understanding of whatever work he happened to be playing. But they were anything but cold. His 1930 recording of Chopin's B flat minor Sonata – the most famous of the work ever made – has, like his equally towering account of Schumann's *Carnaval*, stood the test of more than half a century, due to its technical mastery and freshness of insight. Fortunately, Rachmaninov's entire recorded output has been reissued on CD and with luck should remain in the catalogue forever.

149

Godowsky – the ultimate pianist's pianist of the 20th century.

Cortot by Matisse. Cortot's capacity for feeling and intensity of vision were remarkable.

Josef Hofmann

Hofmann's recorded output is neither so extensive nor so consistent as Rachmaninov's, and he remains today very much a connoisseur's pianist. One of the most exploited of child prodigies (and equally gifted in mathematics, science and mechanics), Hofmann (1876–1957) toured the world as both composer and pianist at the age of 7. In 1892 he became the sole pupil of Anton Rubinstein, which he later cited as "the most important event in my life." Hofmann represents, along with Rachmaninov, perhaps the most important transitional figure between the high Romantic era, as exemplified by Paderewski, and the 'objective', musicologically respectful approach which came to dominate 20th-century schools. The influence of his risk-taking technique on fellow pianists was immense. In 1887 he became the first professional musician ever to record (at Edison's laboratory in New Jersey, USA). His repertoire centred on Beethoven, Chopin, Schumann and Liszt, as well as a profusion of salon pieces. He was also a prolific composer (mostly under the name of Michel Dvorsky), an important teacher (and the first director of the now famed Curtis Institute of Music in Philadelphia), an inventor with more than 70 patents for scientific and mechanical inventions, and the author of two books.

150

Josef Hofmann – regarded by his friend Rachmaninov as the greatest living pianist.

Alfred Cortot

Cortot (1877–1962) was never just a pianist, nor even just a musician. In a lifetime of extraordinary industry, he wrote several books, founded and directed for several decades a celebrated school, edited volumes of music still in widespread use, and served in a department of the French government. His repertoire was vast, but in the public imagination he was associated above all with two composers, closely related in outlook and even style. One was Chopin, the other was Debussy.

Cortot's capacity for feeling and the particular intensity of his vision were remarkable, but what singled him out from most of the 'romantics' of his generation was the intellectual discipline with which he clarified the emotional essence of a work – a discipline not always extended to his fingers. Especially in later years, he was almost as well-known for his technical mishaps as for his poetic genius. Despite his later renown as an exponent of the French tradition, his reputation for greatness was first achieved in Beethoven. Nor did he disdain the lighter side of the repertoire. He could be a *saloniste* confectioner with the best of them.

Cortot belonged to the last generation for whom the piano itself was almost an object of worship, but though he loved the piano as much as man, and understood all of its tonal resources, his use of it was always determined by a purely musical purpose. Beauty alone was never enough. It had to express something; it had to have meaning. At the same time, he was an unsurpassed master of characterization. In his hands, music emerged as intrinsically dramatic – continually responsive and developing. His rhythmic liberties were often extreme, and always inimitable, but they were never haphazard.

Cortot combined his activities as a soloist with those of a chamber musician, and in this area too he was outstanding – witness the recordings he made with his friends Jacques Thibaud and Pablo Casals (all transferred to CD).

Artur Schnabel

He came to be known, in some circles, as 'the man who invented Beethoven'. Certainly there was no pianist before him who was so widely associated with Beethoven, not even Bülow or Anton Rubinstein. But Schnabel (1882–1951) might just as well have been called 'the man who invented Schubert'. Amazingly, he was the first pianist who regularly played Schubert's sonatas in public. In 1928, the centenary of the composer's death, no less a pianist than Rachmaninov was able to claim ignorance not only of the works themselves but of their very existence. The situation was not much different in the Vienna of Schnabel's childhood. At one time Schnabel might also have been called 'the man who invented Mozart', or even Bach. It was against this background, so inconceivable to us now, that Schnabel decided early on to devote himself exclusively to those works which, to use his own words, were "better than they can be played."

His reputation as a pianist rests basically on the freshness and communicative depth of his musical insights with regard to five composers – Mozart, Beethoven, Schubert, Schumann and Brahms. While never attempting to be 'different', he was constantly challenging conventional assumptions. Schnabel was never what could be described as a broadly 'popular' pianist.

Schnabel – 'the man who invented Beethoven'; seen here with the violinist Carl Flesch.

Indeed, he became famous almost in spite of himself, playing mostly unfashionable music in a manner rebuked as much as it was praised, and refusing to provide managers with either photographs or press material. In seeking an ever greater "isolation within the music", Schnabel kept his audience at a certain distance. He maintained an indifference to public opinion which was often, and understandably, interpreted as arrogance. The public Schnabel was inevitably more revered than loved, and as much for what he represented as for the way he played.

In his relentless pursuit of musical truth he became increasingly unconcerned with keyboard accuracy, and his technical mishaps, combined with his seriousness, led to his unjust reputation as 'the great Adagio player'. No-one was less bothered by his myriad mistakes than Schnabel himself. It was always the music that came first.

In the 1930s, Schnabel became the first pianist to commit all of Beethoven's 32 sonatas to disc. The results have become a part of musical legend. There are wrong notes, inevitably, but above all there is burning integrity, passionate intelligence, a lofty vision and a profound spiritual insight which remain unsurpassed.

151

Edwin Fischer

Fischer (1886–1960) is remembered first and foremost as a Bach player – and a very great Bach player he was. His recording of the complete 'Well-Tempered Clavier', set down in the early 1930s, is comparable in quality and significance to Schnabel's of the 32 Beethoven sonatas. As in the case of Schnabel and Beethoven, so Fischer could be called, and with more justification, the man who invented Bach – at least where the keyboard is concerned. At the time of Fischer's birth, in Switzerland in 1886, Bach as a keyboard composer was known almost exclusively by a handful of extravagantly romanticized arrangements which turned up in the recitals of bravura virtuosi. The situation was changing when Fischer came of age – romanticism was on the wane and there was a new respect for musical scholarship – but it would be left to him, almost alone among great pianists, to demonstrate repeatedly to a wide musical public that it was possible, on the piano, to breathe life into all of Bach's keyboard music without recourse to the arranger's paintbrush. By the time of his death, Fischer had introduced two generations and more to a Bach who spoke not as a monument, nor as some respectworthy museum-piece, but as a living human being. He did it by combining a highly cultivated musicianship and a profound understanding of his instrument with a passionate awareness that respect is worth nothing in art if it is not born of love. His unbounded reverence for Bach found expression in a unique and unselfconscious sense of joy which radiates from his recordings.

As with Schnabel, there was an element in Fischer's playing which struck certain people as slapdash. There were in his lifetime, as there are now, musicians for whom he was an albeit divinely inspired amateur, a visionary imprisoned by an inadequate technique. True, he was not the most immaculate of virtuosos. True, too, that he sometimes let the rhythm and tempo slip away from him in a kind of seraphic acceleration – but these were symptoms of his personality, not mechanical or conceptual deficiencies. When it came to the control and variation of tone, to the combination and succession of rhythmic nuance, to the long and liquid shaping of a phrase, Fischer's technique was unimpeachable. As a musician and a distinguished editor, he was thorough and highly knowledgeable but he never made the mistake, so prevalent today, of confusing history with musical truth. His public repertoire was almost exclusively Classical – he confined himself, on the whole, to Bach, Handel, Mozart, Schubert, Beethoven and Brahms – but his approach to the piano was eclectic, to say the least, with strong Romantic tendencies and a weakness, as some might see it, for impressionistic sounds. In private he often played Chopin, even Debussy, and friends and pupils were dazzled by his accomplishments in such outwardly un-Fischerish repertoire as Stravinsky's *Petrushka*. Stylistically he was never a purist, in a strictly musicological sense, but he communicated a purity of 'spirit' which has been approached by very few. As both man and musician, he exuded a self-forgetfulness whose radiant humility was an inspiration to all who experienced it. In the words of one pupil, "He made us better than we were". In his best playing, he achieved a synthesis of intellectual and emotional experience through which he managed to convey a sense of infinite spiritual freedom. It is not for nothing that Fischer, like his beloved Bach, was felt by many people to have been, quite simply, 'The Fifth Evangelist'.

Artur Rubinstein

Rubinstein (1886–1982) was very possibly the most famous, and certainly the most popular pianist of his time. His face, his name and even his playing was known to people in most walks of life in almost every country in the world – and for one overwhelmingly simple reason: he made people happy. There were musicians whose fingers worked more infallibly, there were some (though not many) who could match the extent and the universality of his repertoire, and others whose intellects perhaps probed deeper, but none ever took or gave more sheer pleasure in the act of performance. Unlike many of the Romantics with whom he was associated, his every act was

152

Artur Rubinstein – a life-affirming Romantic. Here he is seen in rehearsal with his partners in the so-called 'Million-Dollar Trio', the violinist Jascha Heifetz and the cellist Gregor Piatigorsky.

an affirmation of life. Gifted with a natural facility and a prodigious memory, the young Rubinstein saw little virtue in practising, and right up to the onset of middle-age he regularly indulged his temperament at the expense of the notes. In Latin countries, particularly in Spain and South America, audiences appeared not to mind, and it was there that he enjoyed his most spectacular successes, and it was as an interpreter of Spanish music that he enjoyed his earliest fame.

As he approached his forties, Rubinstein was saddled (rightly, he always insisted) with the reputation of an ageing 'wunderkind' whose self-evident talent remained essentially unfocused and undisciplined. In 1932, however, he married and began to take stock of his situation. Spurred as much by worldly as by artistic ambition, he settled down for the first time in his life to a period of relentless hard work and unflinching self-examination. The results were notable not only in a markedly increased professionalism but in a new seriousness of purpose which was reflected both in his repertoire and in the way he played it.

Rubinstein's temperament, lucidity and deep pianistic instinct found perhaps their most natural, and certainly their most famous, fusion in the music of his fellow countryman, Chopin. For many people, Rubinstein was the greatest Chopin player of the century, and he substantially altered the way in which Chopin was commonly regarded. He was one of the first pianists to challenge the exaggerated Romanticism that characterized the playing of most 19th-century interpreters, though not anything like as single-handedly as he liked to make out. Even as late as the 1920s his Chopin playing was thought by many critics to be unacceptably severe. At home in the music of most composers, he brought to almost everything he played a beauty and variety of sound, and a subtlety of rhythm whose naturalness was as irresistible as it was inimitable.

Very early in his career, he was a dedicated and courageous champion of contemporary composers, both famous and obscure. When audiences booed him for daring to inflict on them Ravel's *Valses nobles et sentimentales*, Rubinstein responded by repeating the entire work as an encore. He was similarly steadfast in his support for Stravinsky, Szymanowski, Prokofiev, Albeniz, Falla and Villa Lobos, whom he all but put on the musical map. And in Paris, where he spent much of his domestic life, he became a kind of unofficial spokesman for that group of composers known as Les Six.

Miecyzslaw Horszowski

Purely pianistic achievements held relatively little interest for the piano world's most spectacular 'sleeper', Miecyzslaw Horszowski (1892–1993). For him the piano was never more than a medium for great art, a means to a purely musical end. Born (like both Hofmann and Godowsky) in Poland, in 1892, Horszowski had the longest career in musical history. An astonishing prodigy, he made his public debut at the age of 5 and retired from the concert platform in 1992, having been before the public for fully 95 years. His diminutive size (barely topping 5 feet) and extraordinary modesty may have accounted for his relative obscurity where the public was

153

concerned. Only in his tenth decade did he become world famous, although he had long been recognized by musicians as one of the greatest of all 20th-century pianists.

Horszowski – the piano world's most gifted 'sleeper' who awoke to world fame at the end of his life.

His repertoire was extensive but he was best known for his interpretations of Bach, Mozart, Beethoven and Chopin. As a solo recitalist he gave cycles of the complete Beethoven piano works, all of the Mozart sonatas, generous helpings of French music, many of the piano works of his friend Szymanowski and reams of Chopin. As a chamber musician, of which he was an outstanding example, he played with the best: Casals, Szigeti, Alexander Schneider and the Budapest Quartet were among his regular partners.

For all Horszowski's much remarked simplicity, there was nothing ascetic about his playing; nor was there any trace of the voluptuary. The tone he drew from the piano was of unsurpassed beauty and variety, but its deployment was governed entirely by the character of the music he was playing. While never conforming to stereotypical notions of the virtuoso, Horszowski was largely a stranger to difficulties. So effortless was his command of the keyboard, and so wholly was it put at the service of music, that one scarcely noticed it.

Walter Gieseking

If Cortot had any rival as an exponent of Debussy and Ravel, it was the German pianist Walter Gieseking (1895–1956). Chiefly remembered today as one of the subtlest miniaturists in musical history, he was himself a great hulk of a figure, six foot three in his stocking feet and tipping the scales at more than fifteen stone. It was only fitting. The man was born with an outsize personality, and an outsize talent. His self-confidence, too, was breathtaking, untainted by any discernible trace of modesty. Born in France to German parents, he never went to school, owing largely to his precocity. At the age of five he could read and write perfectly and was gifted with apparently total recall. "After that," he once wrote, "I never needed to learn anything. I was, from a tiny little chap, very fond of music and I somehow picked up piano-playing by myself." Nevertheless, it was eventually decided that even he could use a little formal instruction and in 1911 he became the pupil of Karl Leimer in Hanover. He made his official debut at the age of twenty, a concert which he quickly followed up with a series of six recitals in which he played all 32 of the Beethoven sonatas. "The most difficult part," he remarked, "was

Gieseking – outsize in all senses and one of the subtlest miniaturists in musical history.

memorizing them – and even that wasn't very difficult." Among his most striking characteristics was a remarkable understanding of pianistic sonorities and a naturally breathing style which led to an early reputation as a Chopin player.

In whatever he played, Giesking gave meticulous attention to clarity of detail, beauty of sound and a precise differentiation of style as between one kind of music and another. In Bach, his brisk vitality, tight rhythm and restricted tonal palette are far removed from the easy freedom and poetic sensuality which animated his Chopin. His Brahms and Beethoven were similarly individual. Despite his apparently unlimited repertoire, it is with the French 'impressionists' that Gieseking was (and remains) most famously identified. With a mind as agile and disciplined as his fingers, and an uncanny and perhaps unequalled virtuosity with all three pedals, he coaxed sounds from the piano which seemed to belie its very nature. His playing of Ravel at his Berlin debut in 1920 reduced the critics to a state of stupefied incredulity. His recording of the complete Debussy *Préludes* is among the greatest of the century, and his playing of *Ravel's Gaspard de la Nuit* and the last two *Miroirs* is hardly less remarkable.

Solomon

At the age of 12 Solomon (1902–88) was already a veteran of the concert platform who had spent a third of his young life as an established fixture on the English musical scene. His surname was Cutner but from the outset of his career he was known to the public by his first name alone. When he was 7 he delighted himself by arranging Tchaikovsky's *1812 Overture* for the piano, a feat which brought him to the attention of Mathilde Verne, a well-known teacher who had herself been a pupil of the great Clara Schumann. In 1909, for better or worse, she became Solomon's teacher. The Schumann connection was important, because she had inherited her own teacher's celebrated mistrust of virtuosity for its own sake. During his five years with her, the young Solomon developed to a high degree all those qualities which became famously associated with his maturity: the apparently effortless technique placed always and withot ostentation at the service of the music, the unfailing beauty of his sound and, perhaps above all, the ability to unfurl the shape of a piece in one continuously evolving line.

From the beginning, one of the most remarkable features of Solomon's playing was its economy. As a measure of his faith in the power of music to express itself, he would hold with an almost metronomic accuracy to his chosen tempi, and he avoided, on the whole, all extremes of contrast. Yet within these apparently strict confines he found an infinite variety of nuance which saved him from sounding mechanical. In one sense he was a true Classicist who found in clarity of form an innately expressive meaning, but he was also, in the best Romantic tradition of the 19th century, a true 'pianist' who loved his instrument not simply as a servant of music but unashamedly for its own sake. He valued and perfected the art of piano-playing to a degree reached by few, but his virtuosity was undemonstrative to a

point which struck many as self-effacing if not downright austere. Unity of form and beauty of sound were always uppermost in Solomon's mind. In his extraordinary recording of the Tchaikovsky B flat minor Concerto he approaches the piece not as the usual bravura confrontation between a percussive soloist and a radiant orchestra but as a kind of symphonic chamber music which sheds fresh light on an almost painfully familiar work. Solomon's repertoire was all-embracing, but no matter what he programmed, he was apt to be described as a 'classical' pianist – precisely because of the clarity, restraint and multi-faceted control which he brought to everything he played, be it Liszt, Tchaikovsky or Sir Arthur Bliss.

It would be too much to expect any man with Solomon's sovereign command of the keyboard to forgo altogether the shallower but no less intense pleasures of sheer, unabashed bravura, and while he never got within hailing distance of vulgarity there is at least one recording – of Liszt's fifteenth Hungarian Rhapsody, made in the early

1930s – in which he came as close as his temperament would allow to letting his hair down.

Solomon rarely fell short of the highest standards in any music, and his recordings of Chopin, Liszt, Schubert, Brahms and Debussy command the respect, and repay the attention, of serious music students. It is as a player of Mozart and Beethoven, however, that he remains, in the view of many people, unequalled, despite the fact that just under forty years have elapsed since his final performance.

In 1956, during a holiday in the South of France, and by general consent at the height of his powers, Solomon suffered a massive stroke that put a sudden and tragic end to his career. He lived on for another three decades, suffering a series of further strokes, discomforts and privations and ending his years unable either to move or to speak. It is said that from the time of his first stroke to his death he was never known to utter a single complaint.

Solomon – a true Classicist and yet a true pianist in the Romantic mould.

Rudolf Serkin

During his lifetime, Rudolf Serkin (1903–91) was regarded by a significant number of people as the greatest pianist in the world, yet he was never really a widely popular one, and he did less than most to court popularity. In one sense, he never needed to. As a man he was almost universally loved, and deeply loved, by audiences, friends, and many who may have met him only once. They loved him for his generosity, his deeply ingrained humility and the seemingly endless time he had for other people. But when it came to Serkin the performer, he aroused, particularly in the latter part of his career, not only controversy but sometimes open hostility. Musically, he could aptly be described as a passionate puritan, who had little interest in the lighter side of the repertoire, and whose uncompromising search for artistic truth made no concessions to his listeners.

Though Serkin himself was born in Bohemia, his parents were Russian. His father was a largely unsuccessful Jewish cantor whose poverty was such that the entire family (parents and eight children) were forced to live in a single room. It was in these circumstances that the young Rudi developed his intense powers of concentration and his rigorous single-mindedness. Despite his youth, he soon became part of a circle that included Arnold Schoenberg (his composition teacher), Webern and Berg, the painters Kokoschka and Klee, the writer Hermann Hesse and the architect Adolf Loos.

He was always an unpredictable player. At his most relaxed, he produced playing of unmannered tranquility and a loveliness of tone matched by few. On other occasions, once his shy walk to the piano was completed, he seemed to be locked into a life-or-death struggle with music and instrument alike, in which harsh sounds and rigid, angular lines emerged to the accompaniment of a feverish stamping on the pedals, strained, heavy breathing and an often distracting vocalizing. Arms flailing and sweat pouring from his brow, Serkin demanded from his audiences, not by choice but by virtue of his temperament, a considerable act of will. In the symbolic language of tones, he was always a wrestler with the great issues, and a large part of his power as a performer lay in his ability to make listeners grapple with them too. A Serkin recital was never anything so simple as merely enjoyable, if indeed it was enjoyable at all. It might be uplifting, exciting, even awe-inspiring, or it might be acutely distressing. Serkin never regarded himself as a natural pianist, and the element of struggle was never altogether absent from his playing. It is no accident that the composer with whom he spent most of his many thousands of hours at the piano was Beethoven, or that the work which most obsessed him throughout his life was that most epic of all musical struggles, the *Hammerklavier*. He was mainly identified with the great Germanic repertoire, but in the course of his long career he also played such outwardly un-Serkinesque composers as Chopin, Bartók, Debussy, Ravel, Prokofiev, Grieg, Liszt and even MacDowell.

156

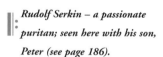

Rudolf Serkin – a passionate puritan; seen here with his son, Peter (see page 186).

157

Arrau – his multi-layered approach produced a sound that was unmistakable.

Claudio Arrau

Arrau (1903–91) was another of that select group felt by a large and significant part of the music-loving public to have been the greatest pianist of his time. His technique was all-embracing, and so, very nearly, was his repertoire. In the earlier part of his career he won extraordinary praise as a player of Bach, whose entire keyboard output he knew by heart. In view of this it is unsurprising that he took an essentially polyphonic view of all music, be it by Mozart, Chabrier, Bartók, Balakirev, Weber, Prokofiev, Schoenberg, Carlos Chavez or Elliott Carter, all of whom were in his repertoire. Perhaps the most fundamental effect of this multi-layered approach was a depth and variety of tone so strangely individual that he could almost be recognized by his sound alone.

Although born in Chile, Arrau was largely German-trained and basically Germanic in outlook, bringing to his performances a depth of analytical insight and musicological study matched by a wide knowledge and appreciation of culture which he saw as essential complements to musical experience. While always

spurning bravura display for its own sake, he could in no way be described as a self-effacing performer. His interpretations were highly individual, reflecting his analytical perceptions in the exceptional character and extent of his rubato and a highlighting of inner voices (those polyphonic strands of melody lying between melody and bass-line). The result could sound very mannered, and sometimes suggested a didactic, 'instructive' intent that worked better in the one-off circumstances of the concert hall than in the recording studio. At the same time, there is no avoiding the fact that his playing was often revelatory. His discography was vast, though not a patch on his repertoire, and included the complete cycle of Beethoven sonatas and concertos (his Beethoven playing is felt by many musicians to have been unrivalled), most of Chopin (his recording of the Nocturnes is one of the glories of the gramophone), much Schubert and Brahms, reams of Schumann and Liszt, and the complete Mozart sonatas. In some ways a definitely acquired taste, his playing has nevertheless occasioned a reverence on the part of his audiences that has rarely been matched.

Vladimir Horowitz

In the space of a single year, 1924, the 20-year-old Horowitz (1904–89) played no less than 25 separate recitals in Leningrad alone, without repeating a single work. In the following year, he left Russia for Germany, and it was there that the Horowitz legend was born. In only a short space of time, this slim, rather dandified youth was playing to sold-out houses of 3,000 and more, and in Paris he roused the audience to such a pitch of hysteria that the police had to be summoned.

In one sense Horowitz was an old-fashioned Romantic for whom the interpreter shared equal billing with the composer (he not only recreated but sometimes substantially rewrote certain works). In another sense he was (or tried to be) a simple, even humble servant of his art. The demonic streak in Horowitz, though it declined in old age, sometimes threatened to engulf much of the music he played. (Rudolf Serkin once accurately described a Horowitz performance of the Chopin G minor Ballade as being "like a fireball exploding".) Perhaps his greatest liability as an artist was his desire to please at almost any cost. One result was a tendency to show off and to play everyone else under the table, which he often did to quite flabbergasting effect. The forcefulness of Horowitz's temperament, and its will to expression, laid him open to widespread charges of misrepresentation. In a typically waspish observation, Virgil Thomson once labelled him "a master in the art of musical distortion".

Many people unfamiliar with the full range of Horowitz's playing were under the mistaken impression that he played almost everything as though it were Liszt. In Classical and pre-Classical music, however, where his supremacy was never universally acknowledged, his playing was often characterized by the utmost restraint, fidelity to every detail of the text and a purity of expression which was never marred by sentimentality.

From the time of his late teens, when he had a working repertoire of over 200 pieces, Horowitz was musically omnivorous. There was virtually nothing that he did not play in private, though his concert programmes, for the most part, continued to represent him as a virtuoso in the grand tradition. Chopin, Schumann, Scriabin and Liszt formed the core of his public repertoire, and his performances of certain 20th-century works (most notably by Rachmaninov, Prokofiev and Barber) were near-legendary. At the same time, his Scarlatti was of a quite breathtaking purity and subtlety, backed up, like most of what he played, by meticulous and scholarly research. For all his Romantic leanings, he was a painstaking stylist, capable of miraculous nuance. Yet ever since his American debut, when one critic dubbed him "that unleashed tornado from the Steppes", Horowitz attracted audiences intent on enjoying some staggering pianistic fireworks, and he never disappointed them. Among his most dazzling achievements was his peerless arrangement of John Philip Sousa's *The Stars and Stripes Forever,* which as well as being a compendium of keyboard virtuosity is a festival of ingenuity, sensitivity and wickedly sophisticated satirical humour.

158

Horowitz – a virtuoso in the grand tradition yet capable of breathtaking purity and subtlety.

159

Lipatti – described by Francis Poulenc as 'an artist of divine spirituality'.

Dinu Lipatti

Lipatti (1917–50) was already composing and giving charity concerts at the age of four. Owing both to his precocity and his always frail health, he never went to school. In addition to receiving private piano lessons he was regularly visited by professors from Bucharest University who took charge of his general education. It was not until 1934, when he was already 17, that he first played outside Rumania. His international debut was quickly followed by concerts in Germany, Italy and France (where he was hailed by Poulenc for his 'divine spirituality'). This was felt wherever he played, and continues to be communicated through his lamentably few but incomparable recordings. His integrity and humility were unimpeachable and uncompromising, but he was in no way austere. His devotion to the ideals of nobility, beauty and grace was untainted by that self-conscious piety which seems to afflict so many serious artists. He was never remotely 'Holier than thou', but inspired in those who heard him an abiding sense of spiritual communion.

There was very much more to Lipatti, however, than 'divine spirituality'. There was also charm (try his recordings of Scarlatti) and, when he saw fit to unleash it, a flamboyant and breathtaking virtuosity (his playing of Ravel's *Alborada del gracioso* remains in a class of its own). He was not easily pigeon-holed, though he was born at a time when musicians, and perhaps pianists in particular, tended to fall into one or other of two opposing camps. There were those who, like Fischer and Schnabel, dedicated themselves to the reaffirming of Classical values in the face of what they saw as recent Romantic excesses, and others, like Moiseiwitsch and Horowitz, who still found much to champion in the great virtuoso tradition which was their historical and cultural birthright. Lipatti was one of the first supreme executants who demonstrated to a wide musical public the intrinsic nonsense of such polarized thinking. He was neither an intellectual nor a hedonist but a musician who brought discipline and an inborn intelligence to the communication of refined emotion and spiritual experience. In his playing of Liszt, for instance (that great bugbear of Classical zealots), he combined all the tonal colours of the Romantic palette with a purity and restraint which in no way conflicted with the character of the music.

The extraordinary balance and sense of proportion in Lipatti's playing derived in part from a perfectionism which could be carried to extreme lengths. When he was asked to perform the Tchaikovsky B flat minor Concerto he replied that he would need three years to prepare it. For the *Emperor* Concerto it was four. Lipatti excelled in many kinds of music, but it was perhaps in Chopin that he found the most perfect synthesis of Classical restraint, Romantic sentiment and the full range of tonal resources afforded by the modern piano. His death from leukaemia in 1950, aged only 33, robbed the world of one of its most priceless treasures.

Freed Spirits

The piano has always played a central role in the enforced domestication of the female sex. The capacity to tinkle prettily away held pride of place among those emphatically female 'accomplishments' long considered an essential part of a 'nice' girl's matrimonial armoury. Once an eligible bachelor had been safely netted, his newly betrothed succumbed more often than not to an attack of pianistic atrophy which settled in for life. And woe betide those few who wished not only to continue their studies but to pursue a musical career. Such things were not done by respectable girls.

Felix Mendelssohn expressed the belief that his sister Fanny was even more prodigiously gifted than himself, and thoughtfully agreed to publish some of her songs under his own name, but neither he nor any of the elders of their distinguished and enlightened family would countenance the idea of her becoming a professional musician. An earlier example is Therese Jansen, a pupil of Clementi and the daughter of a prosperous German dancing master, who was a very considerable pianist. One need look no further for evidence than the difficult and brilliantly inventive sonatas that Haydn wrote for her, yet there is no evidence that she ever once played in public.

Of the young women who did – especially in the 18th century – most were generally disadvantaged in some way. They might be blind, like the noted composer-pianist Marie Theresa von Paradis (1759–1824), or simply ugly, like the brilliantly gifted Josephine Aurnhammer (1756–1820) for whom Mozart wrote his great Sonata in D for Two Pianos ("Augh, she is a very fright to see!" he wrote, with his customary delicacy. "If a painter wished to portray the devil to the life, he would have to choose her face! So horrible, so loathsome and so dirty!").

The overwhelming majority of piano pupils have always been girls and young women, yet the profession of concert pianist remains disproportionately a male preserve. History is rarely so neat, but for purposes of convenience one may trace the liberation of the woman pianist to the influence of a single, towering figure in the story of 19th-century Western music – the daughter of a famous teacher and the wife of Robert Schumann.

Clara Schumann

The eminent if irascible piano teacher Friedrich Wieck had determined even before her birth that his daughter Clara (1819–96) would be an outstanding musician. He must, therefore, have been more than a little disturbed by the fact that she neither spoke nor gave any sign of understanding speech until she was almost five. Once she did, the die was cast. Her father trained her with merciless thoroughness, and

focused her attention so exclusively on music that she was forbidden to read – a deprivation which she lamented throughout her life. Within the bounds of music, however, her education was broad, taking in the serious study of singing, violin, orchestration, score-reading, counterpoint and composition. At eight she was playing concertos by Mozart and Hummel, which set the tone for the stringently 'classical' character of her later career. Considering the radiant puritanism of her later life, though, it comes as a surprise to learn that her repertoire in childhood, extending even into her early teens, contained liberal lashings of froth by such debonair lightweights as Herz, Hünten and Kalkbrenner. By the time she was sixteen she was acclaimed throughout Europe and could count Goethe, Mendelssohn and Paganini among her greatest admirers.

Quite apart from the quality of her playing and the critical response to it, her debut in Vienna in 1837, at the age of nineteen, was historic, being the first occasion on which anyone other than the composer had ever performed Beethoven sonatas for the Viennese public (this fully ten years after the great man's death). And she played not one but three: the 'Tempest', the 'Moonlight' and the *Appassionata*.

She was the first woman to establish a major international career as a pianist, and, even more than Liszt, it was she who most steadfastly pioneered the institution of the unaccompanied recital. She was particularly admired for her playing of Bach, Beethoven, Schumann, of course, and Brahms, but no less exacting a figure than Chopin said of her "She is the only pianist in Germany who knows how to play my music."

When the 20-year-old Brahms first entered the Schumann household in 1853, Robert's mind was already beginning to give way, and within a year he threw himself into the Rhine. Following his rescue, he was incarcerated at his own request at the asylum in Endenich, where he died in 1856 at the age of 46, Brahms devoted himself almost entirely to the support and comforting of Clara, fourteen years his senior, and fell deeply in love with her. More than 20 years later he was writing to her: "I love you better than myself or anyone or anything in the world." The degree to which she reciprocated has been a matter of conjecture ever since, but they certainly became the closest of friends, and throughout his life she offered invaluable advice and comment on his compositions.

She was also greatly respected by Liszt, but in later life refused to return the compliment. "Before Liszt," she was to say, "people used to play. After Liszt, they pounded or whispered. He has the decline of piano playing on his conscience." She was also among the first to perform regularly from memory – an act hitherto deemed disrespectful to the masters. This applied even when master

and player were one and the same. There was a famous occasion when Mozart performed one of his piano concertos before having written out the solo part. Rather than risk offence to the Emperor and his assembled company, he arranged for a friend to turn blank pages for him. Even in the 1830s, playing from memory earned Clara considerable abuse. "With what unendurable pretension she seats herself at the piano and plays without the notes!" quoth Beethoven's friend Bettina von Arnim.

Clara was arrogant only in her humility, and in that she bowed to no-one. In an age when the performer, and particularly the pianist, was ranked at the very least on a par with the composer, Clara Schumann's principled adherence to the text, while not perhaps quite as impeccable as she

made out, was unusual to the point of exoticism. Well before she advanced into stately middle age, she was the self-styled High Priestess of musical integrity, scorning all music that lacked the highest aspiration, and spurning exaggeration in all its forms. Yet she could never have been described as an ascetic, nor did she lack emotional intensity (how could anyone beloved of Schumann and Brahms lack that?). With a minimum of rhythmic elasticity she achieved an eloquence and purity of expression that set her apart from virtually all of her most successful contemporaries.

Combine the comments on her style of those who often heard her and you get a vivid picture of a remarkable artist.

Clara Wieck in 1840, the year of her marriage to Robert Schumann.

162

Clara was the self-syled High Priestess of musical integrity, scorning music that lacked the highest aspiration and spurning exaggeration in all its forms.

Describing her as a "nobly beautiful and poetic player," George Bernard Shaw went on to dub her "the Grail of the critic's quest". Liszt spoke of her "complete technical mastery, depth and sincerity of feeling." But it was the outspoken and controversial Viennese critic Eduard Hanslick who left the most illuminating account. "In one or another aspect of virtuosity, she may be surpassed by other players, but no other pianist stands out quite as she does at the radial point of these different technical directions, focussing their respective virtues on the whole of harmony and beauty. She could be called the greatest living pianist, rather than merely the greatest female pianist, were the range of her physical strength not limited by her sex. ... Everything is distinct, clear, sharp as a pencil sketch."

The extent to which she balanced the rival claims of music, marriage and motherhood was unprecedented in her century and has probably not been equalled since. When she married Robert Schumann in 1840, it was inevitable that her career would be subordinated to his, even before the arrival of children – not because her gifts were any less (they were,

but that was irrelevant) but because she was a woman. This indeed played a major part in her father's implacable and deeply unpleasant opposition to the marriage.

Far from merely withholding his consent, he kept the lovers apart while it remained in his power to do so, slandered Schumann, proclaiming him (not entirely without foundation) a drunk and a moral reprobate, casting (justified) aspersions on his prospects as a breadwinner and eventually forcing the lovers to court. At the time of Schumann's original proposal, Clara was just sixteen and demonstrably on the brink of an unprecedented career. Even before illness robbed him of his reason, Schumann was hardly a model of stability. It could be said that Clara was experienced in motherhood before the birth of her first child. In all, she bore eight children – one of whom died at fourteen months, another of whom was brain damaged from birth – and was expected not only to raise them but to manage the housekeeping and create an environment in which Robert could pursue his own career undisturbed.

Amazingly, she managed to go on performing, playing as far afield as Scandinavia (1842) and Russia (1844). She even found time to compose, though it was to be thirteen years before domestic arrangements allowed her the freedom to practise and compose without fear of disturbing her husband. From the time of his confinement in Endenich, she pursued a performing career which cemented her reputation as the greatest woman pianist of the 19th century. She continued to compose, and became one of the greatest teachers of her time. As a composer she wrote almost exclusively for the piano, and though much of her work was published, from her teens onwards, it was seldom performed by anyone else – an unjust fate, since it contains many excellent pieces, including some beautiful Preludes and Fugues (1845), the highly attractive and polished *Soirées musicales,* Op. 6, from 1836, and a generous number of songs, some of which (Op. 23, 1853) are of striking originality and betray a sense of humour never alluded to in contemporary accounts of her personality. The substantial Piano Concerto of 1834 is a remarkable work to have come from the pen of a fifteen-year-old, especially in its expert handling of the orchestra, and the G minor Trio of 1846 is still occasionally played, and recorded, today.

Clara's Legacy

Of Clara Schumann's many pupils, four, all women, ventured into the recording studio, with very variable results. Natalie Janotha (1856–1932), an extravagantly dramatic and most un-Schumannesque performer, is better remembered for her ostentatious placing of a prayerbook on the piano and her refusal to play without the presence on stage of her dog Prince White Heather than for her actual playing. Her four recordings from 1905 reveal her as something of a charlatan – an accomplished technician, certainly, but a whimsical embroiderer and 'improver' of other people's music, and just the sort of gratuitous egotist that Clara Schumann abhorred.

Ilona Eibenschütz (1873–1967), Hungarian-born but London-domiciled, was a far more reputable musician – a fluent but self-effacing virtuoso whose style was always scrupulously tailored to the requirements of the music she was playing. Her three recordings from 1903 reveal a sensitive and thoughtful artist if not quite a great one, and are entirely without the mannerisms so prevalent among the pianists of that time. Her reminiscences of Brahms, recorded in 1952, and illustrated with demonstrations at the piano, open a fascinating window on the past. Further amplification is provided by her recording ten years later of a Brahms waltz and intermezzo in which the playing is surprisingly undated.

The same can be said of the Schumann recordings of Fanny Davies (1861–1934), an artist of great stature, whose account of the A minor Concerto and the *Davidsbündlertänze,* Op. 6, dating from 1928 and 1930, respectively, are among the finest and most beautifully integrated performances ever recorded.

The extensive recordings of Adelina de Lara (1872–1961) have aroused more controversy, and it must be said that she was well past her prime (in her late 70s and early 80s) when she made them. But the playing is full of vigour, poetic insight and rhythmical unity and should be studied by anyone seriously interested in the history of musical interpretation. Among de Lara's compositions are two piano concertos, an orchestral suite, an Idyll for tenor and orchestra, two song cycles and many vocal ballades with piano accompaniment.

Clara Schumann's example was followed by many who were not actually her pupils, and of these a goodly number played an important part in promoting the cause and encouraging the acceptance of women pianists. Arabella Goddard (1836–1922), for instance, born in France to English parents, conformed to no-one's idea of what a 'lady pianist' should be. Unlike her teachers Kalkbrenner and Thalberg, she spurned the lightweight elements of the repertoire in favour of such then uncommon feminine fare as the last five sonatas of Beethoven. Indeed, she even offered the titanic *Hammerklavier* Sonata at her London debut in 1853. Her technique was by all accounts immaculate, and she enjoyed considerable celebrity in Britain. Elsewhere, however, she was widely felt to be a rather severe, unemotional player.

Not so the brilliantly gifted Camille Marie Moke (1811–75) who in 1831 became the wife of her Christian-namesake Camille Pleyel, one of the greatest figures in the history of piano manufacture and a remarkable musician himself (see page 25). Only three months previously his young bride had been engaged to the flamboyant Hector Berlioz, then in Italy reaping the somewhat questionable fruits of the Prix de Rome, awarded to him on his fourth attempt. On hearing of her surprise betrothal to Pleyel, Berlioz returned post-haste to Paris, acquiring en route a brace of pistols and the costume of a ladies' maid, in which disguise he aimed to kill his faithless fiancée before turning the second pistol on himself. Needless to say, he came to his senses in time to avert the disaster. As it happened, Marie's marriage to Pleyel was short-lived and she later moved to Brussels where she taught at the Conservatoire, establishing, in the words of its director, the renowned scholar and critic François-Joseph Fétis, "the first true school of piano playing in Belgium." For Fétis, her playing achieved a unique perfection, and he was not alone in his enthusiasm. Mendelssohn greatly admired her, Chopin dedicated his Op. 9 Nocturnes to her, and Liszt his *Réminiscences de Norma* and the *Tarantelle après 'La Muette di Portici' d'Auber.*

Liszt's Pupils

After Clara Schumann, there was no woman pianist of the German school more admired than Liszt's pupil, Sophie Menter (1846–1918). As far as Liszt himself was concerned, there was not another woman pianist who could touch her, Clara included. Famous for her broad, 'singing' projection and a technique that saw off all difficulties, she aroused in audiences the kind of adulation normally associated with the greatest prima donnas, and even became known in Paris as 'l'incarnation de Liszt'. Pretty, pert and of unshakeable self-confidence, she had a chance-taking bravura style all her own and an enviably thick skin when it came to the opinions of the critics. Not that she had much to complain of. Typical was George Bernard Shaw's judgement that "she produces an effect of magnificence which leaves Paderewski far behind ... Mme Menter seems to play with splendid swiftness, yet she never plays faster than the ear can follow, as many players can and do; and it is the distinctness of attack and intention given to each note that makes her execution so irresistibly impetuous."

Other notable women who enjoyed Liszt's benediction included the remarkable Adele aus der Ohe (1864–1937). At the age of ten she became one of the very few prodigies he accepted as pupils, and grew to become a formidable virtuoso, introducing Tchaikovsky's Piano Concerto No.1 to New York under the composer's own baton at the opening celebrations of Carnegie Hall in 1891. She regularly played both Brahms concertos, among the most colossal and demanding in the repertoire (even today, few women play the B flat in public). Then, too, there was the diminutive and beguiling Russian, Vera Timanoff, another super-virtuoso (described by Liszt as "la crème de la crème"), but one who wilfully turned her back on a performing career and became a noted teacher in St. Petersburg.

In terms of influence, none of Liszt's female pupils surpassed the remarkable American Julie Rive-King (born in Cincinatti in 1857), whose repertoire was as apparently boundless as her energy. In the two decades following her return from Europe she gave more than 4,000 solo recitals and more than 500 concerto appearances, in the course of which, as Harold Schonberg has remarked, she made the kind of contribution to American musical life that Gottschalk could have done but did not. No pianist before or since has done more to raise the standard or expand the range of America's musical life. Sadly, although she performed until the year before her death in 1937, she appears never to have made any recordings.

Teresa Carreño

Sadder still, though less surprising, is the absence of any recordings by the volcanic Venezuelan Teresa Carreño (1853–1917). One of the most sensational virtuosos of the 19th century, she seemed to have everything and then some – except in her private life. Beautiful, breathtakingly self-assured and possessed of a fiery temperament, she was an accomplished composer, a pioneering conductor and a very creditable opera singer. Of her four husbands, the second and the last were brothers, and the third was the tempestuous Eugen d'Albert, a pint-sized giant of the keyboard (a pupil of Liszt) and an admired composer who seems to have had a sobering effect on his wife's approach as an interpreter. Whereas in her earlier years she took major liberties with the scores she scorched, she emerged from her three years with d'Albert exercising an altogether greater control and self-discipline. She had always been a great pianist, and from this time onwards she was increasingly regarded as a great musician, maintaining her popularity to the end. Even before the d'Albert years, however, she had been described by no less exacting a judge than Hans von Bülow as "the most interesting pianist of the present age". He went on to hail her as "a phenomenon. She sweeps the floor clean of all piano paraders who, after her arrival, must take themselves elsewhere." One gets some measure of her rugged independence from the fact that when the legendary Liszt himself offered to teach her, the thirteen-year-old Carreño declined. And why? She did not fancy being in Rome. Perhaps she was getting a little world-weary. After all, she had played at the White House for President Lincoln when she was only nine and was already tiring of being hailed as a genius.

Leschetizky Protégées

Hardly less impressive, though very much less flamboyant, was the Russian-born Annette Essipoff (1851–1914), widely but needlessly identified as the second wife of the great Leschetizky, probably the greatest piano teacher of the age. Essipoff, however, was too good to need anyone's coat-tails. A technician with few rivals, she was no barnstormer in the Carreño mould, but a cool, collected mistress of all she surveyed. Her playing won the equal admiration of critics and fellow-artists alike. To Paderewski, the most famous product of the Leschetizky school, her playing was "in many ways perfect", though he felt that, when it came to the major monuments of the pianists' repertoire, she lacked the power of a Carreño. Other accounts of her playing speak of her "faultless technique", her "cat-like strength and subtlety", "the beautiful movement of her hand and wrist, which is worth watching for itself". Shaw wrote of her "terrible precision and unfailing nerve; her cold contempt for difficulties; her miraculous speed, free from any appearance of haste; her grace and finesse without a touch of anything so weak as tenderness." "All these," he continued, "are subjects for awe rather than criticism." In the light of such comments it comes as no surprise to read that she was entirely without platform mannerisms. With Essipoff, the poetry and drama were concentrated in the music. She came, she played, she conquered, and then "vanished as calmly as she had appeared" (Shaw again).

Another great witness to Leschetizky's inspirational genius was the Austrian-born American pianist Fanny Bloomfield-Zeisler (1863–1927), who studied with the master for six years. Long regarded as the greatest American pianist of the 19th century, she was, in the words of one critic, a "small, slight, frail, delicate woman, who appears more to need assistance for walking than for playing. How can she dare attempt the gigantic task she often does of playing two or even three great concertos in one evening?" When she retired after a performing career of half a century, she bade the public farewell by playing the Chopin F minor and the Schumann concertos, with the Chicago Symphony Orchestra, as well as a number of taxing solo pieces. Her technique was apparently electrifying, her repertoire virtually limitless and her stamina extraordinary. In San Francisco she once played eight major recitals in a little over a fortnight

165

*The explosive Teresa Carreño,
who added musicianship to her
phenomenal virtuosic gifts.*

Amy Beach – the American composer-pianist who toured Europe with her own Concerto.

without once repeating a work.

It was for the Scottish pianist Helen Hopekirk (1856–1945), however, that Leschetizky reserved his highest praise, calling her "the finest woman musician I have ever known". It was as a teacher and composer, however, rather than as a performer that she was to be best known. She wrote more than 100 songs, many of which enjoyed great popularity at the time, several large-scale orchestral works, two violin sonatas, some chamber music and, of course, a great many piano pieces.

After Julie Rive-King and Fanny Bloomfield-Zeisler (curious that they should both be double-barrelled), the most significant woman composer-pianist in the United States was the redoubtable Mrs. Beach (1867–1944). Amy Marcy Cheney was her maiden name but it was specifically as Mrs. H. H. A. Beach that she chose to identify herself professionally. Her husband, a quarter-century older than his 18-year-old bride (they married in 1885), was a well-to-do surgeon, like herself a Boston Brahmin. From her music, however, she might have laid some claim to be a Boston Brahmsian as well. She had made a very public debut at the age of 16, playing the G minor Concerto of Moscheles with

the Boston Symphony Orchestra, but was prouder of her return engagement in 1900 as the soloist in her own Piano Concerto, a work with which she subsequently toured Europe to great effect. She was also the first American woman to compose a symphony, but despite her large-scale orchestral and choral works, and some durable chamber music, it is as a piano composer that she is best remembered – a skilled and attractive though not perhaps a very adventurous one, drawing equally on the heritage of Brahms and Wagner. In her day, however, it was her songs that found the greatest favour, two of her Browning settings in particular enjoying very considerable popularity.

In the 20th century the number of women admitted to the pianists' Hall of Fame is still small. Very few have been accorded the highest accolades of critics and public alike, and of those, most are dead. The names that spring to mind most readily include Tatiana Nikolayeva and Annie Fischer (both very great artists), and Gina Bachauer and Guiomar Novacs (both borderline cases). Thereafter the mind begins to grope. Three women in particular, however, have reached the highest echelons of popular favour in the mid to late 20th century, and their posthumous reputations have happily kept their names alive – none more so than that of Myra Hess.

Myra Hess

When asked, near the end of her life, to reflect on her many and popular recordings, there were only two which Dame Myra (1890–1965) would acknowledge as having even come close to giving her pleasure, let alone a sense of pride. One was of Schumann's *Carnaval*, made in 1938, the other was of Beethoven's E major Sonata, Op. 109, made some sixteen years later. Dame Myra was an artist whose exacting standards and deeply entrenched humility withstood a lifetime of public adoration, and a performer whose mistrust of machines culminated in a positive hatred of microphones. The essence of her art lay in the act of direct, personal communication, and for all her sometimes agonizing pre-concert nerves she thrived on the presence of an audience. Her attitude to music-making was essentially religious, in that she saw herself not simply as a seeker but as a transmitter of the spiritual truth which is enshrined in the work of all the greatest masters. For most of her career, she confined herself, like Schnabel and Edwin Fischer, to a repertoire dominated by Bach, Mozart, Schubert, Beethoven, Schumann (occasionally Chopin) and Brahms. From the beginning of her career, she was both a gifted and an enthusiastic teacher who quickly discovered that there is in fact no better way of learning.

In later years, with the combination of her repertoire, the warm dignity of her platform manner and her habit of always wearing black, she was widely seen as a kind of High Priestess of music, the very embodiment of simplicity, grace, beauty and nobility. But while she scorned empty virtuosity, she had a masterful technique and a lightness of humour nicely captured for posterity in her now very rare recordings of Scarlatti. There was an element of toughness, too, and an exuberant energy which could be both formidable and infectious, as in her superb recording of the Brahms C minor Piano Quartet.

During the Second World War, Dame Myra became a household name with the now famous series of lunchtime concerts which she organized throughout the war at the National Gallery in London. Countless musicians took part, but the guiding light behind it remained Myra Hess, who had set the keynote at the very first concert by playing her own arrangement of Bach's 'Jesu, Joy of Man's Desiring'. For many people Myra Hess and this piece became synonymous – to the extent that they forgot what a multi-faceted artistic temperament she had.

If 'Jesu Joy' was the theme song of her middle years, it was with Beethoven, and his last three piano sonatas in particular, that she became most widely associated at the end of her career. Her recordings of these bring to mind a creed enunciated by her friend Casals: "When we stop beginning, we stop altogether".

Myra Hess – her recordings of Beethoven's last three piano sonatas bring to mind a creed enunciated by her friend Casals: "When we stop beginning, we stop altogether."

Eileen Joyce

Hess was by no means the only one, of course, who gave of her best during the war. Another was the Tasmanian-born Eileen Joyce, whose career was strangely at variance with the quality of her art. An outwardly glamorous, even spectacular virtuoso, she became much identified with the popular cinema, and with such tabloid-worthy mannerisms as changing her dress several times in the course of a single concert (in accordance with her admittedly idiosyncratic theories concerning the relationships of colour to music). Such things easily distracted people, and music critics in particular, from the fact that she was also a great artist whose Mozart was of impeccable taste and feeling, a Bach player of commanding authority, clarity and proportion, a Lisztian of both poetry and bravura, and a *saloniste* confectioner, when required, whose winning blend of sugar and cream was deliciously seductive.

Throughout the Thirties and the Second World War, she broadcast, recorded and gave concerts at a prodigious rate, amassing a repertoire of some 75 concertos and more than 500 solo works. Her many recordings became immensely popular, especially in Britain, Australia and North America (where she did not appear in person until 1950, when she was dubbed by the New York critic Irving Kolodin "the world's greatest unknown pianist").

Her popularity increased still further in the post-war years, when she was known to play in a single season as many as fifty sold-out concerts in London alone. Eventually the strain took its toll, and she announced her retirement very suddenly in the midst of a Far Eastern tour in 1960, reappearing only once, for a charity concert in 1966. She took part in eight feature films, one of them the story of her own life, and will be best remembered for her work in *The Seventh Veil*, the most popular British film of its time, and *Brief Encounter* (both 1945), where her playing of the Rachmaninov Second made more converts to the work than any number of concert appearances or gramophone records. She died, largely forgotten, in 1991.

Eileen Joyce – according to one critic, "The world's greatest unknown pianist". Her glamorous looks tended to take attention away from her wide-ranging gifts as a player.

Clara Haskil

How different was the career of the Rumanian Clara Haskil. Known throughout her life as 'a musician's musician' and 'a pianist's pianist', she was, in fact, very much more than this, and in the last decade of her life she played to packed halls wherever she went. Yet the labels do fit. No public performer was ever less demonstrative in manner, or less rhetorical in style. Indeed, there was an air of privacy about her playing that rendered the listener almost intrusive. In the decades since her death in 1960 at the age of 65, she has achieved cult status in some quarters, yet it is probably true that most music-lovers, certainly of the younger generation, are unfamiliar with anything but her reputation, if that.

Many listeners, coming to her playing for the first time, may be disconcerted by a selflessness and simplicity which border at times on the deliberately ascetic. Then-unfashionably sparing with the pedals, she was never primarily a tone-painter, though her fingers could conjure from the piano a remarkable range of colours, discreetly applied, as in her vivid evocation of Falla's 'Nights in the Gardens of Spain'. Her playing was unique, inimitable and entirely without mannerism. In overall character it might be said to resemble a kind of amalgam of Horszowski, Lipatti and Richter, with the spirits of Mozart and Chopin hovering like guardian angels over everything she did. She also had a way of bringing out the best in all who worked with her. The violinist Arthur Grumiaux, for instance, was never quite so wonderful as when he played with Haskil, and their partnership in Mozart and Beethoven constitutes one of the great treasures in the history of recording.

169

Adefinitive list of important pianists and composers of piano music to supplement the information given elsewhere in this book is next to impossible, given the constraints of space. The entries below are wide ranging and are designed as a reference source rather than as a running narrative. That said, the section can be read through from A to Z, some of the entries being meaty enough to catch and hold the attention on grounds of purely human interest.

ALBENIZ, ISAAC *(1860–1909)* Spanish composer and pianist. Exploited, like Mozart, at an early age, he made his concert debut at the age of four and was composing fluently at seven. For his childhood appearances, his mother dressed him as a French musketeer, complete with rapier. He tried repeatedly to run away from home but was invariably apprehended and returned. At nine he hopped on a series of trains, playing the piano at various destinations to earn himself some money, and at twelve, carrying only the musketeer's costume he was wearing, he stowed away on a ship travelling across the Atlantic to Puerto Rico. He played for the passengers, who established a fund for him (one can hardly guess at the tale he must have spun to the captain), and on disembarking began a vagabond life throughout the Americas, often sleeping rough and begging on the streets, but finding opportunities to play as well, often in saloons and the like, where he would amuse the public by playing popular numbers with his hands upside down and depart with a new infusion of money in his pocket. A year or so later his father finally ran him to ground in Cuba, but the child clearly had persuasive powers beyond the reach of ordinary mortals: the father returned to Spain empty-handed, while his thirteen-year-old son made his solitary way first to New York and then to San Francisco. At fourteen, he returned to Europe for a year or two, but his riotous way of life led to trouble with the authorities and he decamped once again to America. Finally, he returned home and in 1878 became a pupil of Liszt. In 1893 he settled in Paris, where he counted among his close friends Dukas, d'Indy and Fauré. A prolific composer, mostly for the piano, he always drew on the folk traditions of his native Spain. His immortality is guaranteed by the work on which he laboured almost obsessively during the last three years of his life. Published in four parts, under the title *Iberia*, this colossal undertaking (twelve pieces in all) was of such complexity and technical difficulty that it was originally

pronounced unplayable. Today it is in the repertoire of many pianists, and is generally conceded to be the foundation of the modern school of Spanish piano literature

D'ALBERT, EUGEN *(1864–1932)* British-born German pianist and composer. Of all Liszt's pupils, two, in Liszt's own view, stood out from all the rest. One was Tausig (see page 148); the other was d'Albert. Diminutive in size, and with an ego of outsize proportions, he was widely known as 'The Little Giant', and for many people he was the greatest Beethoven player who ever lived. Tubby and unprepossessing, he sported a moustache that all but engulfed his chin, and a technique that could unleash sounds of overwhelming power – emotional as well as acoustical. His difficult temperament was legendary and cost him six marriages, one to Teresa Carreño, the most dazzlingly brilliant and charismatic woman pianist of the 19th century (see page 164).

ALBERTI, DOMENICO *(1710–40)* A very minor Italian composer, whose only claim to immortality is his supposed invention of a broken-chord style of left-hand accompaniment that became standard in the Classical era and was much used by Mozart, Haydn and scores of lesser composers. His name has been wrongly attached to a variety of arpeggio-style figures but the authentic Alberti bass presents the notes of any three-note chord in the unvarying order of bottom-top-middle-top (C-G-E-G, for example). A well-known instance occurs at the start of Mozart's so-called 'easy' sonata in C, K. 545 (which, like so much Mozart, is only easy to play badly).

AMMONS, ALBERT *(1907–49)* African-American blues pianist and sometime band leader, mainly associated with the boogie-woogie style. Well known for his dynamic partnerships with Meade 'Lux' Lewis and especially Pete Johnson, with whom he made a number of recordings. His

solo work on *Shout for Joy* (1939) and *Bass Goin' Crazy* (1942) shows him at his best. Thereafter his playing declined, though he went on performing and recording for some years. With good reason, he was known as a 'loud' pianist, and many felt that no recording could really do him justice

ANDA, GEZA *(1921–76)* Hungarian pianist. A virtuoso of commanding authority, he studied with Erno Dohnanyi and became a world-renowned champion of Bartók, whose three piano concertos he played many times all over the world. He spent the years of the Second World War in Switzerland, and became a naturalized Swiss citizen in 1955. He was greatly admired for his Brahms playing and was among the first pianists to record the complete Mozart Piano Concertos, in which he directed the Orchestra of the Salzburg Mozarteum from the keyboard. He also published a volume of cadenzas for those concertos lacking any by the composer himself, and gave seminars in Switzerland.

ARENSKY, ANTON *(1869–1906)* Shamelessly derivative and generally lightweight, Arensky's piano music has nevertheless great elegance and charm. The glitteringly bespangled waltz from his first suite for two pianos is delectable. His piano concerto, heavily influenced by Chopin, is occasionally revived, but he is heard to better advantage in his two piano trios. Excellent modern recordings exist of all these works and are worth seeking out.

ARGERICH, MARTHA *(b.1941)* One of the greatest of all 20th-century pianists, she was born in Argentina but has long since been a citizen of the world. Despite a technique which is one of the wonders of the modern world, she often seems, in the best possible sense, to be the very embodiment of Artur Schnabel's jubilant motto "Safety last!". That sense of living dangerously is one of the hallmarks of an Argerich performance, yet seldom if ever is she reckless. Still, such detractors as she has are all but unanimous in their claims that she is indiscriminately electrifying, that she injects a high voltage level of excitement and tension into music which neither requires nor benefits from such attributes. One pianist, possibly nursing a certain jealousy, described her prize-winning performance of the Chopin E minor Concerto at the 1965 Chopin Competition in Warsaw as "hell on wheels". He remains in a minority.

Her public repertoire is not large but embraces most styles from Bach to the contemporary Rabinovitch. She is a chamber player to the manner born, and her recordings of the Beethoven violin and cello sonatas with Gidon Kremer and Mischa Maisky, respectively, are among the finest ever made. Gifted with a technique so natural that she reputedly never practises, she nevertheless shuns display for its own sake, always putting the music first.

ASHKENAZY, VLADIMIR *(b.1937)* Russian-born pianist and conductor. A virtuoso of sovereign technique, his repertoire is vast. He has played or recorded the complete Mozart piano concertos, the complete sonatas and concertos of Beethoven, the complete piano works of Chopin, Schumann, Scriabin etc.. A charmingly self-effacing man of conspicuous modesty, his playing is entirely without mannerisms or eccentricities. His many chamber music recordings with such friends as Itzhak Perlman and Lynn Harrell are among the finest of their time.

Left: Isaac Albeniz – the founding father of modern Spanish piano literature.
Above: Martha Argerich – high-voltage artistry with intelligence.

AX, EMANUEL *(b. 1949)* Polish-born American pianist. At six he was a violinist, but he soon gravitated to the piano, which he studied with his father. When he was ten, the family moved to Canada and since 1961 he has made New York his home. He combines a virtuoso technique with a searching, musicianly mind and a wide cultural and intellectual background; he received a masters degree in French from Columbia University in 1970. His tastes, in both music and musicians, range exceptionally wide but he has achieved a very special distinction in his playing of Mozart, Haydn, Beethoven, Chopin and Brahms. His ebullient, generous personality and aristocratic flexibility of mind have made him a chamber player of rare quality, as his recordings with Yo Yo Ma, Isaac Stern, Jaime Laredo and others abundantly demonstrate. In 1971 he leapt to worldwide attention as the outright winner of the first Artur Rubinstein Piano Master Competition in Tel Aviv, and was awarded the coveted Avery Fisher Prize in 1979. He has also been a persuasive advocate of much contemporary music.

Ⓑ

BACHAUER, GINA *(1913–76)* Short, rotund and forbidding in appearance, her sleek black hair drawn back across her head so tightly that it looked painted on, Bachauer was one of the very few Greek pianists to gain international acclaim. Her audiences soon discovered the warmth of personality behind the façade, and by the time of her unexpectedly premature death at 63 (she collapsed with a heart attack on the same day that she was scheduled to play with the National Symphony Orchestra of Washington, D.C.) she had a loyal worldwide following. She had an exceptionally powerful technique and excelled in the large-scale Romantic repertoire of the 19th and early 20th centuries, being a particularly admired exponent of the famous concertos by Tchaikovsky, Rachmaninov and Brahms. Stranded in Egypt during the Second World War, she gave more than 600 concerts for the Allied troops, and after her Carnegie Hall debut in 1950, attended by only 35 people, she spent half of every year in coast-to-coast tours of the United States. Her repertoire ranged roughly from Mozart to Stravinsky, but she could be very persuasive in Bach, albeit in arrangements by Busoni and Tausig. A former law student at Athens University, she studied in Paris with Cortot and also had lessons with Rachmaninov.

BACKHAUS, WILHELM *(1884–1969)* German-born pianist. He made his debut at the age of eight, and went on to establish a reputation as one of the supreme exponents of Beethoven and Brahms. By all accounts, his many recordings do him scant justice.

BADURA-SKODA, PAUL *(b.1927)* Best known in the latter part of his career for his scholarly championing of period instruments in the Viennese classics (Haydn, Mozart, Beethoven, Schubert), his enthusiasms are, in fact, very wide-ranging and his repertoire includes such unusual works as the Rimsky-Korsakov concerto. He has recorded extensively on both period and modern instruments, and has composed cadenzas for many 18th-century concertos, most notably Mozart's. With his wife Eva, herself an outstanding scholar, he wrote a landmark book on Mozartian performance practices (*Interpreting Mozart on the Keyboard*, 1957) and another with his once-frequent duo partner Jorg Demus on the sonatas of Beethoven. Like Demus and Alfred Brendel, he cites the Swiss pianist Edwin Fischer (see page 152) as a formative influence.

BARBER, SAMUEL *(1910–81)* American composer. A natural pianist and a born melodist, Barber allied himself with the more conservative wing of 20th-century music. His *Adagio for Strings* has become one of the most frequently played of all 20th-century works. Barber's piano works are surprisingly few, but three have found a place in the active repertoire of contemporary pianists: the brilliant Piano Sonata of 1949, introduced by Vladimir Horowitz, the Piano Concerto of 1962 and the witty and superbly crafted *Excursions* of 1945. These works are by no means as instantly accessible as the *Adagio*, and both the sonata and the concerto, while generally adhering to the European Classical/Romantic tradition, are full of thoroughly 20th-century modernisms. All of his writing for the piano is supremely idiomatic, though by no means easy, and his delightful piano duet version of the 1952 ballet *Souvenirs* is well worth looking into.

BARENBOIM, DANIEL *(b.1942)* Israeli pianist and conductor. Already a very distinguished pianist in his boyhood, when he played most of the Beethoven sonatas, Barenboim achieved his first great international reputation in his 20s, giving complete cycles of the Mozart concertos and Beethoven sonatas and conducting many of the Mozart symphonies. His knowledge of the repertoire seems to be comprehensive, and he has excelled in virtually every corner of the performer's art, from bravura solo works and most of the great concertos, to the chamber music repertoire and the 'accompaniment' of such great singers as Dietrich Fischer-Dieskau and Jessye Norman, and the direction of the major symphonic and operatic repertoire. His platform manner is businesslike and aloof, and his playing tends to be conceived on a very broad scale. His most consistent successes as a pianist have been in the Germanic repertoire (Bach, Mozart, Beethoven, Schubert, Schumann, Mendelssohn, Liszt and Brahms), though he has distinguished himself in Chopin too.

BARERE, SIMON *(1896–1951)* One of the most stupendous technicians of all time, the Russian-born Barere was more renowned for his virtuosity than for his interpretative insight and is best known today for having died onstage in the middle of a Carnegie Hall concert with the Philadelphia Orchestra. Strictly speaking, he died backstage, after falling senseless to the platform while playing the Grieg Concerto. This was at least a more decorous exit than that of an overweight English organist whose vast bulk suddenly sank to the pedals mid-service, releasing a thunderous cacophony which continued unabated until worshippers succeeded in dislodging him.

BELGIOJOSO, CHRISTINA *(1808–71)* An Italian aristocratic of pronounced republican sympathies, she financed political insurgency in her native land and lent lavish support to a number of musicians and writers from her beautiful Paris residence in the Faubourg St. Honoré. An accomplished amateur pianist, she enshrouded herself in a mist of excessive sensibility, proceeding from rooms decorated with black velvet and studded with silver stars, to the Opéra, where, dressed in the habit of a nun, but with lilies in her hair, she would allow herself to succumb so intensely to the powers of music that she had frequently to be carried, with insouciant conspicuousness, from her box to an awaiting carriage. She was widely known, and not flatteringly, as 'The Romantic Muse'.

BENNETT, *(SIR)* **WILLIAM STERNDALE** *(1816–75)* Often cited as the leading English composer of the Romantic school, he was a brilliantly accomplished pianist and a more than competent violinist who earned first the admiration and then the friendship of Mendelssohn, who wrote of him "I am convinced that if he does not become a very great musician, it is not God's will but his own." Schumann shared the feeling: "Were there many artists like Sterndale Bennett," he wrote, "all fears for the future progress of our art would be silenced." Bennett's work has not stood the test of time particularly well, but his considerable volume of piano music contains many attractive and noteworthy features, and uses the essentially percussive nature of the instrument as a means of creating a highly individual sound-world while most piano composers were striving after the ideal of the human voice.

BERMAN, LAZAR *(b.1930)* Russian pianist. Despite an early start (he made his first record at the age of seven), Berman's international career really dates from the 1970s, when a recording of Tchaikovsky's First Concerto with Karajan made the world sit up and take note almost overnight. Equipped with a staggering technique, he is most at home in the works of Liszt, Schumann, Rachmaninov and Scriabin, but has proved himself a probing interpreter of Schubert and Beethoven as well. The most formative influence on his development was his teacher Alexander Goldenweiser, with whom he studied from the age of nine.

BLIND TOM *(Thomas Greene Bethune)* *(1849–1908)* Blind American pianist and composer. Born into slavery in the southern American state of Georgia, 'Blind Tom', as he was generally known, acquired his surname from a Colonel James Bethune, who bought him as part of a package deal including his parents, Charity and Mingo Wiggins. His musical talent was quickly spotted by the Colonel's wife, who undertook to foster its development. Although apparently a mental defective in most respects, he began to compose at the age of five, and was said to memorize long and difficult pieces after a single hearing. From an early age he was a skilled improviser on operatic and popular tunes, and was first publicly exhibited at the age of eight, when he was marketed as 'The Greatest Musical Prodigy Since Mozart'. A year later, the Colonel 'leased' him to an impresario for a three-year period during which he played throughout the United States, not excluding the

Barenboim – excellence in every corner of the pianist's art.

White House, where he performed for President and Mrs. James Buchanan. His programmes included works by Bach, Liszt, Chopin and Gottschalk, as well as fashionable salon pieces and pot-pourris by himself. Reliable information on this curious phenomenon is hard to come by. A pitiful description, published in the *Atlantic Monthly* in 1862, invites a certain scepticism. The boy, we are told, would each time be publicly induced to play by his manager with promises of cakes and sweets, and when he had finished would violently applaud himself. "Some beautiful, caged spirit, one could not but know, struggled for breath," we read, "under that brutal form and idiotic brain". For several decades he made regular appearances in Europe as well, earning a substantial fortune for his owner, who thoughtfully stayed on as his guardian and manager following the Great Emancipation. Among his many compositions, some published under the interesting pseudonym of François Sexalise, were *Rainstorm* (1865), *Wellenlänge* (1882), *The Battle of Manassas* (1894) and the straightforwardly entitled *Imitation of a Sewing Machine*.

BOLET, JORGE *(1914–90)* Born in Cuba, he received most of his musical education at Philadelphia's Curtis Institute of Music, studying piano with Leopold Godowsky, Moritz Rosenthal and Josef Hofmann, and conducting with Fritz Reiner. A virtuoso of the first order, Bolet was appreciated mainly by connoisseurs until the latter part of his life when, helped by a series of outstanding recordings, he was belatedly discovered by the musical world at large. Widely considered to be one of the last exponents of the great Romantic tradition, he combined extraordinary pianism with a self-effacing personality, reflected both in the Old World courtesy of his manner and in the style of his playing which embraced the most hair-raising difficulties with an extraordinary lack of flamboyance. Unlike more narcissistic exponents of a largely Romantic repertoire, Bolet never cheapened the music he played, but rather imbued it with an unaccustomed dignity and grandeur. He excelled in the music of Liszt, made his way with insouciant ease through Godowsky's notoriously difficult arrangements of

Victor Borge – preparing to begin a concerto like no other.

Chopin, and earned widespread praise for his Schumann and Brahms, he was seriously underrated as a Beethoven player. He was in no sense an intellectual musician, though he succeeded Rudolf Serkin (who succeeded Josef Hofmann) as Principal of the Piano Department at the Curtis Institute, but a deeply intuitive performer. Among his more unusual claims to fame are that he served as Assistant Military Attaché to the Cuban Embassy in Washington D. C. from 1943 to 1945, and in 1946 conducted the first performance of Gilbert and Sullivan's *Mikado* in Japan.

BORGE, VICTOR *(b.1909)* Born in Denmark as Borge Rosenbaum, Victor Borge has spent a lifetime concealing his gifts as a pianist with his gifts as a comic. Trained in Copenhagen, Vienna and Berlin, he made his concert debut in 1926 and first attracted widespread notice seven years later in various Danish musical revues, before moving in 1940 to the United States where he became a familiar figure on radio and television. In 1951 he was named 'Funniest Man in Music' and between 1955 and 1957 he broke all previous records for a one-man show with a series of daily entertainments on Broadway.

BRAILOWSKY, ALEXANDER *(1896–1976)* Greatly beloved Russian-born pianist. In 1911 he was taken to Vienna to study with the great Leschetizky. He made a speciality of Chopin, whose complete works he performed in six-concert cycles in Europe and America.

BRENDEL, ALFRED *(b.1931)* Austrian-born pianist. He is particularly renowned for his playing of Haydn, Mozart, Beethoven and Schubert, but is also a noted exponent of Schumann and Liszt. His recordings of the complete Mozart piano concertos and the major piano sonatas of Schubert are widely regarded as being among the greatest ever made, but it is with Beethoven, above all, that his name will always be associated. In the 1960s he recorded the composer's entire keyboard works, and his subsequent recitals and recordings of the complete sonatas and the so-called 'Diabelli' Variations are felt by many to be of unequalled quality. Highly intelligent and widely cultured, he brings to his playing a keen analytical mind which is sometimes reflected in a rather didactic approach to performance.

BRITTEN, BENJAMIN *(SIR) (1913–76)* Regarded by many people as the greatest English composer of the century (his rivals for the claim being Elgar, Vaughan Williams and Tippett), he was a remarkable pianist from a very early age, and ripened into a great one. His appearances as a soloist were rare, but his partnership with the tenor Peter Pears, and his more occasional collaboration with colleagues such as the cellist Mstislav Rostropovich and the pianist Sviatoslav Richter were unsurpassed in their musical insight and technical finesse. His works for solo piano were surprisingly few (the most notable being the Piano Concerto of 1938 and the scampering little suite *Holiday Diary* of 1934) but his use of the instrument in his many songs and arrangements was

supremely imaginative and resourceful. As a composer, he stood apart from the modernist trends of his time and his music, while strikingly individual, is in a conservative and highly accessible idiom.

Alfred Brendel – an analytical approach to music-making.

BRUBEK, DAVE *(b.1920)* Outstanding American jazz pianist and composer. Classically trained (he studied with Darius Milhaud and had one lesson with Arnold Schoenberg), he used a sophisticated, often contrapuntal idiom, combining jazz with elements of Baroque styles. In 1951 he formed the Dave Brubeck Quartet (piano, alto sax, bass and drums), which rapidly became world-famous and featured loosely fugal improvisations by Brubeck and his saxophonist Paul Desmond. The complexity of his harmony, his use of unusual, non-binary metres and his sometimes heavy, 'unswinging' piano playing aroused heated controversy in the 1950s, but by the mid-60s he was safely installed as a classic.

BUSONI, FERRUCCIO *(1866–1924)* Italian-born composer and pianist, regarded by some as the greatest pianist of his time. Gifted with a phenomenal technique and a penetrating intellect of exceptional brilliance, he was especially renowned for his playing of Beethoven and Liszt, and for his many piano arrangements of organ works by Bach, which became standard issue for pianists well into the 20th century. He had a weakness for epic structures, and his gargantuan piano concerto calling for piano, full orchestra and male voice choir takes more than an hour and a quarter to play.

Ⓒ

CARMICHAEL, HOAGY *(1899–1981)* American jazz and popular pianist and composer. The only well-known jazzman to have a law degree (from Indiana University), Carmichael had a distinctive, almost insolently relaxed style of playing, long on atmosphere and character, short on virtuoso pianistics. He also had a respectable career as a character actor in Hollywood and was one of the most successful song-writers of his time. His best-known hits include *Georgia on My Mind, Riverboat Shuffle, Stardust, Lazy River, In the Cool, Cool, Cool of the Evening* and the humorous, quirky *Hong Kong Blues.*

CASADESUS, ROBERT *(1899–1972)* Distinguished French pianist of exceptional elegance and culture. Internationally famous as an exponent of French music, he was also among the most admired exponents of Mozart's piano concertos, Beethoven's sonatas and Chopin's Ballades.

CHABRIER, EMANUEL *(1841–94)* French composer and pianist. Chabrier qualified as a lawyer and worked for many years as a civil servant for the French government. He was unusual, for a composer, in combining a sense of humour with a reverence for Wagner, whose music he wittily mocks in one of his piano pieces, *Souvenirs de Munich.* Although best known for his orchestral rhapsody *España* (1883), he wrote highly idiomatic piano music which

César Franck cited as forging a vital link between modernism and the Baroque traditions of Couperin and Rameau, and which Poulenc ranked in importance with the *Préludes* of Debussy. No less a composer than Ravel stated that he had been more influenced by Chabrier than by any other composer. His style is marked by a wide range of mood and colour, and a fondness for juxtaposing extreme contrasts. Among the works which helped to usher in the age of Impresssionism are the *Dix pièces pittoresques* (1881), *Bourée Fantasque* (1891), the solitary *Impromptu* (1873), the three *Valses romantiques* (1883) and the *Habañera* of 1885.

CHAMINADE, CÉCILE *(1857–1944)* French composer and pianist. Equally successful in both roles, she wrote many charming and polished piano pieces which enjoyed a great vogue for many years on both sides of the Atlantic.

CHERKASSKY, SHURA *(b.1909–95)* Russian-born American pianist. As a child prodigy, he was admitted to the Curtis Institute of Music in Philadelphia as a student of Josef Hofmann and made his debut in Baltimore at the age of 11. One of the last exponents of the great Romantic tradition, his performances are marked by a fabulous technical control and a colouristic range bordering on wizardry. His interpretations are frequently characterized by a capricious imagination best suited to the more flamboyant works of the great 19th-century pianist-composers.

176

Hoagy Carmichael – his playing was long on atmosphere and short on virtuoso pianistics.

CLIBURN, VAN *(b.1934)* American virtuoso. He made his recital debut at the age of four, won his first competition at thirteen, and made his Carnegie Hall debut a year later. Although his talent was never doubted, it was not until he won the Tchaikovsky Competition in Moscow in 1958 that he gained widespread recognition. The Cold War was at its height and the United States, piqued by the Russians' recent launching of *Sputnik*, the first satellite, made the most of their homegrown boy made good. Cliburn was given a tickertape parade in New York on his return from Moscow and became overnight the most famous pianist in the world. Always at his best in the big Romantic repertoire, he was able to produce tremendous volume with an unfailingly beautiful tone (a rarity in any age) and brought to his playing an innate sense of grandeur coupled with a warmth and directness of spirit that endeared him to millions. Worn by the public demands made on him, and the incessant requests for the same restricted repertoire (mainly the Tchaikovsky First and Rachmaninov Third Concertos), he largely withdrew from concert-giving in the late 1960s and has appeared only sporadically since. In 1962 he established the Van Cliburn International Piano Competition in Fort Worth, Texas, which is now ranked with the most important competitions in the world. A simple patriot of impeccable sincerity, he used to begin every recital with *The Star-spangled Banner*.

COREA, CHICK *(b.1941)* Extraordinarily accomplished American pianist and composer. He has won equal admiration as an exponent of avant-garde, jazz and classical music. His recording of Mozart's Double Concerto with Friedrich Gulda and the Royal Concertgebouw Orchestra under Nikolaus Harnoncourt is among the most exhilarating ever made.

CRAMER, JOHANN *(John)* **BAPTIST** *(1771–1858)* German-born English pianist, composer and publisher. 'Glorious John', as he came to be known in England, was one of the most admired and influential pianists and composers of his day. Despite his conservative tastes (like Chopin, he really loved only Mozart and Bach), he was one of the pioneers of a truly idiomatic piano style, and his many studies have remained in continuous use from his day to ours. He counted Haydn and Beethoven among his greatest admirers, and was one of the first itinerant pianists to include the works of others in his programmes.

CURZON, *(SIR)* **CLIFFORD** *(1907–82)* English pianist of world renown. Pupil of Schnabel, Landowska and Nadia Boulanger, and one of the most elegant and intellectually penetrating pianists of the mid-century. He was especially noted for his interpretations of Mozart, Schubert, Liszt and Brahms.

CZERNY, CARL *(1791–1857)* Austrian pianist and composer, a pupil of Hummel, Clementi and Beethoven. Czerny was one of the most industrious musicians who ever lived. Despite a busy teaching schedule (his pupils included both Thalberg and Liszt), he composed a fantastic amount of music, most of which has fallen into oblivion. In addition to his string quartets, concertos, masses and many other works, he published 861 opus numbers of music for piano alone, each of which contained many individual pieces. He was also a busy arranger with a taste for extravagance which was nowhere evident in his lifestyle. His arrangement of Rossini's *William Tell* Overture calls for sixteen pianists playing four-hands on eight pianos. For the deprived multitude that boasted but one piano per household, Czerny could provide alternative arrangements for only three pianists playing six-hands on a single keyboard. Astoundingly prolific, he had several writing desks in his study, each supporting a different work in progress. While the ink dried on one, he moved on to the next desk, thus becoming music's first one-man assembly line.

DOHNANYI, ERNO *(1877–1960)* Hungarian composer, pianist, conductor and teacher. One of the greatest pianists of his time, he is mainly remembered today as the composer of a single work, the *Variations on a Nursery Song* ('Twinkle, twinkle, little star'), Op. 25 (1914), for piano and orchestra. He brought into the central repertoire many then-neglected works by Mozart, Beethoven and Schubert and was the first world-famous pianist to appear regularly in chamber music. His importance in the history of music in Hungary can hardly be exaggerated. In the years 1919–21 he gave over 120 concerts each season in Budapest alone. In 1920 he became the first person to perform the complete piano works of Beethoven, and in 1941 the complete Mozart piano concertos. Among his many distinguished pupils were Georg Solti, Annie Fischer and Geza Anda.

DREYSCHOCK, ALEXANDER *(1818–69)* Bohemian pianist and composer, reputed to be the loudest pianist of his day. Obsessed with technique, he would practise left-hand exercises and passage-work for sixteen hours a day and got to the point where he could play Chopin's 'Revolutionary Etude' in octaves, a feat which still defies belief.

ELLINGTON, EDWARD *('Duke')* *(1899–1974)* American jazz pianist, bandleader and composer. Believed by some to have been the greatest American composer in any genre, Ellington's significance and influence cannot be overstated. He once said that "Bach and myself write with the individual performer in mind". He learned jazz piano from the great James. P. Johnson and Willie 'The Lion' Smith in New York's Harlem, the cradle of urban blues music. Less flamboyant than either, his own piano style owed something to the spare, economical playing of Count Basie, and can be heard to best advantage on the recordings of his own works which he made in 1960 with Louis Armstrong.

Duke Ellington – the king of jazz musicians (see entry on preceding page).

178

EVANS, BILL *(1929–80)* Outstanding and highly influential American jazz pianist and composer. His introspective, highly sophisticated style owed a lot to the French 'impressionists' (Debussy, Satie), and was characterized by a wide-ranging tone and a ruminative, sometimes melancholic lyricism, such as you find in his bewitching *Peace Piece*. Other typical Evans numbers are *Turn Out the Stars, Waltz for Debby* and *Blue in Green*. He died prematurely from drug abuse.

FAURE, GABRIEL *(1845–1924)* French composer. A pianist of very limited abilities, Fauré had to rely almost entirely on others to introduce his solo works, though none of them is particularly challenging from a technical point of view. Their difficulty lies in the subtlety and textural insight required to do them justice. His most important piano works, the earliest of which are deeply influenced by Chopin, are the Nocturnes, Impromptus and Barcarolles, which he composed between 1880 and 1921, but much of his most inspired piano writing lies in the accompaniments to his many exquisite songs, notably in the cycle *La Bonne Chanson* (1894). Also noteworthy are his two works for piano and orchestra, the *Ballade* of 1881/1901 and the *Fantasie* of 1919. Fauré's best works yield more delights and beauties on each successive hearing.

FISCHER, ANNIE (1914–95) Hungarian pianist. A searching and profound musician, she won especial fame as an interpreter of Mozart and Beethoven but was an outstanding advocate of such other masters as Schumann and her compatriots Liszt and Bartók.

FRANCK, CESAR *(1822–90)* Belgian composer, organist and pianist. Despite touring at the age of 11 and winning many prizes, including the Grand Prix d'Honneur for piano at the Paris Conservatoire, Franck never really regarded himself as a concert artist. In adult life he was far more interested in the organ, but he brought an organist's sense of resonance and grandeur to his piano writing. His significant works with piano are the Prelude, Chorale and Fugue (1884), still very much in the repertoire, the lesser-known Prelude, Aria and Finale (1887) and the great Sonata for Violin and Piano of 1886. A series of early bravura works has long since sunk into obscurity.

FRIEDMAN, IGNAZ *(1882–1948)* Polish pianist. Friedman was one of the most urbane, elegant and individual performers ever to have trodden the boards. His tempos and rubato were often extreme and highly idiosyncratic, as was his weakness for highlighting inner parts, but his best playing, particularly of Chopin and Mendelssohn, remains peerless to this day. His complete recordings have been reissued on CD.

GABRILOWITSCH, OSSIP *(1878–1936)* Russian-born pianist, conductor and son-in-law of Mark Twain. Like his teacher Anton Rubinstein, he had a phenomenal repertoire and gave 'historical' series, tracing the line of development from Bach to Rachmaninov, as well as enormous concerto marathons. He was particularly noted for the beauty of his tone and the subtlety of his virtuosity.

GOODE, RICHARD *(b.1943)* American pianist. Regarded by many as the greatest Beethoven player of his generation, he has recorded and frequently performed the complete cycle of Beethoven's 32 sonatas. His solo career was late in blooming. For 30 years he was known as a superlative player of chamber music but only as he approached his fifties did the musical world at large awaken to his true importance. His repertoire is wide, but his reputation is based principally on his magisterial and vital playing of the great Germanic classics (Bach, Haydn, Mozart, Beethoven, Schumann and Brahms). He commands a tonal palette of exceptional variety and is also an illuminating interpreter of Debussy.

GOULD, GLENN *(1932–82)* Canadian pianist. Renowned for his eccentricity as much as for his genius, Gould was perhaps the most provocative and iconoclastic pianist who ever lived. Claiming that Mozart died "not too early but too late", he then recorded the complete sonatas by way of substantiating his point. This cycle predictably includes some of the most gratuitously murderous, but at the same time some of the most illuminating, assaults on a great composer ever set down. Gould had fingers second to none, and a memory that embraced very nearly the entire output (and not just pianistic, either) of Byrd, Gibbons,

Fauré – his works yield more delights on each successive hearing.

Alexander Glazunov, photographed in 1930.

179

GARNER, ERROLL *(1923–77)* American jazz pianist and composer. Self taught, he made his debut on American radio at the age of seven and went on to play on riverboats and in restaurants and nightclubs. Musically illiterate, he needed an associate to write down his many songs (more than 200). His style was unique, heavily chordal in the left hand, full of syncopated bounce and embellishment in the right. So small he needed to sit on a telephone directory, he was a tremendously appealing figure, with a joky side reminiscent of Fats Waller, whose Harlem 'stride' style had a formative influence on his own. He made a number of European tours and in Paris was dubbed "The Picasso of the Piano". Among his most famous songs are *Misty, Blues Garni, Solitaire, Dreamy* and *That's my Kick.*

GILELS, EMIL *(1916–85)* Russian pianist. His sovereign technical command and glorious sonority were matched by immense intelligence and deep thought. A virtuoso to rival any, he was phenomenal in Liszt and the mainstream Russian repertoire, but will probably be best remembered for his many powerful and revelatory performances of Beethoven, whose complete sonatas he was in the process of recording when he died.

GLAZUNOV, ALEXANDER *(1865–1936)* Like his compatriot Tchaikovsky, Glazunov is far better known for his orchestral than for his piano works, though in the case of his piano concertos, the two are one (which has not saved either from neglect). His real *pièce de resistance* is the Grand Concert Waltz, Op. 41, an entrancing and taxing showpiece rich in humour, style, exuberance and polish.

Glenn Gould – a provocative iconoclast.

Bach, Richard Strauss, Mahler, Schoenberg and many more. After his premature death from a stroke, he became a cult figure and looks likely to remain so. He retired from the concert platform in his early thirties, apparently at the very peak of his form, thereafter confining his musical activities to the recording studio. A prolific and sometimes verbose writer of increasingly streamlined prose, he also made radio and television documentaries on subjects both musical and otherwise. His best playing, perhaps particularly of Bach (the composer with whom his name has always been most closely linked) is widely regarded as being among the greatest ever heard, despite rather than because of the exaggerated mannerisms which so often disfigure it.

GRAINGER, PERCY *(1882–1961)* Australian-born pianist and composer. A brilliant pianist of extraordinary individuality, he was a student of Busoni's, a friend and famous interpreter of Grieg, and a great and illuminating player of music he admired. He could also be cavalier and slapdash. His best recordings of Bach, Chopin, Schumann and Brahms, are all now reissued on CD and have an almost uncanny spontaneity and inner grandeur. He was an enthusiastic champion of Debussy, Ravel and Albeniz when their music was still freshly minted but had little time for Haydn, Mozart or Beethoven. His own piano music is heavily influenced by folk music (of which he was a pioneering scholar) and has an infectious lilt to it, though much of it is extremely difficult to play. He was also a resourceful and loving arranger of songs by Fauré, Gershwin and others. Eccentric and flamboyant, he married his wife in a spectacular ceremony staged at the Hollywood Bowl. He also proposed that his skeleton should be preserved and possibly displayed at the Grainger Museum in Melbourne, but this wish was not fulfilled.

GRANADOS, ENRIQUE *(1867–1916)* Spanish composer, pianist and teacher. As suggested by his music, Granados was a thoroughly equipped virtuoso with an exceptional flare for rhythmic vitality and drive, and an almost impressionistic tonal palette. He was a famous exponent of the Grieg Piano Concerto and often played chamber music with such luminaries as Thibaud, Casals and Saint-Saëns. Multi-talented, he was an accomplished writer and painter. His most important piano works are the suite *Goyescas* (1911), based on paintings by Goya and by general consent his greatest achievement, and the earlier *Danzas espanquolas*. Both works were among the first by a native composer to enshrine the national heritage of Spain in instrumental music, and *Goyescas* remains in the central piano repertoire today. Granados drowned in the English Channel while attempting to rescue his wife after their ship was torpedoed by a German submarine in 1916.

GRIEG, EDVARD *(1843–1907)* Norwegian composer and pianist. Grieg's best-known work for keyboard is the Piano Concerto in A minor, one of the most popular pieces ever composed. Of his solo works, the most substantial is the Ballade in G minor, the most popular is undoubtedly the loosely Baroque-style 'Holberg' Suite (written for the bicentenary of the writer Ludwig Holberg, sometimes called 'the Molière of the North', and best known today in its orchestral form), followed by the ten books of Lyric Pieces. These, along with his three sets of folksong arrangements, span virtually the whole of his creative life and provide a fascinating survey of his developing style. Almost all of Grieg's music is intensely national and the closer he gets to his folk roots the more interesting and original his music becomes.

GULDA, FRIEDRICH *(b.1930)* Austrian pianist and composer. Hailed in the 1940s and 50s as one of the most brilliant and penetrating performers of Bach, Beethoven and Mozart, he later turned his back on the classical music scene and devoted himself primarily to jazz, and jazz-oriented compositions, including a reworking of famous Viennese waltzes in blues style.

HALLE, CHARLES *(née Carl)* *(SIR)* *(1819–95)* German-born Anglicized pianist and conductor. He made his concert debut at the age of four, conducted Weber's *Der Freischütz* and Mozart's *Die Zauberflöte* when he was eleven, and at seventeen went to Paris where he introduced the Parisians to the sonatas of Beethoven and became friends with Chopin, Liszt, Berlioz and Wagner. He was the first pianist ever to perform the complete cycle of Beethoven's sonatas in public. In 1848 he moved to England where he founded the symphony orchestra that bears his name to this day. A more peripheral claim to fame was his invention of the automatic page-turner.

HENSELT, ADOLF *(1814–89)* German pianist and composer. Reputed to be the shyest great pianist of all time, he was greatly admired by Liszt and Schumann. Once, on being recognized by the band in a café, he leapt up with a look of sheer terror on his face and exited at high speed through the kitchen. On the rare occasions when he appeared in a concerto, he would hide in the wings until just before the piano entry, at which point he would race onto the stage, play his part and then dash away again without once looking at the audience. In the last thirty-odd years of his life he gave a mere three concerts. He was obsessed with the piano and with technique, practising regularly for ten hours a day long after achieving a level of virtuosity that put him on a par with Liszt. His speciality was wide stretches, and by means of various self-torturing devices he developed the ability to play at one time C-E-G-C-F in the left hand and B-E-A-C-E in the right. The independence and strength of his fingers was unique and he could unleash greater volume from the knuckles than other virtuosos could manage from the shoulders. A much-feared teacher, he dressed entirely in white, save for a bright red fez, and would wield a fly-swatter with unerring accuracy throughout the lesson. His pupils were not amused.

HERZ, HENRI (*originally Heinrich*) (1803–88) Brilliant if lightweight Austrian virtuoso and composer, whose playing, teaching and compositions were all the rage in France, England and the United States (his works fetching three or four times as much in sales as those of his most superior colleagues).

HINES, EARL (*'Fatha'*) (1903–83) Superlative jazz pianist, bandleader and composer. Endlessly inventive, effortlessly sophisticated and benignly nonconformist, he did much to liberate jazz piano from its more confining stereotypes, and his highly individual rhythmic patterns were widely copied. His recordings with Louis Armstrong are among the classics of the age and reveal the evolution of his distinctive 'trumpet piano style', with its sharp accents, Lisztian octave tremolos in the right hand and artfully repeated melodic figures. In the 50s and 60s his foreign tours took him to Europe, the Soviet Union and Japan.

Earl Hines, putting on the style as 'fatha' of jazz piano.

181

HUNTEN, FRANZ *(1793–1878)* German pianist and composer. A polished and accomplished lightweight, his *saloniste* confections included reams of facile waltzes, variations on operatic themes, fantasies and other glittering trifles. With Henri Herz, he became a focal point of Robert Schumann's war against the 'philistines'. He made a fortune from teaching and the sales of his 267 published soufflées. The vast popularity of his pieces is partly explained by their relative ease. His approach to teaching is illustrated by the *Méthode de piano*, Op. 60. He wrote mainly for amateurs and in the late 1830s was commercially the most successful piano composer in the world. Unlike his colleagues Herz, Kalkbrenner & Co., he never performed in public.

JARRETT, KEITH *(b. 1945)* American pianist and composer. One of the most sophisticated, lyrically introspective, classically oriented jazz pianists ever, he has drawn on the styles and character of Africa for much of his inspiration. Uniquely, he has achieved equal success as a classical pianist and harpsichordist. His recordings of Bach's 'Well-Tempered Clavier' (Book I on piano, Book II on harpsichord) have been highly praised on both sides of the Atlantic.

KABALEVSKY, DMITRI *(1904–87)* Russian composer. Among his prolific output Kabalevsky's piano music reveals both craftsmanship and fertility of invention. Much of his keyboard output was written for children (the charming Sonatina in C becoming very well known in the West), but he also wrote three very accomplished piano concertos, of which the second is particularly rewarding. His most successful piano works include three sonatas (of increasing conservatism, by dint of Soviet decree), 24 Preludes and 6 Preludes and Fugues.

KALKBRENNER, FRIEDRICH *(1785–1849)* German pianist, composer and teacher. One of the most polished and accomplished virtuosos of his day, he earned the wholehearted admiration of the 20-year-old Chopin, who seriously considered studying with him but wisely thought better of it (he himself was already one of the greatest pianists of all time). His approach to technique, set forth in his *Méthode* of 1830 and evident in his many études, many for the left hand alone, was highly influential. He amassed a considerable fortune through teaching and writing.

KATCHEN, JULIUS *(1926–69)* American pianist. Prodigiously gifted, he graduated with highest honours in philosophy and English literature at the age of nineteen. He made his nationwide radio debut, playing Schumann, when he was eleven. His technique was all-embracing and his repertoire vast. He was a great interpreter of the Russian repertoire but excelled equally in the Germanic Classical tradition. He was particularly associated with the music of Brahms, most of whose piano works he had recorded by the time of his premature death from cancer.

KEMPFF, WILHELM *(1895–1991)* German pianist, composer and arranger. A musician of wide culture, Kempff was acclaimed as a Beethoven player of unsurpassed quality. He was also a distinguished interpreter of Bach, Mozart, Schubert, Chopin, Schumann, Liszt and Brahms. His piano arrangements of works by 18th-century composers are of extraordinary beauty and ingenuity.

LESCHETIZKY, THEODOR *(1830–1915)* Polish-born Austrian pianist, composer and teacher. One of the two most important teachers of the piano in the 19th century, he numbered among his pupils Paderewski, Schnabel, Friedman, Moiseiwitsch, Gabrilowitsch and Horszowski.

LEWIS, JOHN *(b.1920)* A founder member of the Modern Jazz Quartet, he was one of relatively few pianists to reach stardom in the bebop era and one of the more conservative jazzmen of the Fifties, though the Bop orientation of his piano style was always audible. With a classical training and university education, he was among the most sophisticated of jazz composers and devoted a major part of his time to teaching and to bridging the gap between jazz and classical styles. In 1984 he recorded Book I of Bach's 'Well-tempered Clavier'.

LHEVINNE, JOSEF *(1874–1944)* Self-effacing Russian-born virtuoso who brought a classical restraint to his playing of the great Romantics. His technique was prodigious and his playing of octaves and double-notes induced a state of stunned disbelief in all who heard it. His recording of Schumann's *Toccata* belongs in the 'Ripley's "Believe it or Not"' category, as does his habit of taking the glissando octaves in the Brahms 'Paganini' Variations, prestissimo, pianissimo and staccato.

LIBERACE, WLADZIU VALENTINO *(1919–87)* The most outrageously flamboyant 'classical' pianist in history, he gave a whole new dimension to the term 'camp'. Prancing onto the stage in a designedly preposterous suit of white mohair, beaming, double-dimpled, at his audience and frequently invoking the figure of his mother and 'my brother George', he would seat himself at an all-white concert grand, bedecked with his trademark candleabra, and proceed to mingle Beethoven's 'Moonlight' Sonata with Rachmaninov's C sharp minor Prelude in a manner calculated to reduce the pious to a state of gibbering indignation. A showman of near-genius and inspired vulgarity, he made a fortune on television, and installed a gigantic piano-shaped swimming pool at his California mansions. Serious musicians had to admit that underneath the froth and glitz the man was actually quite a pianist. Though his Polish name was genuine, he was American born. He began playing at the age of four, was encouraged by the great Paderewski and made his debut with the Chicago Symphony Orchestra at fourteen. Briefly forsaking the concert platform, he turned for his livelihood to the nightclub circuit, using the name of Walter Busterkeys. In 1982 he was unsuccessfully sued to the tune of $380,000,000 by his bodyguard-chauffeur for services rendered 'in an exclusive non-marital relationship'. He died of AIDS in 1987.

LOGIER, JOHN *(1777–1846)* More notorious than famous, this German pianist is best remembered for his grotesque invention, the 'chiroplast' – an elaborate medley of rods, wires, springs and metal rings designed to keep the hands properly positioned while practising. He was also the world's first assembly-line piano teacher, instructing roomfuls of aspiring virtuosos simultaneously. Curiously, his methods enjoyed a considerable vogue in England, Germany and France.

LUPU, RADU *(b.1945)* Rumanian pianist, most famous for his exceptionally poetic and refined playing of Mozart, Beethoven, Schubert, Schumann and Brahms. He is nevertheless very far from being just "a lyricist in a thousand". While never remotely a barnstormer, he is a master of dramatic pacing, for example in the monumental First Piano Concerto of Brahms. It is doubtful whether he has ever played an ugly note.

MARX, CHICO *(real Christian name Leonard) (1891–1961)* The piano-playing member of the Marx Brothers. His unique technique has to be seen to be fully appreciated and defies description. As he plays in every one of the Marx Brothers' much-revived movies, this is no problem. Essentially a cocktail of glissandos and pistol-trigger finger-flicks (in which the index finger scores a succession of graceful bull's-eyes) mixed with a throwing of the hand at the keyboard like a kind of animated beanbag, it should be studied daily by all pianists who suffer from excessive tension in the hand, wrist and forearm. If more pianists played like Chico, piano recitals would be a lot more fun – even for the pianist.

MATTHAY, TOBIAS *(1858–1945)* Distinguished English pianist, composer and teacher. He devised a special method of teaching and learning which for a time earned widespread currency in England, on the Continent and in the United States, but is probably best remembered today as the teacher of Dame Myra Hess.

MEDTNER, NIKOLAI *(1880–1951)* Medtner stood apart from all forms of musical nationalism and cultivated a generally conservative style, deliberately drawing on what he saw as the best traditions of the Western classical and Romantic traditions. The main influences on his style were not his fellow Russians but Schumann and Brahms. Apart from 100-odd songs, he wrote almost exclusively for the piano. His music is highly sophisticated, even 'intellectual' in its elaborate melodic weave, its almost obsessive rhythmic ingenuity and its tightly integrated structures. While his music has always been prized in Russia (despite his defection to the West, where he spent the last

thirty years of his life) it has never found widespread favour outside it, even in England, where he lived for almost twenty years. His most important music includes three piano concertos, twelve piano sonatas, and a large collection of *Fairy Tales* and *Dances*.

Radu Lupu – poetic refinement par excellence.

MEYER, LEOPOLD DE *(1816–83)* The self-styled 'Lion Pianist' was reputed to be the loudest pianist in history. His assaults on the keyboard were generally preceded by several attempts to move the piano into a position acceptable to the Lion, who invariably declined to change the placement of his seat. While this charade was being enacted, he would make speeches to the audience, and when a satisfactory arrangement had been achieved, he would begin to play, on some occasions using thumbs alone, on others, an invincible combination of fists, forearms and elbows. Mercifully, he played only his own compositions.

MICHELANGELI, ARTURO BENEDETTI *(1920–95)* Italian virtuoso, notorious for his last-minute cancellations and his severely restricted public repertoire (barely more than a dozen works, including, most famously the Brahms Paganini Variations, Ravel's *Gaspard de la Nuit* and G major Concerto, the Bach-Busoni Chaconne and Rachmaninov's seldom heard Fourth Piano Concerto. His technique and accuracy were all but infallible. It is unlikely that he played more than a dozen wrong notes in his entire career. A colourist in a million, his playing was nevertheless criticized for its coldness and aloofness, one great musician referring to him as the 'Great Mortician'.

MOISEIWITSCH, BENNO *(1890–1963)* Russian-born virtuoso. Moiseiwitsch was a mysteriously underrated interpreter, although he achieved great popularity. His glorious, multi-hued sound was a reminder of the Golden Age of pianism, and indeed he was one of the last remnants of that era. Undemonstrative in manner, he was nevertheless one of the warmest and most generous of players, and was

Moiseiwitsch – a mysteriously underrated artist.

especially rewarding in the works of Mendelssohn, Chopin, Schumann and Brahms, the great Romantic repertory which he seldom strayed beyond.

MONK, THELONIUS *(1917–82)* Highly influential jazz pianist and one of the founding fathers of bebop. Monk's advanced style, exceptionally bold in harmony and rhythm, prevented him from becoming a really popular figure. Raised in the 'stride' piano tradition of New York's Harlem, he was later associated with such jazz greats as Coleman Hawkins, Charlie Parker, Dizzy Gillespie and Art Blakey.

MOORE, GERALD *(1899–1987)* Great English pianist, and the first to win equal billing for accompanists, a breed once considered so lowly that their names did not even appear on record labels. The great musicians with whom he was most closely associated include Dietrich Fischer-Dieskau, Victoria de los Angeles and Elisabeth Schwarzkopf. He was the author of several books, the best-known being *The Unashamed Accompanist* (1943).

MORTON, FERDINAND *('Jelly Roll') (1890–1941)* The first pianistic jazzman to leave an indelible stamp on the early New Orleans school, Morton was the most important link between ragtime and the mainstream jazz of the 1930s. Preferring to work in small groups, he was virtually forgotten as a pianist during the Big Band era of the 1930s, but many of his original compositions became jazz standards. These include *King Porter Stomp, Mr. Jelly Lord, Shoeshine Drag,* and *Doctor Jazz.* Among the great figures with whom he was associated were Louis Armstrong, King Oliver and Duke Ellington.

MOSCHELES, IGNAZ *(1794–1870)* Much loved Czech-born pianist, composer and teacher. In the matter of technique, he was a pioneer in the use of touch to modify tone, and undoubtedly influenced Liszt. He was a teacher and close friend of Mendelssohn, and much of his music, polished, inventive and attractive, is undeservedly neglected

MOSZKOWSKI, MORITZ *(1854–1925)* German-born pianist and composer. He is best known for his virtuoso miniatures and his colourful evocations of Spain, particularly the two books of Spanish Dances for piano and piano duet.

Ⓝ – Ⓟ

NIKOLAYEVA, TATIANA *(1924–93)* Prodigious Russian pianist. Particularly noted for her luminous interpretation of Bach, she was equally distinguished in Mozart, Beethoven (all of whose sonatas she recorded) and Shostakovich, whose famous Preludes and Fugues were written for and dedicated to her.

NOVAES, GUIOMAR *(1895–79)* Brazilian pianist. The seventeenth of nineteen children, she won the praise of Fauré and Debussy and became particularly identified with the music of Chopin, Schumann and other Romantics, as well as South American composers.

PACHMANN, VLADIMIR DE *(1848–1933)* Polish pianist and Chopin specialist. He became as famous for his eccentricities as for his interpretations, commenting quite audibly on his own performances, making jokey or rude remarks to the audience as he played, and climbing under the piano at the end of his recitals "to search for all the notes that he dropped". He was at his best in miniatures, and prided himself, rightly, on the range and tonal subtlety of his soft playing. Widely known as 'the pianissimist', 'the Chopinzee' and 'the Clown Prince of Pianists', he made a serious assessment of his art particularly difficult.

PERAHIA, MURRAY *(b.1947)* American pianist. Widely considered as one of greatest pianists of this century, his playing is marked by a combination of extraordinary finesse and dazzling brilliance. His recording of the complete Mozart piano concertos (conducting the English Chamber Orchestra from the keyboard), like his Beethoven cycle, is unsurpassed, and he is widely regarded as peerless in the music of Chopin and Schumann.

PETERSON, OSCAR *(b.1925)* Canadian jazz pianist and composer. One of the most recorded artists in any genre, he established himself as perhaps the greatest virtuoso jazz pianist since Art Tatum, whose playing was a formative influence. Associated with many of the greatest names in post-World War II jazz, he was best known for his work with various trios, and became in the 1970s one of the few jazz pianists to give entirely solo recitals.

PETRI, EGON *(1881–1962)* German-born pianist. He was one of the relatively unsung titans of the piano, bringing to his playing a combination of intellect, virtuosity and passion rarely encountered. He was particularly famous for his playing of Liszt, was closely associated with Busoni, and though he was notably erratic in his later years, he was also a formidable Beethoven player.

PLETNEV, MIKHAIL *(b.1957)* Brilliant Russian pianist and conductor, gifted with a technique and individuality of style reminiscent of Horowitz. Best known for his interpretation of Russian works, he has also proved a compelling player of Scarlatti, Haydn and Beethoven, and a transcriber of genius.

POLLINI, MAURIZIO *(b.1942)* Italian pianist, and one of the most formidably equipped virtuosos in history. Scorning bravura display for its own sake, he is a scrupulously meticulous interpreter whose performances are entirely without mannerism. A tendency to four-square phrasing has nourished his reputation in some circles as a 'cold' pianist. His vast public repertoire ranges from Mozart to the contemporary avant-garde, but he is perhaps most readily associated with Beethoven, Schubert and Chopin. Like his teacher Michelangeli, he has seldom if ever played a wrong note.

POULENC, FRANCOIS *(1899–1963)* French composer and pianist. The most distinguished of that group of French composers known as Les Six, he wrote a quantity of delightfully elegant and tuneful piano music which owed little to the modernist developments of his time. He was basically a neo-Classicist like Ravel, his music being essentially anchored in the more conservative traditions of the 19th century. His *Mouvements perpétuel* has found a place in the repertoire of many amateur pianists.

PRESSLER, MENAHEM *(b.1923)* German-born American pianist. Although a soloist of outstanding quality, he is best-known as the pianist of the superb Beaux Arts Trio, of which he is now the only remaining founding member.

PREVIN, ANDRÉ *(b.1929)* Outstanding and exceptionally versatile pianist, conductor, composer, television presenter and chat-show host. He was scoring Hollywood films while still in his teens and established a great reputation as a jazz player before winning recognition as one of the most brilliantly gifted and accomplished classical pianists and conductors of his age.

Ⓡ–Ⓩ

RICHTER, SVIATOSLAV *(b. 1915)* Russian pianist with a technique that is one of the marvels of 20th-century pianism. He appears to have memorized the entire piano literature, and has recorded much of it. His Bach recordings are of a remarkable purity, his Schubert and Schumann are legendary, his Debussy is of near-miraculous subtlety, and in the works of Russian composers, particularly Rachmaninov and Prokofiev, he is generally spellbinding. For many years he never played a recital without including in the programme a piece that was new to him. With advancing years came an increasing austerity, and some highly eccentric choices of tempo. In a London performance of Schubert's G major Sonata, he took longer over the first movement than most pianists take over the whole work. His epic vision of gigantic structures, however, is almost unequalled.

RIFKIN, JOSHUA *(b.1944)* American pianist, musicologist and conductor, whose scholarly expertise ranges from the 17th century to the present. During the 1970s he did more than anyone else to popularize the music of the great ragtime composer Scott Joplin.

185

Tatiana Nikolayeva – noted for her luminous Bach readings.

Richter – his technique is one of the marvels of 20th-century pianism.

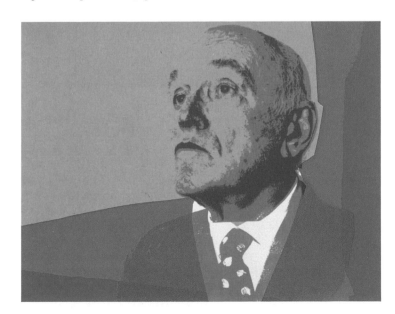

Saint-Saëns, with one of his long-eared personages.

ROSENTHAL, MORIZ *(1862–1946)* Polish pianist. A pupil of Liszt, he had a colossal technique, a sound that ranged from the subtlest pianissimos to the most thunderous fortissimos, and an ego to match. He specialized in the Romantic repertoire, achieving particular renown as a Chopin player. Famous for his barbed wit, he was notoriously ungenerous about his colleagues.

SAINT-SAENS, CAMILLE *(1835–1921)* Prodigiously gifted French composer and pianist. He gave his first public performance at the age of five, and was seriously composing by the time he was seven. At the age of ten he could play the entire cycle of Beethoven piano sonatas from memory. In his tastes and repertoire he was exceptionally conservative, a fact reflected in his brilliantly polished piano music, which includes five concertos, of which the Second is the most popular, the 'Carnival of the Animals' (for two pianos and sundry other instruments), and a number of taxing études.

SATIE, ERIK *(1866–1925)* Iconoclastic French composer and pianist. One of the great snook-cockers of all time, he composed in a highly personal idiom, characterized by a kind of simplistic melancholy alternating with an almost childish playfulness. His best known piano works include the three *Gymnopèdies* and the *Trois pièces en forme de poire* (Three Pieces in the Shape of a Pear), which are neither three nor perceptibly pear-shaped. His music enjoyed a considerable revival in the late 20th-century.

SAUER, EMIL VON *(1862–1942)* German pianist and composer. A pupil of Nikolai Rubinstein and Liszt, he was every inch the complete virtuoso, although not naturally drawn to the blood-and-thunder school of piano lions. His playing was notable for its smoothness and clarity of texture.

His compositions have been almost entirely forgotten, though his Piano Concerto still gets an occasional airing.

Sauer – every inch the complete piano virtuoso.

SCHIFF, ANDRAS *(b.1953)* Hungarian pianist. Celebrated for the beauty, polish and crystalline clarity of his playing and for the wide range of his repertoire and affinities, he has become especially identified with the music of Bach (all of whose most important keyboard works he has recorded), Mozart (his complete cycle of the concertos is among the finest integral recordings ever made), Schubert (most of whose piano sonatas he has recorded) and Beethoven. He is also a distinguished Mendelssohnian and a compelling performer of the music of his compatriots Bartók and Kurtag.

SERKIN, PETER *(b.1947)* American pianist of immense distinction. The son of Rudolf Serkin, he is a completely equipped artist whose public repertoire extends from Bach (most notably the 'Goldberg' Variations) to Takemitsu. He has made remarkable recordings of Beethoven's 'Diabelli' Variations, Mozart's middle-period concertos, Chopin's Ballades, Bartók's First and Second Concertos and Messiaen's *Vingt regards sur l'Enfant Jésu*s.

TATUM, ART *(1910–56)* Probably the most astoundingly virtuosic jazz pianist ever, he can be compared to such classical counterparts as Liszt and Horowitz. He brought to its pianistic peak the so-called 'stride' piano style pioneered by James P. Johnson, Fats Waller and Willie 'The Lion' Smith, with an elaborately decorative style which sometimes all but buried the tune it was embellishing. The fact that he was blind only added to the incredulity occasioned by his technical wizardry.

TURECK, ROSALYN *(b. 1914)* American pianist and harpsichordist. Most famous as a scholarly and brilliantly accomplished Bach player (she has recorded most of his major keyboard works on the piano, maintaining that it and not the harpsichord is the ideal vehicle for Bach's music), she was a formidable exponent in earlier years of such Romantic epics as the Tchaikovsky First and Brahms Second Concertos.

UCHIDA, MITSUKO *(b.1948)* Japanese-born pianist. She is particularly noted for her performances of Mozart (whose complete piano concertos she has directed from the keyboard), Beethoven (whose complete sonatas she plays), Chopin and Debussy (her recording of whose *Etudes* is widely regarded as the finest ever made).

VINES, RICARDO *(1875–1943)* Spanish pianist, who became an ardent, brilliant and imaginative champion of the modern French and Spanish schools (most notably Albeniz, Ravel, Granados, Falla and Debussy).

WALLER, THOMAS *('Fats')* *(1904–43)* The Artur Rubinstein of jazz piano, Waller probably gave more sheer pleasure and fun to more people than any jazz pianist before or since. His jokey presentation, with verbal asides, sometimes distract from the masterly and individual style that puts him well into the pantheon of jazz greats. Waller also showed himself to be a gifted composer. Among his output of some 400 pieces are the songs *Honeysuckle Rose* and *Ain't Misbehavin'*.

WILD, EARL *(b.1915)* Extraordinary but erratic American pianist, whose repertoire and approach hark back to the heyday of the 19th-century Romantic virtuoso. His

transcriptions and arrangements call to mind those of Liszt, Thalberg, Tausig and Godowsky.

Zimerman – a performer of exhilarating vitality.

187

ZIMERMAN, KRYSTIAN *(b.1956)* Polish pianist of aristocratic cast. His combination of sovereign technique, penetrating insight and warmth of imagination have paid rich dividends in Chopin, Liszt, Schubert, Beethoven and Brahms. Very occasionally his interpretations can seem a little didactic and mannered, but they are always of unfailing interest and exhilarating vitality.

'Fats' Waller – an exuberant performer who blended a dizzying array of pianistic styles. He probably gave more pleasure to audiences than any jazz pianist before or since.

Index

189

191

ACKNOWLEDGEMENTS

The publisher would like to thank the following for their kind permission to reproduce the photographs and illustrations in this book:

AKG London 10, 45(tl), 52, 54, 56-57, 58, 68, 72, 73, 91, 102, 103, 104, 113, 114, 118, 120, 124, 136, 143, 161, 179(b); APR 155; BFI stills 38; The Billie Love Historical Collection 15, 45(b); Blüthner 23(t); Bösendorfer/Stefan Jankubowski 2, 5, 17, 17(tl), 19; Broadwood Trust 40; Bridgeman Art Library 47(r), 64, 65, 67, 69, 75, 78, 80, 85(t), 100, 107, 116, 123, 127(b), 128; Burghley House 98; Calderdale Leisure Services, Halifax (Shibden Hall) 13; Jean-Loup Charmet 27, 29, 92, 150(t); Christies Images 18; Corbis/Bettmann 6, 24, 33(b), 83(t), 85(b), 88, 101, 110, 111, 126, 135, 142, 148(t), 152, 154, 156, 158, 180, 178, 186(l), 187(b); David Dear/Kate Ryder 42(b & t); Decca/Heiya Okada 183; Deutsche Grammophon 187(t), (Susesch Bayat) 171; Peter Feuchtwanger Archive 168(l & r); Cobbe Collection, Hatchlands Park 11(br); Hulton Getty 34, 35, 37, 89, 94, 97, 146, 147, 148(b), 162, 167, 179(t); The Lebrecht Collection 8, 9(br), 23, 30, 32, 33(t), 46, 51(t), 59, 60, (Nigel Luckhurst) 62, 66, 74, 77(t & b), 79, 84, 86, 87, 90, 99, 105, 106, 109(br & tl), 112, 115, 119(b), 125, 129(bl & tr), 130, 131(tl & br), 133, 137, 132, 139(t), 144, 150(b), 151, 153, (Suzie Maeder)157, 159, 167, 166; Mansell Collection 49, 61(bl), 76, 93, 95, 121; Maureen Gavin Picture Library 14(l); Mary Evans Picture Library 11(tl), 12(bl), 20, 28, 36, 48, 50, 51(b), 53, 55, 61(tr), 63, 70, 81, 108, 117, 119(t), 122, 127(t), 134, 139(b), 149, 165; Metropolitan Museum of Art, New York 9; Nettle & Markham/Upbeat Management 41; Peter Newark's Pictures (Military Pictures) 26, (Western Americana) 82, (American Pictures) 83(b); Olympia Records 185(l); Philips Classics Productions 175, (Lia van Hengstum/Alecio de Andrade) 185(r); Pictorial Press 141, 174, 176, 181; Popperfoto 31(br), 184, 186(r); Ronald Grant Archive 39(l & r); Steinway & Sons 25; Tate Gallery Publishing 71; Warner Classics 173.